# Roads and Trackways of
## WESSEX

# Roads and Trackways of
# WESSEX

MPC

British Library Cataloguing in Publication Data

Wright, G.
Roads and trackways of Wessex.
1. Roads and trackways, history
I. Title
388.1-09423

ISBN 0 86190 248 3

Published by
Moorland Publishing Co Ltd,
Moor Farm Road,
Ashbourne, Derbys DE6 1HD

Printed in the UK by
Billings & Sons Ltd,
Worcester

# Contents

# Introduction

Although the history of roads and trackways has for long been a subject of interest to anyone curious about the past, very few regional studies have been produced dealing with roads in specific areas. Wessex has, probably, received more favourable treatment than most parts of Britain in this respect, largely due to its rich legacy of presumed prehistoric downland tracks which have fascinated generations of antiquarians, archaeologists, historians and field-workers. Indeed, I freely acknowledge the debt I owe to three books in particular: *Ancient Trackways of Wessex*, by H.W. Timperley and Edith Brill; *The Old Roads of Dorset*, by Ronald Good, and *The Lost Roads of Wessex*, by C. Cochrane.

The approach adopted here is a chronological one, starting with prehistoric tracks and working through to the turnpike roads. It must be emphasised, however, that it is almost impossible to maintain such an approach strictly throughout, for with the exception of some Roman roads and the turnpikes deliberately created in Wessex from the early eighteenth century, most roads and tracks visible in the landscape are both undated and undatable. It is not uncommon in Wessex to follow a delightful green lane across the downland, apparently linking prehistoric sites, or to trace a winding, hedged lane between villages or towns of medieval importance, without ever being able to prove prehistoric origins for one, and medieval beginnings for the other. As Christopher Taylor has pointed out, once a track is made, or, more accurately, has evolved, it tends to be used by succeeding generations.

The history of roads is inextricably linked to the growth or decline of population, the development and success (or failure) of towns and trade, fluctuation in agriculture, and the changing influences of royalty, monasteries and the Church. All these may determine how many roads there are, and their relationships with one another, but it is the physical landscape which determines their routes.

Companion volumes to this have dealt with the Peak District, the Lake District, the Yorkshire Dales, and Wales, all areas within Britain's 'highland zone', characterised by upland landscapes, and having a rather dispersed pattern of settlement. Wessex is vastly different, and within the area covered, no land reaches 1,000ft (305m). Much of it is chalk downland which, in pre-Roman times, was probably the most densely populated in Britain. Today its settlement pattern is very largely one which evolved during early medieval times: the Industrial Revolution had remarkably little impact on most of Wessex; the story of its roads and trackways is very different from that of the other areas mentioned above.

Only where it meets the sea has Wessex any finite frontier. Even during the centuries of its own independent existence it expanded or contracted according to the powers of its rulers or to the strength of assaults made on it by neighbouring tribes and kingdoms. But the name implies a unity, perhaps one which owes more to geology than to history or Hardy. For the purposes of this book Wessex embraces the whole of Dorset, Wiltshire as far north as, roughly the line of the old A4, the eastern fringe of Somerset, the western part of Hampshire, and a bit of Berkshire.

Although a number of maps are provided to illustrate the text, potential explorers of Wessex trackways are advised to look at, and use in the field, the appropriate Ordnance Survey 1:50,000 Landranger maps, or — better still — the larger scale 1:25,000 Pathfinder Series of maps, published in increasing numbers. Most of Dorset is now covered by these, but maps for much of Wiltshire still remain to be produced. Grid references are given throughout the book to places not immediately obvious, but the prefix letters are omitted in the belief that readers' commonsense will lead them to the right 100km grid squares! Incidentally, an important High Court ruling (11 December 1987) relating to a section of the Wildlife and Countryside Act 1981 confirms that the showing of a path on the definitive map — as given on the OS maps quoted — is conclusive evidence of its existence as a public right-of-way, except in very limited circumstances such as the loss through erosion as with the old coach road between Lyme Regis and Charmouth. This is good news for walkers of Wessex tracks.

This book has two objectives: to tell the story of some aspects of the history of the road network of Wessex, and, more importantly, to encourage local research, and persuade readers to explore some of the roads and trackways of their own parishes or parts of Wessex with which they may be reasonably familiar. As Brian Hindle wrote in the introduction to his book about the Lake District in this same series, 'Anyone who has an interest in roads, local knowledge of an area, and above all imagination, can help to expand the sum of human knowledge'. To this end, a car and a pair of good walking-boots are almost as important as the maps.

My interest in Wessex tracks developed during my 25 years' residence near Bradford-on-Avon. However, I am painfully aware that the geographical area covered by this book is such that it is impossible to treat all parts, and all aspects of the subject, as fully as I would have liked. Only a small fraction of the hundreds of miles of roads and trackways are represented, so that this book claims to be little more than an introduction to a subject of which even one facet can offer material for individual local research and the rewards of fieldwork in countryside rich in the humus of history.

Many people have helped in the making of this book. The staff of the County Record Offices at Dorchester and Trowbridge, and of the reference departments of local history sections of libraries at Bath, Chichester, Dorchester, Salisbury, Sherborne, Trowbridge and Winchester, have all shown the kindness and patience I have come to expect at such storehouses of knowledge. Special thanks are due to my friend and former colleague, Mrs M. Bignell, of St Laurence School, Bradford-on-Avon, for allowing me access to local history material from the school library. The County Councils of

Dorset, Somerset and Wiltshire have kindly allowed me to reproduce certain items from the collections in their record offices, and the Library of the Wiltshire Archaeological and Natural History Society has been a source of great help to me. Special thanks are due to Mr R. Haynes for making available his unique observations and research about Wiltshire milestones.

The use of two cars has made easier the walking of many miles of Wessex tracks, and in this respect I must express my warmest thanks to my Sussex friends, Pat and Pearl Mitchell, of Chichester. My sister-in-law and her husband, Margaret and Roy Wilcox, have also shared in some enjoyable 'two-car' explorations of trackways in the heart of Dorset as well as having investigated in the field on my behalf, the Roman roads of west Wiltshire and north Somerset.

As with previous books my wife Jean's contribution is incalculable. She has undertaken much of the research and planning, accompanied me on most of the fieldwork trips, prepared many of the maps and diagrams, and coped with the problem of typing from a rough and sometimes illegible manuscript. At all times she has been a constant source of help and encouragement. My deepest thanks are due to her and to all who, often unknowingly, helped in any way. All the photographs, like any errors or omissions, are my own.

*G. Wright*

# 1 • Prehistoric Roads

A time-traveller journeying into the past and alighting, perhaps, around 8000BC, would find some aspects of life comparable with those of today. Much of Wessex was an area of open landscape whose gently undulating, river-intersected uplands never reached 1,000ft. Grazing stock ensured that woodland and scrub did not wholly cover the downland. From this broad mass of shallow-soiled and relatively dry downland four main natural land passage routes radiated through the marginal forests and clay vales of the north and east giving access to much of the rest of Britain: the Thames-Avon divide in north Wiltshire leading to the Cotswolds; the Test-Loddon divide near Basingstoke leading to Surrey and the North and South Downs; the Thames gap at Goring separating the Berkshire chalk from that of the Chilterns which itself continues to East Anglia; and the downland ridge running from Winchester to Butser Hill and the South Downs into Sussex. These, together with other lesser forest ways, tended to determine the subsequent lines of trackways.

Migratory animals about 10,000 years ago probably used these tracks. Modern television films about wildlife, especially in Africa, often show huge numbers of animals on their migratory movements, almost invariably as a broad, untidy straggle, and not a narrow, follow-my-leader, single-track trail. There is no reason to think that Britain's migrating herds behaved any differently. Equally, these long-distance movements probably acquired others on the way, where smaller groups joined or left the main migration. Additionally, more localised tracks would be made by animals moving from pastures to drinking points which, in the chalk country of Wessex, would almost always have been in river valleys. Thus, from evidence discovered by palaeobotanists and palaeozoologists, by as early as 8000BC Britain may have been intricately networked with animal trackways, both local and long-distance. Palaeolithic and Mesolithic man (10,000-5000BC), as hunter-fisher-gatherers, probably followed these broad zones of communication.

However, from about 4000BC, new arrivals from Europe brought new ideas and a technology which included the ability to make pottery and use better tools such as stone and flint axes. They had also learned how to domesticate herds of animals — cattle and sheep — as well as how to grow primitive types of cereals and certain other crops. Extensive forest and woodland clearance was done by fire and axes, but more importantly so far as trackways are concerned, livestock husbandry and a settled rather than a nomadic life necessitated permanent tracks of a local and functional nature, from farmstead to pasture, from one farmstead to another. The Neolithic farmers of from 4000-2000BC were a well-organised society, with the mobility to travel distances in order to locate and trade flint, chert and stone, and also with the motive and organisational skill to construct huge monuments such as the Avebury and Stonehenge temples, the henges at Durrington Walls, also in Wiltshire, Knowlton and Mount Pleasant in Dorset, and Stanton Drew in north Somerset.

Although many miles of Neolithic tracks were used it is impossible to prove their existence. As Christopher Taylor reminds us, once a track has evolved, and continues to be used by later generations, its beginnings can no longer be recognised. Centuries of wear and subtleties of minor changes can render even archaeological excavation an inconclusive exercise. Thus some of our Wessex lanes and main roads may follow Neolithic routes.

## Neolithic Tracks in the Somerset Levels

However, Wessex can provide proof of some Neolithic tracks, not, as one would expect, on the dry upland ridgeways of downland, but in the marshy, low-lying landscape of the Somerset Levels west of Glastonbury. Two important factors have contributed to the discovery and dating of over a dozen miles of elaborate, constructed trackway. First, Neolithic farmers on 'islands' of sand or hard rock amid the surrounding marshes needed to build tracks across the marsh; second, the marsh has not only preserved these tracks but contains in its natural constituents the materials which allow them to be accurately dated. Forty trackways, from 3200-2000BC, have now been discovered, partly as the result of major drainage work, and more recently through large-scale commercial digging for garden peat.

Most of the tracks were on Edington Heath, Catcott Heath and Shapwick Heath between Burtle and Westhay, and the Polden Hills to their south, an area of about 10sq miles. The earliest-discovered track, named The Abbot's Way, was excavated in the 1960s and dated to late Neolithic times (2000BC). Subsequent discoveries have unearthed what is believed to be the oldest known road in the world, certainly in Britain. The Sweet Track is dated to 3200BC and extends for about 2 miles from Westhay (433422), south-south-westwards towards Shapwick. Much of its southern part has been destroyed by peat-cutting and other sections are drying out. One good stretch is within the Shapwick Heath Nature Reserve, where the Somerset Levels Project has arranged for the Reserve to be kept wet to ensure the preservation of the Sweet Track 1m beneath the surface.

This track, and others built around or soon after 3000BC, were all similarly constructed. Bundles of brushwood, mainly birch, were laid across the marsh, held in place by pegs driven into the ground on each side. Where the ground was very marshy transverse timbers were sometimes laid first to provide a firmer foundation. About 2000BC more elaborate constructions were introduced, in which planks or split logs of alder were laid transversely along the lines of the track, peg-held at the sides as before, but with the pegs fixed to the logs by longitudinal stringers to make a much more stable track.

Estimates suggest that for a mile of this type of track about 20 miles of split logs and at least 80,000 pegs up to 3ft long would have been needed, an indication of the woodland which had to be cleared and of the organisational skill of Neolithic farmers to arrange this, and transport the timber from the Polden and other nearby hills. Reconstruction of short lengths of these Neolithic tracks are shown at the Somerset Levels Project display, together with a small archaeological and natural history exhibition at The Willows Garden Centre near Westhay (427415).

## Neolithic Ridgeways

In addition to the broad, swathe-like tracks left by animals and men in their pastoral travels tracks must also have existed by which were brought to Wessex the polished stone axes originating in Cornwall, Wales and the Lake District, and flint tools from East Anglia. Other long-distance routes linked separate and often distant communities to causewayed camp meeting-places as well as to the great ritual monuments.

Windmill Hill (086714), near Avebury in Wiltshire, is one of the most famous of the causewayed camps, so called because they were neither defensive nor, apparently, permanent settlements. A series of concentric rings of banks and ditches on a low grassy hill has gaps in its banks and causeways across its ditches, and the camps appear to have been seasonal meeting places where traders and farmers met to exchange goods, commodities and stock — the forerunners, as it were, of medieval fairs. Even today, five bridleways converge on Windmill Hill from all points of the compass, and the downs to the south and east are criss-crossed with tracks. Interestingly enough there is no present track making a direct link between Windmill Hill and Avebury, although the camp was probably in existence when work started on the stone circle 1½ miles away.

The great circles of standing stones at Avebury and Stonehenge were probably associated with some form of ceremonial. They, and one or two other 'henge' monuments, have distinctive, presumed processional ways connected with them, and these must be among the earliest known Wessex tracks. The West Kennet Avenue runs for 1½ miles south-eastwards from Avebury, and is known to have comprised at least 100 pairs of large stones along the sides of a broad green corridor 50ft wide. The northern third of this has been restored, and the southern end terminated on Overton Hill (118680) at a small stone circle called The Sanctuary which was excavated in 1930, and the positions of its vanished stones identified. Stonehenge had a cursus extending to its north-east — the beginnings of a long avenue course has been identified as swinging eastwards and southwards in a big loop towards the Avon. By far the most important of these cursus monuments or processional avenues was in north Dorset extending over 6 miles from Thickthorn Down (969124) north-eastwards to near Woodyates (039191), the largest known cursus in Britain.

Ridgeway routes are, or were, alleged long-distance prehistoric trackways. They could be regarded literally as highways because they tended to follow watersheds, descending to cross valleys only when there appeared to

*Part of the avenue at Avebury
(1600-1800BC)*

be no practical routes round valley-heads. But it cannot be emphasised too much that because the remains of our pre-Roman populations and their likely tracks are most widespread on the chalk uplands this does not mean that people had not lived in and used the lower land in valleys. Indeed, aerial photography supplemented by extensive field work in recent years has proved a much greater range of site-occupation on the gravel terraces along many southern and Midland valleys than had hitherto been known. Centuries of subsequent land-use and settlement have, however, obliterated most of the surface evidence.

Names of the various 'ridgeway' routes are post-Roman. Some occur in medieval and later documents, while many have simply acquired names through familiar use or local place-name associations. Undoubtedly the normal wear and tear of human and animal tread will have confirmed their continued use over many centuries. During the enclosures, particularly from the eighteenth century, low banks and hedges were constructed to define the limits of old downland tracks, both to mark their course and to prevent travellers and animals from encroaching on private land adjoining the highways. Many such highway boundary hedges survive and flourish, but in too many places barbed wire has replaced the living hedge. Sometimes, hedges down the sides of an old track have gradually grown inwards and flourished to produce an almost impenetrable linear thicket, as in the case of parts of the Great Ridgeway in Wiltshire, near the Wansdyke, and a little farther on, where it descends into the Vale of Pewsey.

# The Great Ridgeway

By definition there can be no records of prehistoric tracks so one can merely surmise that the Ridgeway, and its continuation beyond the Thames at Goring gap, the Icknield Way across the Chilterns and into East Anglia, forms the oldest road in Britain. We are here concerned with its Wessex section along the northern edge of the Berkshire Downs, then swinging more southwards by the Marlborough Downs towards Avebury. This extent of the Ridgeway now forms part of an official long-distance footpath and bridleway. South of Avebury its line becomes less apparent, but is believed to continue across Pewsey Vale and the western part of Salisbury Plain, following the downland scarp above Warminster, before taking a southwards course to Shaftesbury, and a generally south-westwards one across Dorset to the coast near Axmouth.

The fact that the Great Ridgeway passes scores of burial mounds, tumuli, Iron Age hillforts and other aspects of prehistory does not prove its prehistoric origins or importance, but merely suggests these. Artefacts found along its route certainly indicate its trading use, while prehistoric field systems near it probably relate to its significance as a route across the country. It is worth noting that the Great Ridgeway does not actually enter Avebury but passes it 2 miles away; it goes nowhere near Stonehenge, and except for that at Barbury Castle near Swindon it touches no other hillfort, although it passes close to many. The Romans found it inconvenient for their road system, and its use seems steadily to have declined since Saxon times, except for purely local needs, and as a drove road in later centuries.

Unfortunately, the Ridgeway as a long-distance footpath is defined as a byway open to *all* traffic, including motor-cycles, cars and heavy farm vehicles, all of which appear to use various sections from time to time, in spite of its being — except for a few miles near Swindon — an unsurfaced road. For much of its length from the Thames to near Avebury it is a green lane between hedges or wire fences, sometimes sunken, as near Uffington, sometimes firm, often rutted. Perhaps the stretch below the scarp of the Berkshire Downs — Blewbury Down and East Hendred, behind Segsbury hillfort and Uffington Castle, with the wooded section by Wayland's Smithy (285845) — best evokes the sense of the past. In Wiltshire the 4 miles section over Hackpen Hill (130750) southwards to Overton Down above Avebury are equally rewarding. Here, the Great Ridgeway ignores the great 'temple', while four apparently unprehistoric routes converge on it. They are just as likely to represent Neolithic approaches to the complex.

The Great Ridgeway continues to the Sanctuary on Overton Hill (118680), by the A4, where the modern long-distance footpath ends (or begins). The course continues across the Kennet, joins a metalled road through East Kennet village, but where this bends south-east (121671) the Great Ridgeway goes ahead, first as a lane, then as a grassy track. On the crest of Furze Hill the way, overgrown by brambles and thorns, crosses the Wansdyke and descends to the col between Walker's Hill and Knap Hill where it briefly joins the modern road (115638). In half a mile it leaves the road and as a very overgrown track descends by a hedge (apparently *in* it) into the Vale of

*The Ridgeway descending Hackpen Hill, near Avebury in Wiltshire*

Pewsey at Alton Priors (110623).

Its course across the Vale cannot be traced with certainty although it may have been on or near the line of the present cross-valley road through Honey Street to Broad Street (106591). Saxon charters of North Newton and Beechingstoke as translated by Dr Grundy suggest that the footpath southwards, across the next road, and heading across the fields towards Puckshipton House and a tiny brick bridge over the infant Avon, marks the ancient way. It follows a parish boundary, and the charter refers to it as 'Way to Wivelsford', and 'Highway through the Brushwood'. Wivelsford is now Wilsford, and the path enters the west of the village by a lane. This, and the path from Broad Street, according to Grundy, were 'probably part of a great highway of pre-Saxon times'.

South of Wilsford the route to the crest of the Plain is uncertain, but it probably climbed by Broadbury Banks to the tumulus on Wilsford Hill (094548), where it turned abruptly westwards. From here for the next 6 miles, to St Joan à Gore's Cross (009509) on the Devizes-Salisbury road, A360, the route crosses Ministry of Defence land and has been surfaced to take military vehicles. It remains a right-of-way and can be used as such when the red warning flags are not flying. At the top of Redhorn Hill (060554) the Ridgeway crosses the Wilton-Devizes turnpike of 1760-1, but there is no sign of the 'Red Horn Turnpike Gate' shown on the 1773 map. Nor is there any sign of the gibbet on Gibbet Knoll (026535) above Market Lavington, nor a cross at St Joan à Gore, where the 1773 map names 'Gore Cross Pond', with six tracks converging on it, including the Ridgeway. The route of this now continues south-westwards as a surfaced lane for a mile and then enters Ministry of Defence land again, with no public access. Which of the many downland tracks marks the main prehistoric route we cannot say, although the way through Imber and past Ladywell Barn (935488) and its associated tumuli could be as likely as any. Such a route would continue, crossing the Wylye valley near Bishopstrow and Norton Bavant, and heading for Sutton Veny. One alternative could have struck south-westwards from Imber, towards Heytesbury, over the Wylye to Tytherington, and southwards on to the downs. A second alternative though less direct course could have kept the Ridgeway to the edge of the northern scarp of the Plain, by the present road from St Joan à Gore's to Littleton Down (974510), then north-westwards along the line later adopted by the Salisbury-Bath coach road over Stoke Hill to Coulston Hill, passing a couple of late eighteenth-century milestones on the way.

While the later coach road descended Coulston Hill the Ridgeway route is more likely to have swung south-westwards and, keeping fairly close to the scarp edge, looped round a succession of combes along a route now followed by farm lanes to the tumulus (900512) south of Bratton Camp, thence to Beggar's Knoll and Upton Cow Down, descending to Biss Bottom on the A350, the present road adopting the old way into Warminster, continuing to the Wylye at Longbridge Deverill. The downland character would be regained on Lord's Hill, but where the A350 turns southwards there (888384), a bridleway straight ahead passes behind a copse and in a short distance reaches a point on the lonely downs (897365) where many tracks meet, two of these being the west-east arms of the Roman road from the Mendips to Old Sarum (Salisbury). Nothing in the landscape today, nor in the tracks themselves, of which only the north-south one is at all obvious, hints at the earlier importance of this site. But it is here, or hereabouts, that the various alternatives of the Great Ridgeway converge. The fact that the boundaries of seven parishes meet here is surely significant, and of the converging tracks only the Roman ones do not coincide with boundaries. The Ridgeway's course may be subsequently represented by a sketchy track running south-westwards to join the main road at 883356 continuing through East Knoyle into Shaftesbury. Alternatively it may have kept farther east along a course now marked by wriggling lanes through Donhead St Mary and across the Nadder to become a downland route near Win Green (925206).

From Win Green both Professor Good and H.W.Timperley, basing their speculations on landscape features and prehistoric sites, agree on the probable course of the Great Ridgeway across Dorset — if it ever was a continuous trackway. The minor road south-west from Win Green takes it to the upper Shaftesbury-Blandford road which it follows south to 889120, where a track known as Smugglers Lane takes it, gently at first, then more steeply as a good hollow way with a rough stony surface, down to the Iwerne valley which was probably crossed near the present main road bridge. Passing behind Hod Hill the track probably approached the River Stour by what is now a sunk and overgrown bridleway through woodland, fording the river at the apex of its large bend (852110). Although the only evidence of a crossing here is the

*Smuggler's Lane, part of the presumed Great Ridgeway above the Iwerne valley, Dorset*

name of nearby Hanford House, it should be remembered that the river's course and flow will have changed over the centuries. In the meadowland opposite a short green drove is significantly called Hodway Lane, and this continues south of the main road A357 at Gain's Cross to climb through the afforestation on Shillingstone Hill to reach open country again on Turnworth Down (813094). South-westwards from there a 2-mile length of chalky-flinty track runs along the scarp-crest of Bell Hill, with its ancient settlement sites to the south, open views to the north, and Bulbarrow ahead, and joins the modern road coming up from Okeford Fitzpaine.

On a northern spur of the Dorset chalk, Bulbarrow's 900ft crest is focus for at least eight roads and tracks, and was of undoubted significance in prehistoric times. Present roads converge on the broad hilltop at the points of a large triangle of ground left open after its occupation by a small RAF unit. Each branch splits and sub-divides to link villages, hamlets and farms. Any or all of three tracks descending south or south-westwards could be the Ridgeway's course; one follows the road down to Ansty Cross (771036) from where a bridleway runs west to Dorsetshire Gap; a second goes down as far as Moots Copse and cuts across to Breach Wood; a third starts by going westwards to Rawlsbury Camp and then descends the hillside, fords the stream near Crockers Farm (757052) and heads for the western end of Breach Wood, then by a drove-like lane to Melcombe Park Farm before climbing along the ridge to Dorsetshire Gap.

Insignificant in the distant view from the north, the Dorsetshire Gap (744031) seems to have been an important way through the northern chalk scarp. How it got its name is not known, nor is the cause of its formation,

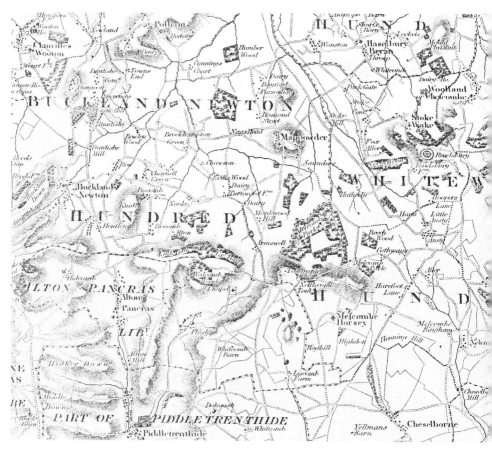

although this is presumed to be natural. As a skyline nick it may have been a useful landmark for route-finding. Deep hollow ways radiate from it, and the west-bound one may be the Ridgeway, going through woodland before reaching open plough and pasture and turning westwards into another hollow way, bluebell-beautified in spring, leading behind Nettlecombe Tout to Folly (728032). Until about 50 years ago this was The Fox, one of the remotest inns in Dorset, an indication that the minor crossings of routes here must have seen more travellers than it does today.

From Folly the alleged Ridgeway ascends Ball Hill as a steep, flinty hollow way, past the edge of Watcombe Wood and some prominent ancient enclosure banks, along the crest of Church Hill and down to the Piddle valley road, B3143, latterly its course marked by a hedge and parish boundary. The route continues westwards, climbing steadily along Barnes Lane to the old Sherborne road at 673036. Beyond this it runs northwards as a pleasant field path along the crest of Little Minterne Hill, descending as a gravelly lane to the road, A352, at Dogbury Gate (656053). On the way it throws off two old tracks which swing down to Minterne Parva and Minterne Magna, the former entering the hamlet by a medieval cross.

Dogbury Gate marks another gap in the chalk, commanded by Dogbury

Camp and High Stoy, and the Ridgeway's course was up the now-wooded slopes of this before heading south-westwards over Telegraph Hill, its line marked for $2\frac{1}{2}$ miles by the road along Gore Hill and Batcombe Hill, passing on the way, on the north side, the grey stone stump of the Cross in Hand (635037), whose origins and purpose are not known, although a connection with Cerne Abbey has been postulated. From the western end of Batcombe Hill various routes have been suggested by which the old way crossed the Frome valley. A northern one represented by the present Haydon Lane to Holywell, continuing through Evershot and by Horsey Knap and Benville Lane to Toller Down crossroads (524032) is certainly the most direct, and is favoured by Good. Timperley points out that this crosses several streams and is off the chalk for some distance, and could have been a summer route. A winter one may have kept to the south, staying on the chalk longer, by Long Ash Lane to Stagg's Folly (613005), then westwards, keeping north to Cattistock before joining the Roman road, now A356, north-westwards to Toller Down Gate.

This is conjecture. Perhaps less so is the westward continuation of the Ridgeway, which Professor Good prefers to call the Northern Trackway throughout its course from Win Green to the Channel coast. The main road north-west from Toller Down Gate forks at the Hore Stones (517035), huge slabs of grey stone embedded in the triangle of ground and grasses at the junction, which Dr Grundy suggests were Saxon boundary stones. The road westwards, following initially a parish boundary, and heading for Beaminster Down, marks the prehistoric route for 3 miles. On the Down (498034), the Harroway coming in from the north-east, by Corscombe and Yeovil, joins the Ridgeway in an area of rough pasture, brambles and gorse.

At 471053 where the modern road swings north the old way goes ahead through beech trees, over the tunnel cut in 1830-2 to take the Bridport-Beaminster-Misterton turnpike through Horn Hill. Hedgerow vegetation and tree growth have encroached on the track which winds and descends the wooded scarp of the chalk as a stony hollow way. At the foot it leaves the woodland and, as Common Water Lane, heads for Broadwindsor. It may have continued into the village, entering from the east and leaving westwards along the line of the present B3164, or it may have looped southwards at 450024 to Stoke Knap and westwards by the sunken lane running across the northern flank of Lewesdon Hill to pick up the road at 425017. Near Stoke Knap, the hollowed track passes close to Waddon Hill, and the Ridgeway route from there along the northern rim of Marshwood Vale, by the present B3164, seems to have its age emphasised by linking the Iron Age hillforts of Pilsdon Pen and Lambert's Castle.

Beyond Lambert's Castle the modern road continues as a fine ridge-road, doubtless on or close to the prehistoric track to Monkton Wyld Cross (328970). The high triangular plateau to the south-west must formerly have been a meeting-place for many tracks, for even today roads fan out in all directions. Which was the Great Ridgeway is impossible to conclude, but it may be that marked by a minor road running south-westwards over Trinity Hill (305957), south over Hargrove Hill and Shapwick Hill (303933) to Charton Cross, then west as a high-banked lane through Dowlands and Bindon to the mouth of the Axe.

As Professor Good has pointed out, from Win Green to Lambert's Castle this Dorset part of the Great Ridgeway covers over 50 miles, with some form of track or road almost the whole way, with very few gaps. It may not be a proven prehistoric continuity, but its route does stick mainly to the higher land and passes many Iron Age hillforts and ancient settlements on the way.

# The Harroway

This is the name given to the westward extension from Guildford in Surrey, through Hampshire and Wiltshire, of the ancient trackway from Kent known since medieval times as the Pilgrims' Way, derived from association with pilgrims to Canterbury's shrine of St Thomas à Becket. Much of it is now the A31 trunk road between Guildford and Farnham, while westwards from there it follows a succession of lanes and winding country roads. West of Basingstoke its line is probably marked from north of Oakley by a minor road north of the railway and roughly parallel to it, crossing the Kingsclere road at 514517, and the Newbury road at 465496. Crossing the River Test at the significantly-named Chapmansford Farm (430486) it then runs parallel to and just south of the railway before becoming lost in the sprawl of Andover.

Further west it may be represented by the minor road leaving A303 at Thruxton, and continuing by Lains Farm (273444) and Cholderton (225423) to resume its course on or close to the modern trunk road, A303, keeping north of Amesbury and taking the southern fork near Stonehenge. From here the course of the Harroway across Salisbury Plain is a succession of green lanes and chalky, flinty tracks away from traffic's roar.

Near Stonehenge it heads south-westwards (117418), across the densely tumulated Normanton Down, to the A360. Crossing this at Druid's Lodge (100390) it follows a farm lane down into the valley of the River Till which could have been easily forded at or near the present road bridge at the southern end of Berwick St James. About 300yd north in the village street a track leaves on the west by a farm, where two large upright sarsen stones suggest an ancient waymarking — or merely give protection to the corner of buildings — and the Harroway here is known as the Langford Way. Keeping south of farm buildings (a private farm road keeps north) it climbs as a narrow grass-grown track between hedges, then fences, and at 053385 crosses the broad track of the old Salisbury-Bath coach road coming up from Stapleford. Passing a small plantation, the Harroway drops down a spur as a chalky lane into Steeple Langford and crosses the River Wylye to Hanging Langford, where a cottage named 'Harroway' conveniently marks its route to the south.

After a steep climb as an overgrown hollow way, the old road reaches open downland, first as a hedged, stony lane, soon swinging south-westwards at 027362. The next mile, gently ascending, then contouring, West Hill below the earthworks of Hanging Langford camp with its peculiar, useful, modern seat in the form of a tiny trilithon, is perhaps the best part of the whole way, skylarked and sheepy, joyous with butterflies and summer flowers, and wide Wylye views.

Joining the Grovely ridge road at the beech-clad crest the Harroway crosses the Dinton-Wylye road at 005349, winds uncertainly through the trees, and acquires a metalled surface before emerging on the west as a concrete lane heading eagerly westwards between hedges. This was an old coach road from Salisbury and Wilton to the west, and a 1750 milestone in the southern hedgebank, with its

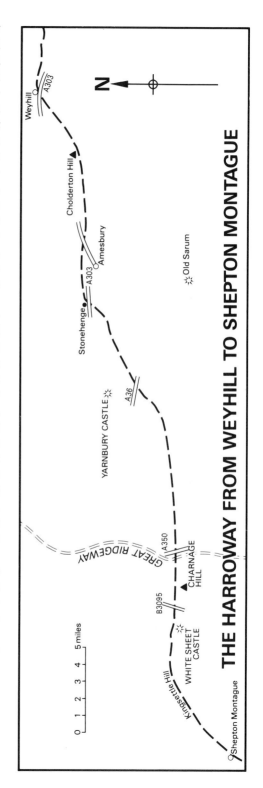

THE HARROWAY FROM WEYHILL TO SHEPTON MONTAGUE

21

*The Harroway, looking east towards Berwick St James in Wiltshire*

'SARUM X MILES' inscription facing south, substantiates this use of an ancient track. The surfaced Harroway continues slightly south of west, broad-verged, crosses two minor roads coming up from Teffont and Chilmark, and beyond the second of these (980346) regains its gentle, grassy surface. At 968343 it passes another milestone ('SARUM XII') by a barbed-wire fence and then climbs gently past the southern edge of a long shelter-belt, crosses pasture, and descends by a hedge to rejoin the familiar A303 in Chicklade Bottom (939342).

For the next 5 miles ancient and modern roads coincide, but about 2 miles west of the important A350 crossroads (now an underpass) the trunk road bends southwards on Charnage Down (853338), while a wide green lane maintains a north-westerly alignment. Thus does Harroway regain its silence, gradually swinging westwards and continuing at about 700ft for the next $3\frac{1}{2}$ miles. Near its crossing with the B3095 north of Mere (826344), and again on the northern flanks of the Iron Age White Sheet Castle, more 1750 milestones remind of the road's coaching days. These high-level miles are some of the most spacious and most lonely of the Harroway's course before it descends the western edge of Salisbury Plain by a steep, winding, rutted track. Crossing the Maiden Bradley road at 787353, it becomes a narrow, hedged lane, and, south of Kilmington Common, as a surfaced road it approaches the county boundary between ancient banks and fine beeches

*The Harroway on White Sheet Hill above Mere, Wiltshire, looking east. The turnpike milestone is dated 1750 and reads 'XXII miles from Sarum, C miles from London'*

along the northern edge of the Stourhead estate. Ahead, the massive bulk of Alfred's Tower, built in 1772 to perpetuate the memory of the great Wessex king, is the most prominent landmark on the Wiltshire-Somerset boundary. Hidden in the undergrowth on the north side of the road at the top of Kingsettle Hill is the stump of a far older boundary-mark by the side of the Harroway which here finally leaves the chalk for the intimate landscapes and winding lanes of Somerset.

Older editions of the OS map name the next few miles to Redlynch as 'Hardway', probably another name for 'Harroway', and where the road crosses the River Brue is the hamlet of Hardway. Continuing as a minor road to Shepton Montague, the course of the Harroway southwards becomes increasingly a matter of speculation. Timperley suggests it is marked by a series of minor roads and lanes, initially by Cattle Hill, across the Wincanton-Castle Cary road and the A303 to Compton Pauncefoot. From there the minor road by the east side of the park leading to Wheatsheaf Hill and the county boundary (642217) suggest a reasonable line. Wheatsheaf Hill may well have been a meeting-point of several tracks, with the Harroway marked by the present road running southwards over Holway Hill to Red Post, where it starts the descent to Sherborne.

Beyond the town one could surmise that the old road coincides with the main Dorchester road A352 for 2 miles, and then at 645135 takes the western branch of the fork past Holme Bushes and Bailey Ridge to Totnell Corner (628085). From there one route goes by Long Bridge Drove, Crocker's Knap and Wriggle River Lane through Batcombe and up the Stile Way to join the

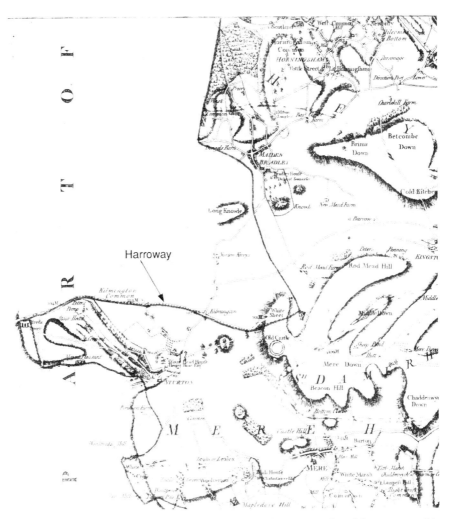

*Andrew and Dury's map of Wiltshire, 1773, showing the western edge of the county, with the Harroway cutting across the centre of the map and the milestones along its route*

Great Ridgeway on the Dorset chalk, and another continues the main road south-eastwards to the foot of High Stoy where, at 645057 a good track leaves the road to climb the western side of Telegraph Hill and join the Great Ridgeway at 642046, on a parish boundary. An alternative to these routes would have started back at Compton Pauncefoot and followed a succession of winding lanes through a landscape of small hills and streams, by South Cadbury, Sutton Montis and the Corton Ridge, then roughly along the county boundary westwards to the main Yeovil road at Mudford. South of Yeovil Sutton Bingham Reservoir hides the route, to be picked up farther south by the minor road through Halstock. At the south-west end of the village Common Lane is a pleasant green track taking the probable course of the Harroway over Woodfold Hill into Corscombe. It leaves the west end of the village opposite Knap Farm, as Ryan Lane, makes a slight 'jink' in crossing the A356, and continues south-westwards by a hedge and then a parish boundary, over Beaminster Down to join the Great Ridgeway on Minterne Hill (492035).

# Dorset Coastal Ridgeway

In Dorset the Great Ridgeway's southern counterpart has been called by Timperley the Dorset Coastal Ridgeway, and by Good the Southern Trackway. Timperley's name places it more correctly in its Wessex context, and this lead shall be followed. Both writers point out that it differs from the Great Ridgeway in two important respects. First, that throughout its length of about 33 miles from Abbotsbury Castle (555866) eastwards to the end of the chalk at Ballard Point (048813) there are only three major hillforts — Abbotsbury Castle, Chalbury and Rings Hill, although Maiden Castle is close — and few other settlements, but tumuli are very numerous, particularly along the western half. Since many burial-mounds have probably been destroyed in the past, the original total must have been enormous, suggesting a dense occupation of the southern arm of the Dorset chalk in Bronze Age times, with fewer people in later pre-Roman or Roman centuries when hillforts would have been occupied. The second point is that a 'blind' ending of the coastal ridgeway at the east, and an indeterminate one at its west, indicate that the track served no purpose as a continuous route throughout its length but is more likely to have linked a series of more localised trackways.

The western end of the Coastal Ridgeway is a few miles beyond the chalk, and the triangular earthwork of Abbotsbury Castle (556866), gravel-capped and largely hidden beneath heather and bracken, lacks the clean, distinctive contours which characterise hillforts on the chalk. From it a grassy track runs south-eastwards, across a surfaced lane, follows the crest of Wears Hill and White Hill on the scarp-edge above Abbotsbury, to join the comparatively modern Bishop's Road at 589867 and continues north-eastwards along the line of this road to Black Down, landmarked for miles by the tall obelisk of the Hardy Monument. Smitten Corner (615877) is a meeting-place for at least six tracks, including the Abbotsbury to Martinstown road. Tumuli on the surrounding heathland testify to early popularity of this upland area, and mark in increasing numbers the course of the Coastal Ridgeway as a well-defined, stony track south-eastwards over Bronkham Hill. On assuming an easterly alignment it becomes a ridge route, remaining so for many miles. Between Corton Down and Great Hill (637867) it leaves the heath and enters chalk country, and tumuli become more green and distinct. Before crossing the Upwey road (663865) the track strides along Ridge Hill, and in another half-mile dips to make a complex crossing of the Dorchester-Weymouth trunk road on Ridgeway Hill.

For the next 2 miles its course is represented by a minor modern road which it leaves at 702853, continuing south-eastwards as a surfaced farm road, and a parish boundary, over East Hill (713845) and White Horse Hill. On the way, Chalbury Hill is passed about a mile south of the Ridgeway track. There seems little doubt that this stretch of the route would have had

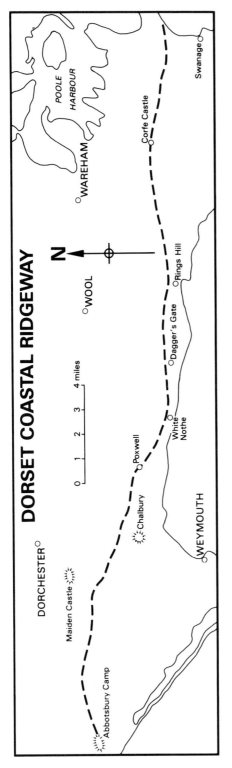

**DORSET COASTAL RIDGEWAY**

N

0 1 2 3 4 miles

strategic importance in times long past, commanding as it does the sheltered anchorage of Weymouth Bay, and the presence of the hillfort at Chalbury is not without significance. The Ridgeway meets the A353 in the woods just south of Poxwell, and there divides into two branches, possibly as a consequence of the more complex topography to the east. The northerly branch goes past ancient earthworks and follows a prominent ridge to the crest of Moigns Down (756836), across the Holworth road.

The main branch of the Coastal Ridgeway, continuing on a south-eastern alignment, crosses a small valley at Poxwell, climbs to the ridge ahead, then as a lane and well-defined track, continues through a succession of gates, past many tumuli, on the downland crest above the coast at White Nothe. As a bridle-way the ridge route pursues its distinctive course past the masts of a WT station and eastwards to Daggers Gate (811814), at a meeting of parish boundaries. Farm lanes beyond Daggers Gate suggest a possible continuation to Burngate, taken up there by the East Lulworth road and its branch which climbs to the western crest of the Purbeck chalk ridge on Whiteway Hill (882811). Timperley, however, favours a more southerly deviation from Daggers Gate, along the minor road to Bewlands Farm and West Lulworth, from where a footpath subsequently follows the edge of an earthwork below the northern side of Bindon Hill.

The ancient route seems to head to the cliff-edge by Arish Mill before climbing to the hillfort and Flower's Barrow on Rings Hill (864805), continuing over Whiteway Hill to join

*The Purbeck Ridgeway at Grange Arch, a folly of 1740, above Creech, Dorset*

the modern ridge road above Tyneham, but military use of the Lulworth ranges severely restricts public access today. However, once West Creech Hill is reached, such problems vanish, and just beyond the Steeple Car Park and Picnic Area (904817) the Dorset Coastal Ridgeway assumes a splendidly spinal character for its course to the sea near Studland.

As a flinty, chalky track it climbs gently, passing the mid-eighteenth-century folly of Grange Arch, continuing as a grassy track along Ridgeway Hill, across the minor road above East Creech, and regaining height on Knowle Hill. Parish boundaries and hedgerows mark its eastwards course, past tumuli, to Corfe gap, with a low-level alternative along the southern foot of Knowle Hill. Corfe is at the main break in the chalk ridge, and the Coastal Ridgeway resumes its true character east of the town, where a well-defined bridleway leaves the Ulwell road near Challow Farm, and, as a distinctive hollow way crosses the contours to the top of Rollington Hill (973823). Brenscombe Hill, Ailwood Down and Nine Barrow Down mark off the miles. Rempstone Stone Circle to the north (995821), a long barrow on Ailwood Down, and at least fourteen tumuli on the grassy, gorsey chalk uplands on Nine Barrows, are good pointers to a prehistoric population hereabouts.

From the crest of Nine Barrow Down (008813), the ancient route may have continued to cross the steep sides of the Godlingston gap in a direct line. Today, a bridleway descends round the southern slopes of Godlingston Hill, possibly an early successor to the ridge route, certainly hollowed into the chalk, and used in medieval times as part of the way from Swanage to Corfe. East of the gap the Coastal Ridgeway runs seawards, past a number of boundary stones along Ballard Down, and although a footpath carries it to the chalk cliffs at Ballard Point, it is probable that prehistoric routes descend north or south into Studland Bay or Swanage Bay.

## The Inkpen and North Hants Ridgeway

This is the name that Timperley gives to a track running roughly parallel to, and several miles south of, the Great Ridgeway which it eventually joins on Wilsford Hill (090550) above the Vale of Pewsey in Wiltshire. Although it can be traced eastwards through Surrey and Kent to the coast, we shall consider its alleged route from White Hill (515565) above Kingsclere westwards to its junction with the Great Ridgeway. Of historic rather than prehistoric significance is that Freemantle, a mile east of White Hill, occupies the site of one of King John's hunting-lodges and local tradition names the south-eastwards continuation of the North Hants Ridgeway from here to Basingstoke, through Hannington and Ibworth as King John's Road.

Westwards from White Hill the Ridgeway contours round the scarp of Cannon Heath Down to Watership Down and is then marked by a bridleway crossing a minor road and heading for the hillfort on Ladle Hill (479567). From there southwards over Great Litchfield Down, formerly an area of medieval hunting forest, the old route is not clear, but it appears to have crossed the main Newbury-Whitchurch road at 462552. A few miles to the north a roadside farm is called Whitway, and one wonders whether this, and the White Hill earlier, may indicate that the north-south routes on which they stand may have been used as salt ways.

The track goes westwards, past woodlands, with the groups of Seven Barrows to the north, and climbs gradually, swinging northwards over Woodcut Down. Shelter-belts and the woodlands of Sidown Hill reveal mature, man-made landscapes, while foxgloves and rosebay willow-herb by the side of the track are sure indicators of the thin clay cover on the downland chalk. From 870ft on Sidown Hill the track drops slightly to 780ft at Three Legged Cross, where it crosses the A343 Newbury-Andover road. Beyond, it maintains a direct, well-defined alignment north-westwards along the downland crest, gradually gaining height over the next 4 miles, to Walbury Hill (376617), at 979ft the highest point on the English chalk. For a short stretch near Pilot Hill the Hampshire-Berkshire boundary coincides with the old track. Steep scarp slopes to the north, and combes deeply cut back on the south, give extensive two-way views. Cultivation detracts from the expected impressiveness of Walbury Hill, but the Iron Age hillfort that follows the contours of the hill and takes advantage of its steep slopes, especially on the north, provides some distinction. The track cuts across the camp from south-east to north-west, crosses a minor road (369620), with plenty of space for car-borne walkers wishing to explore this good stretch of track, which continues westwards past Combe Gibbet, a gaunt reminder of a grisly if relatively recent past, to Inkpen Hill (357620). The northern scarp remains steep as the track leads on to Ham Hill, crosses another minor road and becomes a lane over Rivar Hill, through woods, gradually swinging south-westwards to follow the curve of the land above Rivar Down to the next road (297603).

The escarpment ends here and the course of the Inkpen Ridgeway is

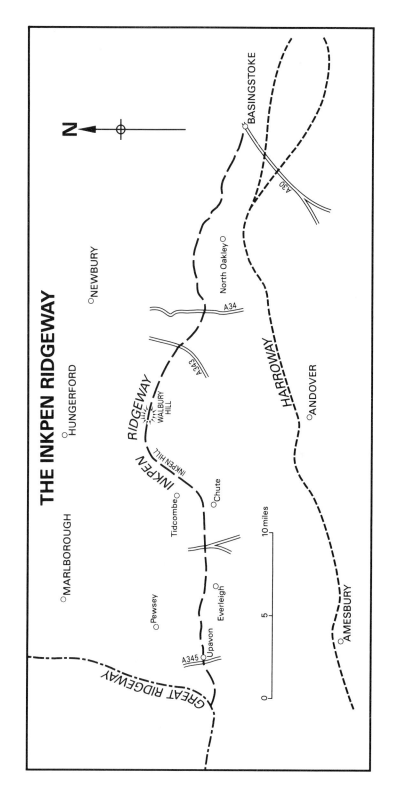

THE INKPEN RIDGEWAY

*Combe Gibbet at Inkpen Beacon, adjoining the Inkpen Ridgeway*

uncertain for the next 3 miles, since Saxon and medieval roads have confused the situation. A wide, overgrown green lane with old hedges, following the line of a parish boundary and passing a long barrow (295599) seems a probable route southwards to Tidcombe crossroads a mile away, and from there a Roman road and modern road mark its course to Scot's Poor (286562), where the former inn is now an attractive red-brick house.

Scot's Poor is the meeting-place for many tracks, with two possible Inkpen Ridgeway routes heading west and south-west. The former, a higher-level route, starts as a lane but, near a group of tumuli, becomes a footpath, crosses a minor road, and continues as a farm lane past Tinkerbarn to Brunton and Collingbourne Kingston (239558). From there the wide lane called Mill Drove continues over Thornhill Down to meet the Old Marlborough Road north of Everleigh (210553) and may mark a course. Parallel to this and a half-mile south, another lane, becoming a bridleway, heads more directly for Everleigh village, is another possibility. Meanwhile, back at Scot's Poor, the south-western route, which has an older 'feel' about it, goes past Gammon's Farm into woodland and crosses the sandy soils and scattered scrub of Sunton Heath to the Shears Inn at Cadley (255538). There it picks up a lane into Collingbourne Ducis and continues along a minor road westwards into Everleigh.

For 2 miles beyond Everleigh the present main road, A342, may well represent the route, but just past a group of tumuli (176439), a track coinciding with a parish boundary leads north-westwards over Bohune Down, to

Upavon Hill from where a path descends by a golf course to the Avon valley south of Rushall. This is RAF territory, and changes have doubtless hidden the old way. However, it probably crossed the river at or near the site of the present road bridge in Upavon on the A342, but where this road meets the A345 west of the village, a farm lane climbs ahead to regain the height of the downs, and this is likely the Inkpen Ridgeway line making for the northern edge of Casterley Camp (114538). Almost immediately it turns sharply to the north-west and in just under 2 miles reaches the tumulus on Wilsford Hill where it joins the Great Ridgeway.

## Puddletown Ridgeway

Not all ridgeways were necessarily long-distance routes. The Puddletown Ridgeway in Dorset, actually named as 'Ridgeway' on the OS map (Sheet 194), was probably a short-distance track linking the ridgeways running generally northwards from Dorchester with those on the heathland between Dorchester and Wareham. Part of it was used as a coach road in the eighteenth and nineteenth centuries, and survives now as a quiet green lane, in its eastern part enclosed by tall hedges. It is easiest to explore from east to west.

It starts west of Puddletown, running due west from the A35 at 755945, and soon becomes a green lane, with many signs of metalling doubtless from its coach-road days. Making height steadily for a mile, and passing a green drove heading southwards to Beacon Hill, it reaches a crossing of tracks at 736944, with one running south-west to Yellowham Hill and the Dorchester road, the other with a north-westerly alignment suggesting it was aiming for distant Bulbarrow. It then crosses more open downland as a hedged bridle-way with an increasingly compacted chalk surface. Across the B3143 it becomes more flinty and on Waterston Ridge passes remains of tumuli at 710945, the highest point on the route with wide-ranging views. Here a branch leads off south-westwards to Fiddler's Green and Seager's Barn, and becomes Charminster Lane past Wolfeton Eweleaze into Charminster. Meanwhile the main ridgeway descends steadily into a great bowl of cultivated downland , meeting a distinct north-south cross-track, where its westwards course seems to have diverted, probably through enclosures. A bridleway continues westwards across arable fields through gateways, crosses the Old Sherborne Road at 685953, with a lane and farm tracks taking it on into the Cerne valley at Forston.

The main A35 from Dorchester to Bridport is as good an example of a ridgeway as any modern road can be, and almost certainly follows a prehistoric route linking Poundbury Camp north-west of Dorchester and Eggardon Camp about 8 miles to the west. The first 4 miles from Dorchester are on a named Roman road, and it is quite possible that the Roman line continued the prehistoric one from Lambert's Hill (632908) where the modern road swings south-west to cross the Winterbourne valley. But west of Winterbourne the chalk uplands south of this road are littered with tumuli, barrows, and various types of earthworks whose presence would suggest that the ridge was of prehistoric significance.

It may be that there was another ridgeway even more important in Bronze Age times running almost parallel to, and just south of, the main road. On Black Down, near the Hardy Monument, the prehistoric track coming up from the south-east over Bronkham Hill, crosses the Martinstown road (616877) and continues, now as a bridleway, through woodland, joins a minor road above Littlebredy Farm, and continues north-west to the cross-roads near White Hill Barn (596893). From there its course is represented by a bridleway along the edge of arable fields over Pitcombe Down and Martin's Down, passing the site of Long Bredy Hut (575907) named from an inn that was once there, and used when this track formed part of a coach road. A lane leads steeply down into Long Bredy village from here, but the ridgeway continues north and west to the main road. North of the road a farm lane to North Barn Farm appears to carry on its line, although other tracks within the next $1\frac{1}{2}$ miles lead north-westwards from the main road, all tending to converge on the triangle within tracks and roads, where tumuli and parish boundaries indicate historic continuity. The great isolated mass of Eggardon Hill bulks prominently immediately to the north-west, a spur of downland where many ridges meet, and an obvious site for an important hillfort rivalling in size only that of Maiden Castle.

# 2 • Roman Roads

By the time of the Roman invasion of AD43, Britain was a highly-developed land populated by two to three million people living in farmsteads, hamlets, villages and fortified hill-top towns, and organised into tribes and kingdoms. Within their political, economic and ideological aims the Romans pursued a policy of absorbing an existing society into their Empire, protecting it from external enemies, and promoting a framework of law and order. In so doing they enjoyed the benefits of a successful bureaucracy, an efficient military machine, and a high level of technology, agriculture and architecture. With these skills they brought to the landscape three new features — country estates, towns, and, most importantly, a new system of communications to link the towns. Much of this road system, which lasted throughout the Roman occupation and, in some instances for centuries afterwards, is still, in a modified way, in use today.

Roads built during the early years of the occupation formed part of the process of conquest. Later ones were built for more economic purposes connected with the general civilizing of Britain, while a localised network evolved serving villas and rural estates. Of an estimated total of 10,000 miles of Roman roads and tracks it is the early military roads which had the most dramatic impact on the landscape.

The Roman army of four legions, together with large numbers of auxiliary troops, represented a total force of at least 40,000 men. It had to be supplied with food and equipment as well as a communications system. Moving initially from its base at Richborough on the east Kent coast to the London area, then to Colchester, the chief Iron Age capital in south-east Britain, it was there divided into its component legions. One remained at Colchester and was responsible for subduing East Anglia. The Second Legion moved south-westwards from London, the main road arising from its progress becoming the London-Reading-Salisbury road, subsequently extended to Dorchester and finally Exeter. From there the Second Legion turned north-eastwards and headed to Gloucester to join the Fourteenth Legion which had travelled south-westwards from Leicester, and this line, from Exeter to Leicester and Lincoln represented a frontier between the newly-conquered south-east of Britain and the defiant Iron Age kingdoms to the north-west. Along it the Foss Way was built as a frontier road used for military purposes and communications .

The historical evidence for Vespasian's campaign in Wessex rests on meagre details of Suetonius' biography of the man who became emperor. Apparently he 'fought thirty battles, subjugated two warlike tribes, and captured more than twenty *oppida* (hillforts)'. These included Hod Hill near

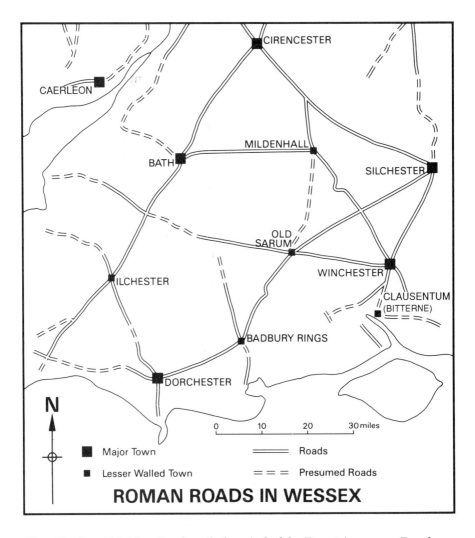

**ROMAN ROADS IN WESSEX**

Blandford and Maiden Castle, tribal capital of the Durotriges, near Dorchester, whose massive ramparts were no match against well-trained troops. Silchester, capital of the Atrebates, became an important Roman town and a nodal point in their road network, with seven roads radiating from it, of which those to London, Cirencester, Salisbury (Old Sarum) and Winchester were early military roads, with the one to Mildenhall and two to Dorchester (Oxfordshire) civil ones.

The military road to the south-west from Old Sarum aimed directly for Badbury Rings before taking a more westerly alignment to Dorchester and Exeter. A civil road ran northwards from Old Sarum to Mildenhall, but one of the most interesting of the Roman roads in Wessex is that believed to have been constructed from the Mendip Hills of Somerset eastwards to the Channel ports. Mineral exploitation was an important objective in the Roman conquest of Britain, and it seems likely that the Mendips were one of the first areas to yield lead, from ores near the surface around Charterhouse.

Mining probably started before AD43, but then, and during Roman working, transport of the metal seems to have been eastwards rather than to the Bristol Channel coast.

The Foss Way has already been referred to, and along it the main Wessex towns, planned as part of Imperial policy, were Bath and Ilchester. These were soon linked to the existing network: Bath to Mildenhall and Silchester; Dorchester to Ilchester, with a southern spur to Weymouth; and Poole to Bath. If these roads were the Roman equivalent of our motorways, thousands of minor tracks were undoubtedly more important to the Romano-British population in the same way as their modern counterparts are to present-day dwellers in the countryside. Indeed, now that it is realised that the Romano-British population was greater than originally thought, living in small settlements sometimes only half a mile apart, particularly in favoured areas of the south, it is probable that much of the present network of rural roads and lanes existed during Roman times. In Somerset, around Ilchester, an area of great density of Romano-British settlement, Roger Leech has pointed out a remarkable correlation between such settlements and the network of known medieval lanes located through individual parish studies. This shows that over 90 per cent of all sites are within 100yd of a medieval lane. Writing of north Somerset — admittedly on the edge of the area of this survey — P.J. Fowler comments that, in an area of 300sq miles based on Bath, the local economy 'revolved round a minimum of about 30 villas and 50 other settlements ... The impression of prosperous self-sufficiency ... is strengthened by the fact that it is bounded by, rather than integrated with, the main Roman road-system, from which ... branched out a system of minor roads for internal communication, linked by tracks to villas, settlements and industries'. This observation needs to be borne in mind as we look at what survives in the field of the more important Roman roads in Wessex.

Roman roads were direct rather than straight. Their surveyors doubtless appreciated that the shortest distance between two points was a straight line but they were far too sensible to follow this principle rigidly where the nature of the land dictated a change of direction to gain some advantage. Thus, they minimised departures from the straightness and constructed roads in series of long straight alignments wherever possible, taking advantage of natural gaps in downland country, using existing fords, and obviously avoiding the few major obstacles. An excellent example of this is at Chute Causeway, on the road from Winchester to Mildenhall, where Roman engineers diverted their road round the edges of a steep-sided combe, using nine short alignments totalling $4^1/_2$ miles, to avoid the steep gradients involved in pursuing a direct route of only half this distance. The main purpose of the major roads was the rapid movement of the legions — men, equipment, pack animals, carts and wagons.

Although Roman roads vary in details of construction, typically they consisted of an agger (a raised central section) of various widths, but rarely exceeding 16ft between ditches on each side. Wherever possible local materials were used, and if suitable material was available, roads were metalled, that is, given a hard surface of quarried stones, flints or even beach pebbles.

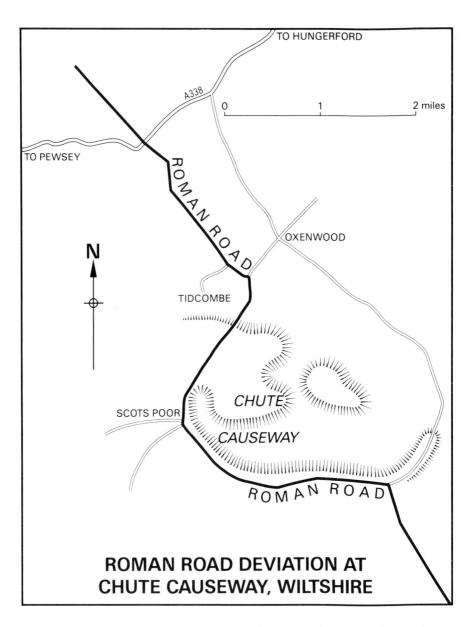

**ROMAN ROAD DEVIATION AT
CHUTE CAUSEWAY, WILTSHIRE**

Many have continued in use over succeeding centuries, with other surfaces superimposed upon them. Others have disappeared beneath the plough, or have had woods grown upon them so that today they may or may not be visible. In any case, where the proven course of a Roman road crosses private land, and is not followed by a public right-of-way, we are not really concerned with it too much here. Nor are we concerned with discovering or proving existence or otherwise of suspected Roman roads!

# Old Sarum – Silchester

Like many old roads this is known as Portway, and this name appears besides its course on the OS 1:50,000 map. In the Dark Ages, or in medieval times, a 'portway' led to a 'port' or market-town. Long sections of this road, especially near Silchester, were abandoned probably in early Saxon times, but around Andover good straight sections remain in use as country lanes.

The road was aligned on the east gate of *Sorviodunum* (Old Sarum), but its course is not picked out now until about half a mile east of the A345, (148334), when the Winterbourne Gunner road adopts its north-eastern alignment for almost 2½ miles, to the corner of the A338, beyond which it forded the River Bourne close to the present mill. For the next mile it cunningly avoided the river's winding course and probably passed through the middle of Porton village at what is now the crossroads. A bridleway, above and close to the railway identifies its straight alignment for the next 5½ miles, showing a distinct agger near the Newton Tony lane-end (227392). Its course departs from the railway near Grateley (252408), along a lane for a mile before deviating slightly eastwards below Quarley Hill, as a modern road through Monxton, and as a minor road to the large roundabout on the A303 between Andover and Weyhill. Modern development obscures it for the next 3 miles until another minor road near East Anton (377477) marks its course towards St Mary Bourne, where it descends towards the river as a field path. In 1879 excavations here identified the Roman road's metalling as 4-8in below the surface, on a width of 24ft.

Beyond St Mary Bourne the map marks its course to and through Bradley Wood, crossing the A34 at Clap Gate (462523). From there, a straight line of hedgerows beside a bridleway, along a parish boundary, indicates the alignment for 4½ miles to near Walkeridge Farm, by which time it has again become a modern road as far as the lane leading to Freemantle Farm. Here on the southern slopes of Cottington's Hill, at about 700ft, the Portway is at its highest point, and the south-western view reveals the impressive alignment arrowing its way towards distant Clap Gate. Ahead, however, the way to Silchester (*Calleva*) is largely lost, and there is little to see or follow on the ground.

# Old Sarum – Winchester

Like the previous road this left *Sorviodunum* by the east gate and the minor road through Ford now represents the first 2½ miles of its course to the crossing of the busy A30. East of the main road its prominent agger identifies it across fields, particularly in Stock Bottom from where, as a bridleway, it heads eastwards for the steep downland escarpment at Middle Winterslow, which it negotiates by a terrace and changes its alignment immediately before entering the western end of the village as a short length of lane (236332). It adopts a slightly more southerly course along the village street until this swings away south-east. As 'The Causeway', the Roman road pursues a direct line behind the main part of the village, becoming a stony holloway between high banks, and emerging at a small recreation field. It

*Roman road, now followed by the Clarendon Way, East of Middle Winterslow*

continues as a bridleway up a hill into Noad's Copse, becoming a surfaced road for the half mile to Buckholt Farm (277322). From Middle Winterslow to this point a modern long-distance footpath, the Clarendon Way between Salisbury and Winchester has followed the Roman road, and the yellow 'bishop's mitre' waymarks are a reassuring guide.

Beyond Buckholt Farm the Roman road is represented by stretches of modern road, and occasionally by field boundary hedges. It probably crossed the River Test near the site of Horsebridge station (341305), and a short length of lane west of the river may represent its course, mirrored by similar short lanes on the east, each side of the main Romsey road. East of Hoplands it descends a steep slope as a well-preserved terrace, becomes a lane for a short distance, enters West Wood, emerging as a lane on a wide agger on Pitt Down, continuing eastwards past a golf course to join the present Romsey road and entering Winchester (*Venta Belgarum*) by the west gate.

## Old Sarum – Badbury Rings

This left Old Sarum in an alignment from the east gate representing a continuation of the road from Silchester. Its course down to and across the Avon valley is not certain, but a farm road near Coldharbour Farm may represent it, and a surburban street 'Roman Road' continues it from the cemetery on the Devizes road to the skew bridge over the railway on the Wilton road, with a subsequent fording of the River Nadder's arms near

# ROMAN ROAD, OLD SARUM TO BADBURY RINGS

Continued at the bottom of the right hand map.

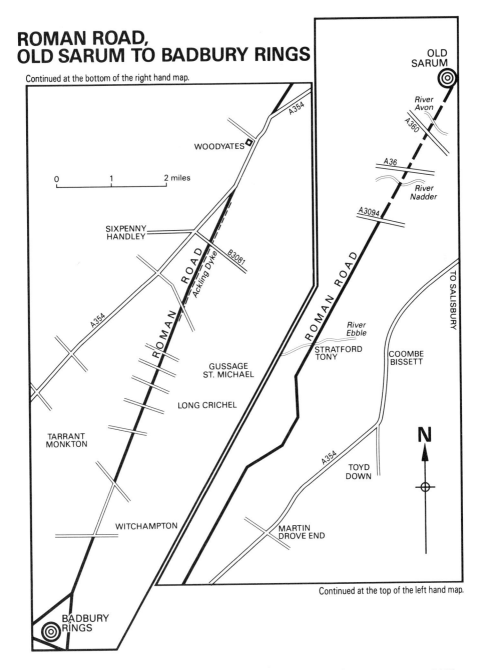

OLD SARUM

River Avon

A360

A36

River Nadder

A3094

A354

WOODYATES

0    1    2 miles

SIXPENNY HANDLEY

ROMAN ROAD

Ackling Dyke

B3081

TO SALISBURY

ROMAN ROAD

River Ebble

STRATFORD TONY

COOMBE BISSETT

GUSSAGE ST. MICHAEL

LONG CRICHEL

A354

TARRANT MONKTON

A354

TOYD DOWN

N

WITCHAMPTON

MARTIN DROVE END

Continued at the top of the left hand map.

BADBURY RINGS

Bemerton old church (St Andrew's, where George Herbert was rector, 1630-2). From there, a direct south-west alignment of 4 miles takes it across the A3094, to climb across the golf course to Racecourse Road on the wooded crest of the downs (103283) followed by a descent to the River Ebble where Stratford Tony (stony ford on the street) marks its crossing. There is a very prominent ford south of the village crossroads (093265), 200yd east of the

*The Roman road from Old Sarum to Badbury Rings, above Stratford Tony near Salisbury*

---

map's conjectured crossing, and on the route of the so-called Wilton Way, an important Saxon track. It would be sensible for later travellers to take over and use an existing ford, although it must be admitted that the nature of this delightful chalk-stream is such that fording places are not uncommon.

Having negotiated three important valleys in the first 5 miles from Old Sarum the Roman engineers faced further problems ahead. From Manor Farm, Throop (087263) the road's course is now recognised as the surfaced farm lane along the east side of a combe but this soon leaves the Roman line which continues across the valley bottom to climb the opposite side, as a terrace, into woodland from which it emerges along a hedgeside to join another farm track, rough-surfaced between high hedge banks with trees (080254).

Here the Roman engineers recognised that if the original alignment were continued the road would need to descend and climb a series of spurs of the chalk downs. So they diverted the route eastwards, then south, and finally west before regaining the old line. The map shows these diversions particularly at 081254 and 070234, with each being about 20°. Thus, steep gradients were avoided. The first part of this Roman engineering is easy to follow on the ground, and for a short while, after the farm lane has left the Roman route, the latter's course takes it to the crest of the downs near a tumulus (076244) on a grassy track summer-rich in wild flowers and grasses. When the author tried to follow it further the course lay hidden beneath tall corn.

On regaining its former alignment, however, the Roman road assumes a new dimension. From the corner of Knighton Wood, shortly after crossing the much older Ox Drove (062232) its course is seen as a very prominent agger. At the southern corner of the wood it crosses Grim's Ditch (052221), forms a county boundary for a mile, and at Bokerley Junction crosses Bokerley Ditch (032198) and enters Dorset on a slightly more southerly alignment. For the next 1½ miles the main A354 Salisbury-Blandford road is superimposed on the Roman one but this then turns westwards to leave the Roman road surging ahead on its magnificent agger. Because this section is on open downland and so splendidly visible, and, more importantly, has not been used since the fifth century, it remains intact as a massive linear bank over 40ft across, raised 4 or 5ft high, running for 2 or 3 miles across country, one of the finest surviving examples of Roman road in Britain. Known here as Ackling Dyke, the best view of it, and access to it, is from the B3081 Ringwood road (016164) a few hundred yards east of the Handley round-about on A354.

From here a cart-track follows it southwards first alongside a wood, then across open country, as a hedged farm lane to the little valley of the Gussage brook (994110), climbing the ridge beyond by means of a distinct S-bend, then as a well-defined field path to the next valley, that of the Crichel stream (989097) where there is a small ford today. From then onwards to Badbury Rings, except for a half-mile stretch north of Sheephouse, the Roman line is clearly identified, easily followed on the ground by a series of lanes, bridle-ways and tracks. The prominent view ahead to Badbury Rings indicates that the alignment was aimed at the eastern side of the great earthwork, thus suggesting, according to Margary, that it was planned to link up with a highway from Poole Harbour rather than continuing south-westwards to Dorchester. North of Badbury the road passes between King Down Farm and an ancient wood called The Oaks, known locally as the Druid Oaks, their predecessors probably being recognised by Leland in his *Itinerary* of about 1540 as 'the famous wood of Bathan'.

At 968035 the alignment changes, and the way to Dorchester swings much more to the south-west, aiming for the western side of the Rings. Lost initially in fields the line is soon picked up at a parish boundary hedge, displaying a wide, prominent agger across pasture, before becoming one of a number of flinty, pebbly tracks used by visiting motorists to the large car-parking space by the Rings. The most prominent of these, leading to the B3082, passes many tumuli and may well be the Roman line.

## Badbury Rings – Dorchester

Most of the 19 miles of this road have been lost, but those parts which survive are still rewarding to follow. Across the Wimborne-Blandford road its course approximates to the present road to Shapwick, where the village street lies on the precise line which subsequently passes south of the church, fords the River Stour, and crosses the water-meadows on a very slight agger. For the next 3½ miles the line has vanished and little more than a line of hedges marks its course to Winterborne Kingston, where it becomes a lane (868978) east of the village. Passing the church it crosses the main village road and for a while is identified on the 1:25,000 map as Bagwood Road, although this quickly deviates from the Roman line which passes through Bagwood

*What is believed to be a Roman milestone* in situ, *near Stinsford, Dorset*

Coppice and the site of a Roman well. Identification is difficult for the next 2 miles, but near Ashley Barn Farm (813955) a prominent hollow way probably marks its course. The modern minor road between Milborne St Andrew and Affpuddle crosses the stream on a course between two right-angled but rounded bends, the intervening 150yd being precisely on the Roman road, presumably to take advantage of its firm foundations and the probable ford used centuries ago, now replaced by a bridge.

Onwards to Tolpuddle the line is marked, though not clearly, as a footpath, but its subsequent course over Puddletown Heath has now become obscured beneath forest plantations. However, where it crosses the minor road from Puddletown to Stinsford (745925), its course into the forest has been adapted for use by forestry vehicles, and this well-maintained surface may not, in a way, be much different from its Roman original! Before emerging from woodland the Roman road, and its modern counterpart, makes a marked swing northwards for about 100yd before the second part of an S-bend enables it to regain the alignment. Across the open expanse of Bhompston Heath it has degenerated into an eroded footpath gradually climbing to the skyline at the southern end of more woodland. Perhaps this is the section described by Hardy in his poem *Roman Road*:

> 'The Roman road runs straight and bare,
> As pale parting-line in hair,
> Across the heath'.

The Roman road crosses public footpaths here which form part of Thorncombe Wood Nature Trail, close to a small pond, and undulations in the heather-covered flinty ground may represent the agger. In Thorncombe Wood itself the line can only be surmised, but farther west the agger can be detected in Kingston Maurward Park, between a bend in the lane and a small chalk pit to the north. The Roman road runs close to the north side of the present road opposite some cottages, continuing to the junction with the main A35. At this point, on the southern bank of the road, a large cylindrical stone $3\frac{1}{2}$ft high, is probably a Roman milestone *in situ*. Although no inscription survives it is significantly just 1 Roman mile from *Durnovaria*, the present Dorchester, which it reached by a route some distance north of the present one and which may well have continued in use until 1748 when the modern eastern approach via Grey's Bridge was constructed. No trace of the Roman crossing of the River Frome and its valley now survives.

*Grey's Bridge, Dorchester, built in 1747, an entirely new structure which changed completely the eastern approach into the town. For centuries this had been over Stockham Bridge and Holloway*

## Dorchester – Axminster

As a Roman town Dorchester was founded about AD70 on the tribal capital of the Durotriges. Although it undoubtedly had military significance, being on the army's main road to the south-west, no structural remains of a Roman fort have been identified. Fragments of a town wall, and remarkably complete foundations of a town house has been discovered in Colliton Park, behind the modern County Hall. Outside the line of the Roman walls the Neolithic earthwork of Maumbury Rings (690899) was adapted for use as a Roman amphitheatre, while the aqueduct which brought water to the town can be traced in places above the south side of the Frome valley as a hillside shelf visible from Poundbury Camp and the Roman road on Fordington Down (670911, 669916, 655917). Dorchester's present street plan, however, is not the Roman one although parish boundaries may relate to the period of Roman occupation.

The road to the west falls into three distinct sections, each related to the different topography it passes through. The first 10 miles to Eggardon Hill are mainly on downland, and the next 16 miles to Axminster negotiating the awkward hill country of west Dorset. Leaving Dorchester by the west gate and following the main Bridport road, A35, there is a stretch for half a mile slightly south of west, followed by a straight alignment of 2½ miles due west as a fine raised highway, a busy modern trunk road. Two short alignments by Hart Hill Plantation swing it north-west, and on Lambert's Hill, where the main road turns to the south-west (632908), a minor road continues the Roman line north-westwards for another 1½ miles, with a deviation at Hogleaze Bungalow to a line slightly south of west. For the whole of this downland course the Roman road forms parish boundaries, and alignments are frequently adjusted to keep it on the ridge, with steep combes to the north near Compton Valence. A 45° turn at 577936 returns it to a westerly course, with the masts of a wireless station ahead. Beyond them, at Two Gates (552938) the Roman road leaves the modern one, as a hedgeside track curving in a gentle arc to meet in half a mile at a gate the modern minor road from Askerswell. From here a bridleway opposite descends the north side of a long spur to South Eggardon Farm probably on the Roman line which continues as a farm lane south-eastwards to Spyway Green.

A course through the broken country of Dorset's Liassic limestone hills, scenically interesting, undoubtedly posed a succession of problems for Roman and subsequent road-builders. The Roman route is by no means certain, one choice being represented by the narrow lane along the south side of the River Asker's valley through Matravers and Uploders to Yondover, followed by footpaths round Boarsbarrow Hill joining a farm lane which reaches the main road half a mile east of Bridport. Alternatively, it may be that of the modern minor road from Spyway, joining the main A35 at Vinney Cross (509928) and continuing as the present road to and through Bridport. In either event it seems probable that the main road generally adopts that of the Roman engineers as far as Morecombelake, since excavations along this section revealed an older stone surface 4ft below the present one.

Beyond Morecombelake the main road follows a modern course, while the Roman route took a course now marked by a surfaced farm lane by Morcombe Farm to Greenlands Farm, then as a terrace running up the hillside below the present farm lane which it joins at the crest of Stonebarrow Hill (390935). Here it keeps a hedge to the north, open downland to the south, as it crosses National Trust property where motorists use its well-drained surface to lead them to crisp turf where they can park and enjoy the glorious seaward view. Descending to Newlands as the present narrow holloway between trees, the Roman road continued through Charmouth along the line of the main A35, but beyond the town its exact course is not proven. A probable route took it inland along the line of the old main road by Fern Hill, Penn Cross and Burrowhayes Cross to Symonds Down. Just beyond Burrowhayes Cross (315965) a line of hedgerows may represent it and lower down, an agger can be identified crossing a meadow, and Woodbury Lane running west-north-west from Symonds Down Farm may well be on or near the Roman road, crossing the Foss Way on the southern outskirts of Axminster at Woodbury Cross (293976) where it becomes a footpath adjoining a hollow way leading towards the River Axe. The alignment from Symonds Down Farm continues across the Axe valley, and west of Yarty Bridge (282980) the straight road up Shute Hill takes it beyond our present survey.

## Foss Way

Since we have now encountered this famous Roman road it seems logical to consider its course next. Its coastal starting-point is not known, although is usually accepted to have been on the tidal inlet of the River Axe near Axmouth, and towards Axminster the present road A358 approximates to its line as far as Woodbury Cross (see above). North of Axminster the main road continues its course to Tytherleigh, north of which the B3167 approximates its route towards Cricket St Thomas and it may be significant that near the farm called Street (353071), where the modern road bends westwards, traces of the Roman road are said to have been identified.

After a 4-mile gap in its known course, the Foss Way resumes its north-eastern alignment at Dinnington as a deeply sunken surfaced lane, narrowing into a cutting at Lopen (424147). Shortly afterwards it crosses another lane and becomes a bridleway for half a mile, very overgrown at its northern

*Foss Way south of Beacon Hill, near Shepton Mallet*

end where it enters Over Stratton and continues as a hedged lane for another mile. From Petherton Bridge , where there is no trace of it, the widened A303 hides the Roman road beneath its modern surface almost to Ilchester. The main road now bypasses the town, leaving the old alignment to be retained as a minor road to the town centre, making a slight westwards bend just after passing the new A37 bypass (520225).

Known by the Romans as *Lindinus*, Ilchester became the capital of one of the Durotrigan tribal areas, probably in the early third century having begun as a Roman fort around AD50. At the peak of its prosperity it is thought to have had a population of 2,000, and the present St Mary's church is roughly above the centre of the Romano-British town, 200yd east of the Foss Way which passed through the heart of the town south of the River Yeo. Evidence of about forty Romano-British structures have been discovered, with another nine or ten north of the river in the parish of Northover.

After a mile further along what is now a minor road the Foss Way continues, almost ruler straight as A37 to Wraxall, and for much of this section modern travellers can recognise that its course is markedly raised above that of the surrounding land. Only near Babcary does the modern road make a strange westward deviation for half a mile. Within the southern part of this enclave the Roman line has vanished, but in the northern half it is identified in a wet, overgrown, hedged lane. At Wraxall (602364) the road climbs 300ft, the modern zigzags probably reflecting those of its predecessor.

*Foss Way running north from Beacon Hill, above Shepton Mallet, Somerset*

Near Pye Hill (617380) the descending gradient for the modern road has been eased, but the line of the Foss Way is continued as a minor road slightly to the east, and from the crest the course of the A37 leaves no doubt as to its Roman origins. Two miles ahead a minor road continues the Roman line diagonally crossing the deviated main road at Cannard's Grave Inn, crossing the A361 at Charlton on the eastern edge of Shepton Mallet (631432).

From here the next 3 miles of the Foss Way are for walkers, and from the turnpike house, embellished with ammonite fossils in its walls, it is a surfaced lane, soon becoming a green one, with occasional paving being evidence of its later use as a coach road. Crossing two modern minor roads the Foss Way continues as a beguiling track between high bushes, and with a distinct agger. At a beech plantation there is a boundary stone, and beyond it the road climbs steeply to the wooded crest of Beacon Hill. After a short descent the Foss Way crosses another important Roman road, the so-called 'lead road' from the Mendip mines to Old Sarum, here adopted by a modern road (638461). From here the Foss continues northwards as a hedged lane to Oakhill, through parkland, to join and align on, the A367 (643477).

This main road crosses the steep Nettlebridge valley by a series of zigzags to ease the gradient, but the Roman road took it more directly, its course down the south side represented by a minor road and up the north side as a field path beside a holloway beside a hedge. Continuing then as the modern main road through Stratton-on-the-Fosse, the Roman road followed a direct course across two more steep valleys, its line identified by tracks as far as Clandown, on a well-preserved agger 15ft wide and 3ft high, although its course is often obscured by overgrown hedges. Beyond Peasedown St John, a bridleway and hedges mark the Foss Way across the Cam Brook valley at Dunkerton, for 2 miles before it rejoins the A367 north of Fosse Farm (725609).

## Mildenhall – Bath

The exact course of the Roman road from Mildenhall (*Cunetio*) to and through Marlborough is not known, although in or near the present town it must have crossed the River Kennet. For the next $3^1/_2$ miles westwards its course is probably approximated by the main road A4, but near North Farm at West Overton (131684) the modern route curves southwards, while the Roman road continues directly across Overton Down on a well-defined agger, across the older Ridgeway about 150yd north of the roadside café. Silbury Hill, to the west, must surely have been used as the next sighting point for the Roman engineers, roughly on the line of the A4, passing the southern base of the great artificial mound. A slight deviation southwards took the Roman road on to a straight $2^1/_2$ miles alignment to Calstone Down. East of the point where it crosses the present Beckhampton-Devizes road (075683) it shows as a conspicuous agger for over 300yd, still traceable westwards as an increasingly faint undulation in the fields, followed by a footpath climbing the downs and picking up a line of hedgerows. Swinging slightly southwards it continues as a well-defined grassy track, climbing on a good contouring terrace towards the plantation to the northern side of Morgan's Hill (029674).

It continues through the Morgan's Hill Nature Reserve, and at 025672 meets the Wansdyke, a great Saxon linear earthwork coming up from the south-east which makes good use of the Roman agger all the way from here to Bath. By heightening the agger and deepening its ditch on the northern side this has had the effect of both preserving the Roman line and making it largely unusable as a road. It has, however, become a parish boundary for many miles, usually identified by hedgerows, occasionally adopted as a farm track, and in some sections, especially near Broad's Green (985672), as a field path. A slight directional change west of this point took the road past Wans House, south of Sandy Lane, where another deviation carried it into Spye Park, emerging near Bowden Hill, where it descended to the Avon valley to cross the river at a place called Lydford (918673). The alignment, indicated by hedgerows, is well identified in the view from Bewley Common, on the road between Lacock and Sandy Lane. Hedgerows, an overgrown ditch, and parish boundaries continue to mark its course westwards to a final descent to Bathford and Batheaston where it joined the Foss Way into Bath.

## Old Sarum – Mendip

Lead-mining was being carried on around Charterhouse-on-Mendip (503565) within a few years of the Conquest, for a lead ingot dated AD49, almost certainly from that area, was found in the valley of the River Test in Hampshire, close to the Roman road from Old Sarum to Winchester. That find, together with others, suggests that the lead was carried eastwards from Mendip, for subsequent shipment from the coast near Southampton. Much

*Line of the Roman 'lead road' from the Mendips on Great Ridge, near Chicklade, Wiltshire*

of the route followed, particularly over the chalk downland, was probably on an older track, and can be regarded as a Romanised ridgeway.

No trace of it exists for the first few miles from Old Sarum westwards, but its course through Grovely Wood has been identified, north of a broad ride, and keeping north of Grovely Lodge (048340). Near Dinton Beeches it joins the Harroway which has come up over West Hill, and for nearly 2 miles accompanies it. The Roman road turns north-west at 988359, joins the main A303 for a mile along Chilmark Down before taking an alignment slightly north of west, adopted as a parish boundary, into the old woodlands of Great Ridge. The OS map marks this section as Roman road (course of), and the broad, grassy ride must approximate to its course. After emerging from the wood it reaches a meeting of five tracks (898365) one of which is the Great Ridgeway. It continues westwards, across arable land, but beyond the Warminster-Shaftesbury road is lost in more arable.

The map suggests it is heading for Monkton Deverill in the valley of the upper River Wylye, but there is no trace on the sloping downland. However, a short stretch of modern road south of the church at Monkton Deverill leads westwards to join the B3095, and a footpath north of this follows what may have been an agger across a grassy field towards the river. At 852373 there is a very good ford taking a lane across the Wylye at Kingston Deverill. In fact, the lane runs into and along the river for several yards where a bend reduces the current's strong flow, and the placid shallow water would have made a safe crossing place. Brian Berry, who explored this area so thoroughly in the early 1960s while researching into the route of the 'lost' Roman road from

*Site of a ford at Kingston Deverill, probably of Roman origin, and shared by the Roman roads from the Mendips to Old Sarum and from Bath to Poole*

Poole to Bath, believes — with some justification — that the 'lead road' and the north-south one met here and shared the ford.

Westwards from here the route of the 'lead road' has not been mapped, but it is reasonable to surmise that its line is that of the present minor road to Maiden Bradley from where Bradley Lane continues it to 792394, where a track leads off into woodland, soon reaching Gare Hill (780401). From there a modern minor road descends the escarpment on the Roman line. At the foot of the hill, where the road bends northwards, the Roman route continues, albeit invisibly, to Walk Farm (762410), but here and for many miles, it is not traceable. Not until it reaches the higher land of the eastern Mendips at Long Cross (650453) does it become apparent again, where a straight alignment of 2 miles takes its modern road counterpart north of Beacon Hill and across the Foss Way to the main A37 north of Shepton Mallet. The next short stretch of minor road to Warren Farm is on or near the old road and a line of hedgerows suggests its line by a golf course north of Maesbury Hill, and more hedgerows continue it to near Whitnell Corner (597487), where the present road carries it to Green Ore and beyond. Its course then deviates from the modern road, but can be identified south of the Castle of Comfort Inn. Further west, Ubley Warren Farm (513553) lies on the presumed Roman line which continues north-west to the site of the former mining settlement at Town Field, Charterhouse.

# 3 • Medieval Routes

Roman colonial rule came to an end in AD410. For some years previously the Roman troops had steadily been withdrawn, and even before then occasions had occurred when the native Britons had elected their own emperors, but 410 represents the time when the Romans abandoned responsibility for defence. However, 350 years of Roman occupation and rule ensured that Roman influence would continue for some time, although for how long is a subject for historical argument. It is known that by about the middle of the fifth century there was an increasing Anglo-Saxon infiltration from the continent which, by the end of the century, had become strong enough in the southern part of Britain to defeat any organised resistance from squabbling British factions.

Neither archaeological nor historical research has yielded much convincing evidence proving the location of early settlements of the post-Roman period. There are certainly no known roads which can be dated to that time. However, Wessex can show, if only in a negative way, one feature relating to the history of roads. Bokerley Dyke is a large defensive bank and ditch running for 4 miles across the downs of Cranborne Chase on the Dorset-Hampshire border, and at one point (033198) it cuts across the Roman road from Salisbury to Dorchester. Excavation at this point dated it to the late fourth century AD and that it must have been intended to block the road, possibly against an attack by Saxon raiders in 367. But the blockage was soon removed and the road re-opened. However, a century later, presumably when a new danger threatened, the dyke was rebuilt across the road, closing it until the turnpike days of the mid-eighteenth century. If this represented an almost instant ending of use of an important Roman road, it is more probable that it was exceptional and that most Roman roads gradually fell out of use. Certainly there would be no repair or maintenance, and there was no justification for use as long-distance communications. Only perhaps when short lengths were used for local traffic did the main roads survive.

Although recent archaeological research has thrown new light upon the pattern and form of Saxon settlement from the late sixth century onwards, there is virtually no evidence for positively dating any tracks to the centuries immediately following the departure of the Romans. However, changes did take place after the establishment of major kingdoms of which Wessex became one in the late seventh century. The church became formally organised, with the creation of the see of Sherborne, and Aldhelm as its first bishop.

The new diocese embraced the whole of Dorset, Somerset and Wiltshire, and Aldhelm's chronicler, William of Malmesbury (where Aldhelm had been its first abbot) tells us that Aldhelm 'diligently travelled throughout his diocese'. While it is known that he visited Frome, Bradford-on-Avon (where he built a church, parts of which survive today), Wareham and Doulting, we know nothing of the routes he followed.

The ninth century saw Wessex threatened and attacked by Vikings, and it was in 878 that King Alfred (of Wessex) ended their domination of the kingdom, as tersely recorded in the *Anglo-Saxon Chronicle*:

'In the seventh week after Easter rode (Alfred) to Egbert's Stone on the east of Selwood. And there came in unto him all the men of Somerset, and the Wiltshire men, and of the Hampshire men such as were yet on this side of the water'

(Which water, and where were the Dorset men, one wonders?)

'And the next day he went on thence to Iglea, and next again to Ethandune. And there he fought against the whole host, and put them to flight, and chased them even unto their stronghold (Chippenham) and there he sat fourteen nights'.

All stirring stuff, but identifying the places poses problems. Alfred had wintered at Athelney, near Lyng, in the Somerset levels (346292). Reference to the Somerset section of the Harroway has already been made, and it may be significant that, although the site of Egbert's Stone has not been identified, one theory places it at Brixton Deverill, a few miles south of Warminster, and another suggests it is near the position now occupied by Alfred's Tower, an enormous triangular brick tower erected in 1772 by Henry Hoare of Stourhead to mark the alleged meeting place for Alfred's men. The author favours this suggestion, for not only is the site at the crest of a conspicuous hill where Wiltshire downland meets Somerset lowland on the ancient and present county boundary in what was Selwood Forest, but the Harroway, traceable for many miles westwards, passes this point. Furthermore, although few writers have pointed this out, there is, deeply hidden in the undergrowth near the north side of the road, the socket-stone of a former cross or boundary-marker (746352). The road up the hill from Redlynch is called Kingsettle Hill, and the wood to the north-east is King's Wood Warren. '*Iglea*' has not been identified, but the outlying chalk hill 'Cley Hill' (838450), 2 miles west of Warminster, and 9 miles — a day's march — north-east of Alfred's Tower, crowned by an Iron Age fort, would have been a splendid vantage point from which Alfred could have observed any Danish advance from the north. '*Ethandune*' has been identified by historians as either Edington in Somerset or Edington in Wiltshire, the more favoured site of the subsequent battle.

Although this is surmise it shows that roads and tracks in use today in this landscape of the Wiltshire-Somerset border may have played an important role at one of the decisive moments in English history. As a result of his victory Alfred consolidated his rule in Wessex and built up a defensive system based on a series of fortified *burhs*, the first towns to be established since the Roman occupation. The sites of these were based mainly on military considerations and whether they succeeded subsequently as towns depended on their developing function as market and trade centres. Badly situated ones declined, good ones prospered and became, for the most part, successful route centres.

Evidence for the existence of Wessex towns in the tenth century comes from the *Anglo-Saxon Chronicle* and the remarkable document known as the *Burghal Hidage*, which lists thirty *burhs* established by Alfred before his death in 899. These included former Roman towns whose defences were still available, such as Winchester, Dorchester and Bath, and others which were newly fortified including Wareham, Shaftesbury, Bridport, Wilton and Langport. All these acquired some degree of economic importance, developing into trading centres and almost certainly causing a new, basic pattern of roads to evolve, linking them with each other and with the scattered settlements between.

Christopher Taylor has pointed out how the road system based on Winchester changed as a result of its becoming replanned as the fortified capital of Alfred's new Wessex Kingdom, 880-6, with new political, administrative and economic importance. Roads radiated from it in all directions. Some Roman ones were revitalised: the roads north-east to London, southwards for some miles towards Southampton, north-westwards to Mildenhall. This was used by the Saxons for 3 miles only, after which it was abandoned in favour of a more northerly and very direct route, now the A34 to Newbury and Oxford. The Roman road to the west, via Old Sarum, was almost completely abandoned, unusually so as it would have given a good route to another important town, Wilton. Presumably, four or five centuries of decreasing use must have erased it from memory, so the Saxons established a new road, now A272, crossing the River Test at Stockbridge. All watersheds around Salisbury have ridgeways, and all are named as thoroughfares in Saxon charters, but only two are still in use as roads, the A360 to Devizes and A345 to Amesbury. The others especially to the west and south-west, are quiet downland tracks between fields of corn, and, as John Chandler emphasises, 'sensible roads ... designed by no-one, belonging to everyone, and costing nothing to maintain.'

During the eighth, ninth and tenth centuries a new pattern of settlement evolved, and the medieval nucleated village began to appear. Historians are not yet agreed why this happened, but it is likely that the newly-appearing villages were related to a road system already in use. New trackways were almost certainly developed, but the documentary evidence for these, and the definition of them, is slight in the extreme.

Many surviving Saxon land charters from the eighth century onwards refer to '*wegs*' or ways along territorial boundaries, and one of the commonest such road names is '*here-paeth*', probably meaning a track used mainly for military purposes, either by troops moving to the sites of important battles, by patrolling forces, or by government officials accompanied by armed escorts. There is no reason why the civilian population should not also have used such tracks when it was necessary for them to travel outside their local area.

One of the best-known *here-paeths*, still called 'Herepath' or 'Green Street', on the 1:25,000 OS map of the Marlborough Downs, runs for about 7 miles between Avebury and Marlborough, across the downs north of the A4. Parts

*Saxon* herepath *above Avebury, Wiltshire*

of it were definitely known as a *here-paeth* in Saxon times, but since its course leads directly eastwards from the Avebury stone circle, and passes innumerable tumuli on the way, it seems likely that it was used in prehistoric times. In fact, its western section running up the downs from Avebury, crossing the Ridgeway at 125708, would have been the obvious link between the Ridgeway and the stone circle. Today, this is a wide, rutted track used by farm traffic. On Overton Down east of the Ridgeway it is an open path crossing a field littered with boulders, part of the 610-acre Fyfield Down National Nature Reserve. After passing training gallops the track descends to a wooded dell before climbing past more, larger, sarsen stones, many hidden among thistles. By now a gravelly track the old way leaves the nature reserve, rises over Clatford Down, with the 'Devil's Den', another burial chamber a mile to the south. After another descent past cornfields, where a track to Hackpen Hill and the Ridgeway leads off to the north-west (152716), the Herepath swings south-east past a series of shelter-belts, continuing as a firm track past grassy gallops, and along more gallops on Barton Down to join the Rockley road across Marlborough Common and eventually into the town.

Another Wiltshire *here-paeth*, also mentioned in a Saxon charter, occurs in the Vale of Pewsey where its existence survives in the name of Harepath Farm (060640) near Bishop's Cannings. Its course may be represented by the present road from Calne towards Bishop's Cannings, becoming a bridlepath and farm track past Bourton and Easton Farm, continuing in this vein past Harepath Farm to join the valley road at Allington. This is a deep holloway for part of its course beneath the downs, indicative of long usage.

*Wilton Way, looking south, on Throop Hill*

In AD827 when Egbert created the English Kingdom by uniting the separate states of the Heptarchy he founded a Benedictine priory at Wilton, later converted by Alfred into an abbey. Before and after the Conquest, and until the founding of New Sarum in the early thirteenth century, Wilton was a favoured place with Saxon kings and nobles and for a while was the capital of Wessex. Its importance, and the outlying estates of its abbey, undoubtedly meant there was much travelling to and from it. Saxon documents suggest it served as a guest-house for noble travellers, and one particular route acquired the name 'Wilton Way'. North of the town we cannot be sure where it aimed for, but to the south it certainly headed in the direction of Wimborne, possibly aiming for Christchurch. Its course as far as Cranborne has a directness suggesting a made route, but some stretches are almost certainly on far older tracks across the downs.

From Wilton to the old racecourse the original line has been obscured by the emparkment associated with Wilton House in the sixteenth century. South of the grandstand the present road to Stratford Tony may represent it, and it probably crossed the River Ebble by the ford just east of the church (093265). Beyond the river a hollowed track climbs ahead through woodland and soon assumes a straight course southwards, a delightful green lane between high, old hedges. A Saxon charter described it here as 'White Way'. It continues as a green lane to the main Salisbury-Blandford road, crosses this and becomes a farm lane, past Toyd Clump, where it forms the county boundary for the next $1^1/_2$ miles over Little Toyd Down. Beyond Toyd Farm it joins another old road, and two boundary stones mark this important junction (089205). One is a low boulder sunk in the grass, and the adjacent one, decorated with a crown-like emblem, bears the date 1895, when the boundary-line between Wiltshire and Hampshire was revised.

Historical and archaeological evidence indicates that by the eleventh century our present road network was virtually complete. Apart from motorways and new roads in areas of urban growth our basic road pattern is very much what it was 900 years ago, and indeed much of it may have been very old even then. From the Norman Conquest onwards an increasing amount of documentary evidence has added to our knowledge of roads and tracks.

With the coming of the Normans and during the following two centuries there was a resurgence of urban life. Roman settlements at Dorchester, Ilchester, Bath, Winchester and Mildenhall (near Marlborough) were supplemented by Saxon *burhs* established by King Alfred or his successors at Wareham, Shaftesbury, Wimborne and Marlborough. Undoubtedly Bristol was the largest and most important town in, or on the edge of, Wessex, a royal possession with a military garrison, a centre of trade and commerce, and comparable, perhaps, with York, Norwich and Lincoln, but tiny by today's standards, with a population of under 5,000 — considerably less than that of Sherborne today. The towns mentioned probably had about 1,000 inhabitants, while a number of other smaller towns existing at the time of the Conquest, with a population of about 500 each (equivalent to a small village today) included Bedwyn, Bradford-on-Avon, Bruton, Calne, Crewkerne, Frome, Langport, Marlborough, Milborne Port, Sarum, Tilshead and Wimborne.

Towns also developed where the Norman aristocracy established castles as at Castle Cary, Corfe, Devizes and Taunton. At these places the natural garrison need for food and other goods stimulated local trade, while the security provided by the castle encouraged visiting merchants. Craftsmen settled beneath the protection of the castle defences so that it would not be long before a small but flourishing market town had developed. Parallel to this urban growth was the founding of many monasteries. For almost six centuries, from AD940 to the Dissolution, Glastonbury Abbey was the wealthiest monastery in England. Lesser, but nevertheless important, Benedictine houses were founded at Abbotsbury and Bruton, and for nuns at Amesbury and Wilton, while the nunnery at Shaftesbury became the wealthiest in the kingdom. The Cistercian Order favoured areas away from the towns and established abbeys at Bindon and Forde in Dorset, while there was a house of Cistercian nuns at Tarrant Crawford, near Blandford. In Wiltshire, Cistercian influence was much less, with two modest foundations at Loxwell and Stanley.

Monastic influence on roads and trackways lay not only at the places where they were established but in the communications between parent abbeys and their distant estates, and from the estates to markets. Glastonbury Abbey owned many estates in Wiltshire, especially in the Deverill valley south of Warminster, at Durrington north of Amesbury, and at Coombe Bissett near Salisbury. The abbey's grain accounts show that pack-

*The twelfth-century walls of the Norman castle and hilltop town of Old Sarum, Wiltshire, within the earthen ramparts of an Iron Age fort*

horses or carting services carried sacks of grain from demesne farms on these and other manorial estates to various markets in Wiltshire, including Salisbury and Wilton, as well as to Cranmore, Fordingbridge and Ditcheat. It appears that distances of 'up to 15 leagues' were acceptable.

Shaftesbury Abbey's estates extended northwards to Bradford-on-Avon, 30 miles away, and Tisbury, much closer, and in both places magnificent monastic tithe barns testify to the richness of the nuns' house, and the vast amounts of grain capable of being stored there.

A list of the more important monastic foundations (including nunneries) shows that more than half had been established before the Conquest.

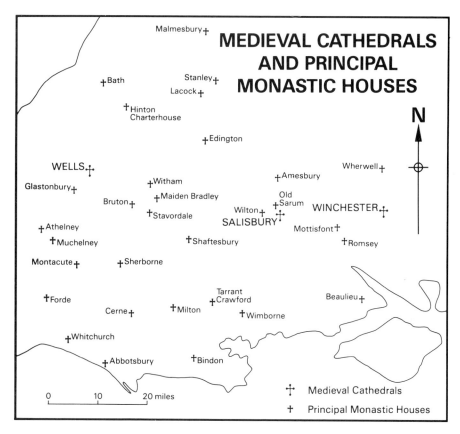

## MEDIEVAL CATHEDRALS AND PRINCIPAL MONASTIC HOUSES

| | | | | | | | | |
|---|---|---|---|---|---|---|---|---|
| H | Winchester | Benedictine | 643+1070 | | W | Wilton | Benedictine (N) | 1065 |
| D | Shaftesbury | " | (N) 888 | | S | Bruton | Augustinian | 1130 |
| S | Glastonbury | " | 940 | | D | Forde | Cistercian | 1141 |
| | | | | | W | Stanley | " | 1154 |
| S | Muchelney | " | 950 | | D | Bindon | " | 1172 |
| S | Athelney | " | 960 | | S | Witham | Carthusian | 1179 |
| H | Winchester | " | (N) 963 | | W | Maiden | | |
| W | Milton | " | 964 | | | Bradley | Augustinian | 1201 |
| W | Malmesbury | " | 965 | | D | Tarrant | Cistercian (N) | 1228 |
| W | Amesbury | " | (N) 980 | | W | Lacock | Augustinian (N) | 1232 |
| D | Cranborne | " | 980 | | S | Hinton | | |
| D | Cerne | " | 987 | | | Charter- | | |
| D | Sherborne | " | 993 | | | house | Carthusian | 1232 |
| D | Abbotsbury | " | 1044 | | W | Longleat | Augustinian | 1235 |
| D | Horton | " | 1050 | | S | Stavordale | " | 1243 |

D=Dorset  S=Somerset  H=Hampshire  W=Wiltshire  N=Nunnery

From the earliest dates monastic houses owned estates not only in their immediate locality, but as granges and outlying estates farther afield. These were large-scale farming and trading units and for most of them the production of sheep and wool formed the basis of their economies almost to the Dissolution. Thus, movement of stock and transport of goods were important, and good lines of communication evolved. Nevertheless it is extremely

*Barton Bridge, Bradford-on-Avon, dating from about 1340, may have been built by Shaftesbury Abbey to give access from their tithe barn (below) to the town*

doubtful if the monasteries were responsible for any road construction as such, although, as we shall see, they built many bridges. Field evidence of routes taken from monasteries to their outlying estates, and from one monastery to another, is very limited. In medieval times roads were not constructed or engineered, so that only positive evidence is often supplied by the existence of bridges. Their provision and maintenance was often regarded, not only as necessary, but also as a pious act. Monastic and church records refer to them, and special taxes were often raised to pay for their repair and upkeep. Early medieval bridges were simple stone structures, wide enough only to accommodate packhorses with their loads. Some replaced fords, many had fords alongside them for use by wagons. The existence of medieval bridges is strong evidence for the presence of tracks which were well used and of some local if not regional importance.

In addition to the monasteries and churches, private individuals and corporate bodies constructed and paid for many medieval bridges. Sometimes they were repaired by owners of local estates, by the church, or through receipts from tolls. White Mill Bridge (958006), near Sturminster Marshall, Dorset, is one of the most beautiful of all Wessex bridges. Believed to date

*White Mill Bridge, Sturminster Marshall, Dorset, known to have been used in the fourteenth century, but probably much older*

from 1175 it is largely unaltered, with a 12ft wide roadway spanning 200ft of the River Stour on eight ribbed arches of superb masonry. In 1341 a Richard Bryan left in his will the sum of 3s a year for its repair. It was decaying in 1713 and more repairs were needed. During recent repairs its foundations were found to consist of oak piles driven into the river bed, supporting a flat raft of oak beams. This had rotted away, leaving tops of piles above the river mud eroded into sharp points, while those parts still submerged in the mud remained in good condition. Modern repairs consisted of back-filling with concrete to move the weight of the masonry piers on to the old oak piles, and to surround the piles with concrete.

These constructional details illustrate the engineering skill and finance needed to build and maintain medieval bridges. The obvious implication is that there was justification for it, yet the road carried by White Mill Bridge is today a minor one, although eight centuries ago it must have been important. The inference is that by early Norman times Badbury, 2 miles north, had become neglected as a road centre in favour of Cranborne, and that Wareham and Corfe, Bindon Abbey and the nunnery at Tarrant Crawford, both important Cistercian foundations by the late twelfth century, were linked to Cranborne by two impressive crossings of the Stour below Blandford. The other, Crawford Bridge (919020), has nine arches in its 225ft span, and was mentioned in a charter of Tarrant Abbey of 1235. In 1506, indulgences for 40 days were granted for its repair. The fact that both these bridges have survived, little-changed, is probably related to the growth in importance of Blandford, where a market was established in the early thirteenth century,

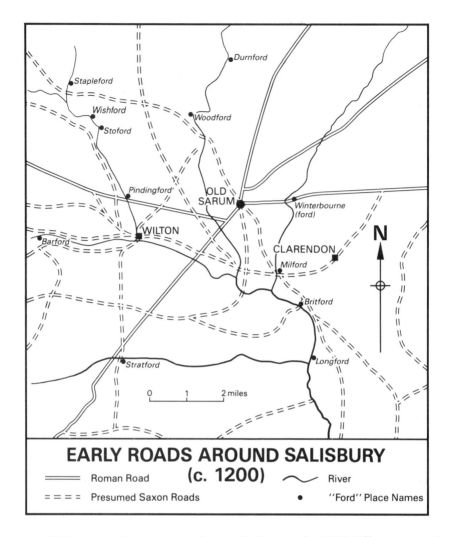

**EARLY ROADS AROUND SALISBURY**
**(c. 1200)**

| | |
|---|---|
| ═══════ Roman Road | ∼ River |
| ═ ═ ═ ═ Presumed Saxon Roads | ● "Ford" Place Names |

and which was sending two members to Parliament by 1307. Offering a good stopping-place on the way between Salisbury and Dorchester, it doubtless took traffic away from the two older river crossings, as it has done ever since.

From the Conqueror's days Norman kings were attracted to the Sarum area. It is possible that the hunting-lodge they added to at Clarendon was on the site of one used by their Saxon predecessors. Clarendon Palace (182302), 2 miles east of Salisbury, became a favourite royal residence during Plantagenet times, retaining its importance until the end of the Wars of the Roses in 1485. It may have influenced the development and subsequent prosperity of the new city of Salisbury, established in the meadows of the Avon near where the Wylye and Nadder joined it, by Bishop Poore about 1220. Written into the city's grant of privileges of 1227 was the right of the bishop to make and alter the roads and bridges leading to the city, thus anticipating the need to attract travellers to New Sarum. Hitherto, they favoured the Saxon capital, Wilton, where, coming from the west by the old Nadder-Ebble ridgeway,

*Milford Bridge, late medieval, on the road between Salisbury and Clarendon Palace*

they crossed the Nadder by the Bull Bridge in Wilton.

Bishop Bingham observed the success of Wilton and in 1244 replaced the existing 'Angel's ford' across the Avon at Harnham by a stone bridge, Ayleswade Bridge, or Harnham Bridge as it is now called. It is still in use, having been widened in the late eighteenth century, and the original six arches can be seen from river level. Repeated references are made to Harnham Bridge, either for repairs or the granting of tolls. Leland, writing in the 1540s, comments pointedly.

> 'Licens was get of the King by a bishop of Saresbyri to turn the kingges highway to New Saresbyri, and to make a mayn bridge for passage over the Avon at Harnham. The changing of this way was the totale cause of the ruins of Old Saresbyri and Wiltoun. For afore this Wiltoun had 12 paroch chirches or more, and was the hedde town of Wileshir.'

To understand why Harnham Bridge made so much difference it is helpful to identify the important trading roads of that time. Although Matthew Paris, a monk at St Albans, drew four maps of Britain about 1250, they are largely concerned with an itinerary from Dover to Newcastle, and ignore Wessex. Far more useful is Gough's map of about 1360 depicting nearly 3,000 miles of roads covering much of England. Who drew the original is not known, and it is named after the antiquarian Richard Gough who discovered it in 1780. Among the five main roads from London one is the route to Exeter and St Ives by way of Winchester, Salisbury, Shaftesbury, Sherborne, Crewkerne and Honiton. It seems clear that, west of Salisbury, the old ridgeway was used, while east of the city, part of the Roman road was in use. Before Harnham Bridge was built there was a choice of fords across various rivers — Stratford-sub-Castle, Britford or Downton.

Subsequently, the road from Winchester came through Clarendon Forest, keeping just south of Clarendon Palace, and entered Salisbury from the east, over Milford Bridge, a fourteenth-century structure still in use, which is really a pair of small stone bridges with a causeway between. The modern Milford Street was formerly Winchester Street, and the main road's western exit from Salisbury was along Drakehall Street, now Exeter Street, which would take it to Harnham Bridge and straight up Harnham Hill to the ridge road. Parts of the medieval and Roman routes from Winchester to Salisbury have recently been incorporated into a long-distance footpath, the Clarendon Way.

The eastern approach to Salisbury throughout the medieval period continued to be by Clarendon, but this fell into disuse by about 1500 when a route from London via Basingstoke and Andover seems to have superseded the Winchester one. The subsequent emparking of Clarendon Forest in Tudor times may have had an effect, while the building of St Thomas' Bridge over the River Bourne (165321) would have improved the north-eastern approach. Strangely, Leland refers to 'Thomas Beketes Bridge of 2 stone Arches', although he makes no mention of Milford Bridge. Perhaps by his time the Milford road from Clarendon had so much declined in use that it was not worthy of mention. The present St Thomas' Bridge is an eighteenth-century replacement, and considerably widened in recent years to accommodate the A30 traffic.

Salisbury reached its height of prosperity in the fifteenth century. One factor contributing to this was its situation on a main route northwards from Southampton, whose Brokage Books for that time show that one-third of all commercial traffic leaving the port headed for Salisbury, probably travelling through Romsey and Whiteparish and entering the city by St Martin's church and St Ann's Street. Westwards the route would have followed the old way to Fisherton and Bemerton to Wilton, and the west side of the Wylye valley to Warminster, heading towards Bristol.

In the early thirteenth century the Bishops of Winchester owned a chain of manors in south-west Wiltshire, from East Knoyle to Fonthill Bishop. Around 1220 the bishop developed Hindon, between East Knoyle and Fonthill, as a market borough, probably intending it as a centre for artisans and of trade in their and other wares. Tenements were planned on both sides of a single main street running north-south which may have been part of an ancient road which by then had declined in importance. The site, on open downland, was probably chosen as far as possible from existing rival centres at Shaftesbury and Mere, and convenient to villages in the Nadder valley, and those along the Wylye between Wilton and Warminster. None of the minor tracks converging on Hindon ever became important, and although the 'town' sent two members to Parliament until 1832 it never became more than a village. Any prosperity it acquired arose from markets and fairs rather than its becoming a local trade centre. The greatest occasion in its history was probably in 1688 when the Earl of Clarendon met William of Orange there. One wonders by which routes they travelled. Perhaps Clarendon came by an old route developed by the medieval bishops to reach Hindon from Winches-

*Part of a medieval and later coach road from Wilton to Hindon, on Crouch's Down*

ter—about which more will be said shortly. From the bishops' estates in West Wiltshire it is known that most of the annual wool crop was sent to their Hampshire palace in Wolvesey, near Winchester.

Contemporary with Hindon was the expansion of Downton, south of Salisbury, on another manor of the Winchester bishops, who also owned Taunton in Somerset. It can reasonably be surmised that a direct route from Winchester to Downton, thence to Hindon, would evolve, probably initially along the pre-Roman ridgeway west of Winchester to Pitt Down, to an early crossing of the River Test at Kimbridge (330256) but subsequently by what is now the A3090 as far as Standon crossways (427267) and then the minor road to Braishfield, curving round the northern ramparts of the once-great hillfort of Merdon Castle. More lanes continue the line to Michelmarsh and Kimbridge.

West of the Test valley the present minor road through Lockerley to East Dean may represent the old course which would have ascended to the old ridgeway route along Dean Hill, either by Dean Hill Barn, or by the White-parish road 2 miles farther west. In any case, the medieval road followed the ridgeway route westwards and south-westwards on Pepperbox Hill (218252), passing the early seventeenth-century brick folly which is so conspicuous a landmark. Where the ridgeway approaches and leaves the crossing of the A36 it is very deeply hollowed in the chalk. West of the main road it is a grassy track curving southwards, becoming a chalky-flinty field track past woodland, and a farm track to Templeman's Farm (203218). Soon afterwards it

*The medieval road from Winchester to Downton, west of Pepperbox Hill*

joins a minor road heading westwards, and at a crossroads a hedged green lane and field path down the hill to Downton marks its course. This latter part of its route from Pepperbox Hill was known as Salt Lane.

Downton was a substantial village on the east bank of the Avon, with a parish church and the earthworks of the bishops' castle close to the site of the Anglo-Saxon hundred moot. The bishops' new town of around 1208 was planned along both sides of a very wide street on the west bank of the river, orientated east-west, and the present spaciousness of the borough retains the original lay-out. Downton's present bridges are modern, but it is likely they replaced medieval crossings of the Avon's three branches. Place-names of Barford to the north and Charford to the south suggest alternative river crossings, although the Avon has been deepened in recent years, making a present ford impossible. From North Charford (198198) a lane leads westwards, soon branching into two, the more northerly one leading to Lodge Farm, and the other keeping due west and becoming a track with fields on the south and woodlands to the north. For a short distance it marks the county boundary, and beyond Searchfield Farm in the valley (179196) its continuation towards the river is represented as a lane which ends abruptly before reaching the river, and a wide shallow trackway suggests a continuation taken up on the opposite bank by a lane past North Charford Manor House, to the main A338 Bournemouth road at 166198.

West of the Avon valley, Gallows Hill (136216) on Wick Down is a significant feature. Grim's Ditch leads up to it from the south-west, accompanied by the county boundary; prominent tumuli are nearby to the south, and on the crest is a triangulation point. Many tracks from the Avon valley between Salisbury and Fordingbridge converge on or close to it. While some may be of recent origin it is apparent that the one from Wick — initially a surfaced road called Wick Lane — is given on Andrews and Dury's Map of Wiltshire, 1776 and on Ogilby's 1675 road map, where it forms part of his London-Weymouth road.

Where the surfaced road ends 2 miles west of Wick (145218), a broad grassy drove between high hedges continues its route westwards, and in half a mile swings towards the south-west as a well-defined track heading for the tumuli and barrows on Tenantry Down and Toyd Down where it joins a medieval road at Tidpit. Meanwhile the bishops' route branched north-west on Wick Down (135218), a good track between arable fields, climbing gently to the southern corner of the ancient woodland of Great Yews (118227). Assuming the route to be aiming for Wilton, the probable continuation was on the good track north-westwards, past Greenacres Farm, across the present Blandford road where the route is lost for a short distance before picking up the Wilton Way on Stratford Tony Down (091242).

Beyond Wilton the present direct route to Hindon, through Barford, Dinton and the Teffonts, was turnpiked in 1761, probably through linking a series of inter-village tracks. However, another track, which was never turnpiked, but which has a series of well-preserved milestones dated 1750 giving distances to Sarum, suggesting its use as a coach road, runs roughly parallel to this valley road but a mile or more to its north, along the downland slopes below Grovely. The 1773 map shows it, even indicating a 'New Inn' just west of the '8' milestone, although this has now vanished.

This track can be easily followed from Wilton to Chicklade Bottom Farm. Soon after leaving Wilton near the railway bridge at Ditchampton, and passing a housing estate, it climbs steeply up Grovely Hill as a wide, deep, double holloway suggesting centuries of use. From Grovely Hill it is a well-defined track between hedges or fences, mainly grassy, sometimes chalky, but not deepened by modern tractors. The milestones, incidentally, are on the south side, with their inscribed faces to the south, away from the track. As it approaches Dinton Beeches and the Dinton-Wylye road (007348) it acquires a metalled surface, retaining this to the Chilmark road where it reverts to grass again. It continues due west, past downland arable and pasture, to join the ancient Harroway, now A303, very briefly, in Chicklade Bottom (935343) where it swings south-westwards as a modern, minor road into Hindon. As with other medieval roads, there is no proof that this route originated in those days. One can only postulate that it may have been used by the Winchester bishops in their journeys to Hindon. Since between Wilton and Hindon it passes through no villages, yet was, presumably, sufficiently used in 1750 to justify the private erection of milestones, this points to an earlier use, and the Winchester connection seems a not unreasonable surmise.

Little documentary evidence survives to throw much light on the state and appearance of roads through the Middle Ages. Law books of the twelfth century mention four 'royal roads' — Watling Street, Ermine Street and the Foss Way from Roman times, together with the far older Icknield Way. As Sir Frank Stenton says 'The tradition is interesting, for it suggests that from a time which was already remote in the eleventh century, these roads had formed continuous lines of travel.' He adds that the importance attached to these roads suggests that the Roman conception of well-defined routes converging on London, from all over southern England, was lost. This probably arose from London's reduced importance, not regained until the fifteenth century. It may have remained by far the largest town, but much of the country's economic life revolved round a large number of local centres, and the roads with which twelfth-century law was concerned were those which led 'from cities to cities, from boroughs to boroughs, by which men go to markets, or about their other affairs.'

By the twelfth century, the king's writ ensured, theoretically, protection for travellers on these highways. An assault committed upon them was punished by a fine of 100s. Some indication of their width was laid down: 'a highway should be wide enough for two wagons to meet and pass there, and for two oxherds to make their goads touch across them, or for sixteen knights, armed to ride side by side. That is called a royal highway which is always open, which no one can close, or divert with walls he has erected, which leads into a city, or fortress, or castle or royal town.' As trade increased, accompanied by an increase in the amount of traffic using other roads which gradually evolved, the authority given the 'royal roads' was extended to embrace most other important thoroughfares.

In 1285 the Statute of Winchester established the responsibility for maintaining the highways on manorial landowners, which included monasteries and churches. The statute also decreed that a zone on each side of a highway should be cleared of any form of cover except for large trees of commercial value. Removal of bushy cover was intended to reduce threats posed by highwaymen and outlaws, and it would also make more practical another stipulation of the statute, that if a track or bridleway became impassable another should be made alongside the original. As a result the most-used medieval roads and tracks tended to become broad zones or corridors of communication, as in prehistoric times, unbordered by hedges or walls. Sometimes even this failed to prevent some medieval roads from becoming eroded deeply into the ground, a process accelerated in prolonged wet weather, forming the many 'holloways' which often signify long-abandoned routes between villages, or leading to villages deserted since medieval times. The state of a medieval road depended on its importance, the extent to which it was used, and on the powers of manorial courts to persuade the local population to accept responsibility for repairs, always providing the necessary materials for this work were available. All available evidence indicates that there was very little new road-building during the Middle Ages. Roads evolved and maintained themselves through usage by horses and carts, by packhorses, by the movement of stock, and by people, from the monarch downwards.

## Royal Itineraries

Various itineraries of medieval times provide evidence of movement of individuals rather than of the physical existence of actual roads. By far the most complete are those of royal journeys. Details of these were not compiled at the time but were worked out by later writers using various sources. Kings and their courts were extremely mobile, visiting palaces, castles, manors, abbeys and market towns, thus not only showing themselves to their subjects, but also gaining an intimate knowledge of them and of the kingdom. The best itineraries are for John, Edward I and Edward II, and it is that for John, a particularly mobile monarch, which gives us a picture of what royal travelling meant: 'In every journey the essentials of government, the *hospitium regis* ... followed the court: a train of from ten to twenty carts and wagons.' These would carry wine, stores, the royal wardrobe, and John, who was very fastidious about personal hygiene, arranged for a bath to be prepared for him in the towns through which he passed.

King John's favourite Wessex resorts, giving access to his hunting grounds, seem to have been Marlborough, Freemantle near Basingstoke, Ludgershall near Tidworth, and Cranborne, and his route from London or Windsor was almost certainly by Silchester and one or other of the Roman roads running westwards from there. He, and presumably the whole court, visited Cranborne fourteen times during his reign, and less frequently was at Bere Regis, Dorchester, Powerstock, Gillingham and Corfe Castle. A century later, around 1300, Edward I, who seemed to move his abode at least eight times a month, was using the Roman highways, and is recorded as having made the Winchester-Clarendon journey via Stockbridge, which had earlier been given royal and ecclesiastical impetus to develop as a market and transport town, with a bridge across the River Test, probably after that at Horsebridge had fallen into disrepair. Edward I also visited the religious houses at Bindon and Tarrant quite frequently, using for these and other Dorset visits the royal palace at Clarendon as his headquarters. None of the medieval kings journeyed beyond Exeter, and even Dorchester was visited only rarely.

## Markets

Although life for most people in the Middle Ages was very localised, centred on manor and village, monastery and castle-town, recent research suggests that by the thirteenth century there was an increasing mobility among the rural population. Exchanges and the trading of excess farm produce and simple manufactured goods, and the carriage of these over short distances, were factors encouraging the establishment and growth of markets. Some commodities such as salt, wool, metals and grain were transported over longer distances, while imported wine, clothes and furs were similarly carried many miles from coastal and river ports. Rural communities then were rarely entirely self-sufficient and for certain things they were dependent on markets, so that a visit to the weekly market was an essential day-trip for a peasant.

A thirteenth-century English lawyer, Henry Bracton, in his treatise. *On English Laws and Customs*, considered that markets, to justify themselves, should not be closer to one another than the distance that could be travelled in a day, and at that time this distance would be 20 miles. But Bracton sensibly realised that it would be necessary to spend some part of the day at the market, and of course to return home afterwards. He therefore concluded that:

*The Corfe Ridgeway, which led to Corfe with its castle and market*

'The day's journey is divided into three parts; the first part, that of the morning, is to be given to those who are going to the market, the second is to be given to buying and selling, and the third part is left for those returning from market to their own homes, and for doing all those things that must be done by day and not by night....'

Thus, the maximum range for a market journey would be one-third of 20 miles, or as Bracton precisely put it, 'six miles and a half and the third part of a half'.

Markets could be established only by charter and can therefore be dated to within a few years of their official recognition. A few surviving charters merely regularised older ones that had grown through custom. In addition to the existing boroughs dating from late Saxon times, and which subsequently gained markets, many new towns came into existence during the period of prosperity and growth during the late twelfth and most of the thirteenth centuries. It is not easy to measure the extent of this urban growth in Wessex where many towns remained small, little different in size or population from their neighbouring villages. Only the weekly market, together with a slightly greater range of crafts and services differentiated them.

We have seen that Downton and Hindon were small, planted towns of the early thirteenth century. Other Wiltshire examples appearing by the mid-fourteenth century include Amesbury, Devizes, Heytesbury, Lacock, Ludgershall, Marlborough, Mere, Trowbridge and Westbury, while the most famous of all, New Sarum, had by then risen to become the ninth ranking English provincial town.

In Dorset, new medieval boroughs with markets had been established at Blandford, Charmouth, Corfe Castle, Lyme Regis, Melcombe Regis, Newton (in Purbeck), Poole, Sherborne, Newland, Weymouth and Whitchurch Canonicorum, while in the area of Somerset concerning us, Chard, Montacute and Yeovil enter the lists. Throughout Wessex, places which we regard as villages enjoyed in medieval times a much greater local importance as market centres: Beaminster, Bere Regis, Cranborne, Frampton, Evershot and Maiden Newton.

Some retain their market-places even if they are no more than small triangles as at Abbotsbury or Steeple Ashton (Wilts), small squares such as Beaminster or Montacute, or road widening as at Cerne, Cranborne, Stockbridge (Hants) and Marlborough. At Sherborne, Bishop Poore of Salisbury set up a new borough at Newland in what were arable fields adjoining the town of Sherborne. Although it gained only meagre success as a borough, it survives today as a single street. Yetminster nearby had a weekly market and annual 3-day fair granted by the Bishop of Salisbury in 1300, but neither prospered, so Yetminster remained a village. While they flourished the markets themselves were bound to one another and to the hinterland they served by a network of roads and lanes. Many of these have developed into motor roads, others are quiet green lanes or field paths, and some have apparently vanished, waiting to be re-discovered.

## Marshwood Vale

To the west and north-west of Bridport in Dorset, Marshwood Vale is a basin of heavy, wet clayland, surrounded by high sandstone hills, with a single opening to the coast afforded by the narrow valley of the River Char. Most farms and settlements in the area are mentioned for the first time in documents of the twelfth to fourteenth centuries, but this does not necessarily mean they were settled at that late date. The vale must always have been difficult country, and Whitchurch Canonicorum is its only village, site of the shrine of St Candida, and hence a place of some importance. Beyond the vale's north-western edge was Forde Abbey, one of the rare Cistercian monasteries of Wessex; and near the centre of the vale, (404976) at Lodge House Farm, there are the meagre remains of the Mandeville's fortified

*Forde Abbey Dorset*

*The road from Pilsdon Pen into Marshwood Vale, probably medieval*

manor house of the thirteenth century.

The vale's pattern of roads and tracks is very likely to be almost wholly medieval in origin. Evidence from the earliest maps suggests that they were never more than of minor significance, but they do suggest two through routes including one between Bridport and Axminster, through Whitchurch. This leaves Bridport by the Charmouth road but soon turns off to Symondsbury. Leaving the village at the north-west by Shute Lane (444936), the track climbs between high hedges, past an isolated cottage, then continues through a narrow defile between sandstone cliffs up to 20ft high, bearing graffiti dated 1801. This quarter-mile stretch is the deepest-cut of any holloway the author has encountered. Keeping left at a fork, the track continues to Quarry Cross at the crest of a hill (434938), descends as another narrow defile between high hedges to North Chideock at Hill Farm. This Symondsbury-North Chideock section is one of the best examples in Dorset of a probable medieval road.

Beyond North Chideock the route continues as a hedged lane by Butt Farm to Ryall and Whitchurch where it forks. The southern branch, for a short distance the Whitchurch-Charmouth road, turns west at Whitchurch Cross, and continues by the old road to Wootton Cross and Champerhayes Cross to Monkton Wyld Cross (328970) and Symonds Down Farm to Axminster. The northerly branch from near Whitchurch Canonicorum's church crosses the Char at Stockham Bridge, goes north as a minor road to Valehouse Farm (392973), then as Prime Lane which becomes a bridleway climbing from the vale to Marshalsea where it joins the Ridgeway road to Birdsmoorgate, and follows the present road north-westwards to Forde Abbey.

There may be significance in the frequency of 'Cross' in place-names in

*Medieval road between high cliffs, near Symondsbury, Dorset*

---

Marshwood Vale. While these may refer merely to road intersections which are especially numerous in this area of an intricate network of roads and tracks (Blackmore Vale has a similar network, but without so many 'Cross' names), they could have a religious association, suggesting the presence of wayside crosses on routes serving monastic granges owned by Forde and Abbotsbury. The Benedictine monastery at Abbotsbury had good communications with its hinterland, and one particular road closely associated with it merits attention.

# Abbotsbury – Cerne,
# a Monastic and Medieval Route

This leaves Abbotsbury by the Black Down road eastwards from the Market Place and from the modern road (Bishop's Road) climbs as a bridleway north-eastwards to Newlands Corner (588866) where it rejoins the present road above the Valley of Stones to the western end of Black Down. The present road to the Winterbourne valley is an enclosure road, and the older route probably lay slightly to the east, possibly represented by the bridleway above Loscombe Wood. Beyond the valley the route followed the existing one by Muckleford Lane, passing two good milestones erected by the Maiden Newton Turnpike Trust in about 1798. At the top zigzag above Quatre Bras, the old road is now marked by a bridleway to Muckleford where a footbridge replaces the former ford across the Frome (640936). The turnpike road crosses the river a few hundred yards to the east by a contemporary bridge recently modernised by re-using the original brickwork. A paved ford beneath may have been the original crossing, for the road northwards runs

*A medieval (and possible later coach road) on Bronkham Hill, with the Hardy Monument on Black Down, Dorset*

on directly as a field path which crosses the railway to a group of farm buildings aligned along the Roman road (644943). Beyond these the track climbs gradually, past tumuli and extensive old settlement boundaries on Grimstone Down and along the western edge of woodland, where Jackman's Cross is now merely a 2ft square stone base with a socket hole for the vanished shaft. Its position close to crossing-tracks points to a medieval importance of these routes (648960).

As late as 1765 this monastic track we are following was named as a complete road, the 'Furzy Down Road', and almost certainly adopted an ancient ridgeway between the Cerne and Sydling valleys. Today it is well-defined, sometimes a broad green lane between hedges, sometimes accompanying a single boundary hedge, sometimes a farm track, along its slightly undulating, airy course, with side-tracks, westwards to Sydling St Nicholas, and eastwards to Godmanstone. On Crete Hill, by an old dewpond (655979) the monastic track to Cerne Abbas branches off north-eastwards as a field path descending past Ridge Barn to join the valley road to Cerne near Lower Barton Farm (665993).

The Furzy Down Road continues on the ridge, past the ruins of Large Bar Barn, and crosses the Cerne-Cattistock road beyond Higher City Farm, maintaining its disciplined course, above Cerne Park, over Ball's Hill and Redpost Hill, to the metalled road on Gore Hill (635038), itself part of the so-called Northern Ridgeway. About 200yd west of the junction, in the grasses on the northern verge stands the 'Cross-in-Hand' (633037). The origins of this mysterious stone pillar are not known, but it may have been a boundary stone of Cerne Abbey's estate. Having been a fine ridge road for almost all the

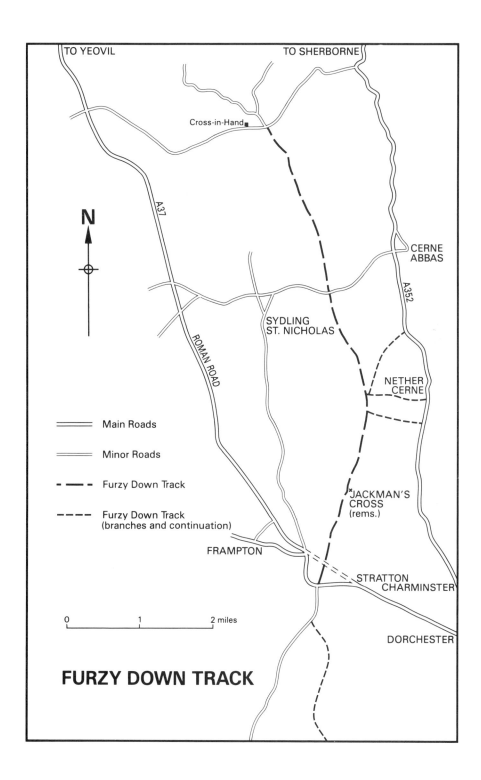

TO YEOVIL

TO SHERBORNE

Cross-in-Hand

N

A37

CERNE
ABBAS

A352

ROMAN ROAD

SYDLING
ST. NICHOLAS

NETHER
CERNE

Main Roads

Minor Roads

Furzy Down Track

Furzy Down Track
(branches and continuation)

JACKMAN'S
CROSS
(rems.)

FRAMPTON

STRATTON
CHARMINSTER

0          1          2 miles

DORCHESTER

**FURZY DOWN TRACK**

*On the Furzy Down Road above Cerne Abbas, looking south*

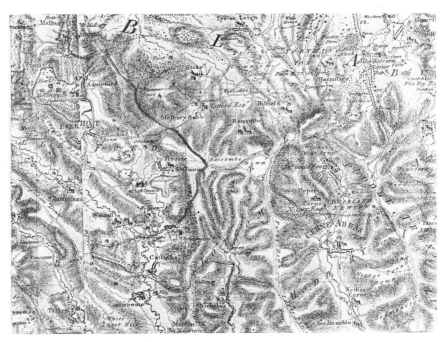

*Taylor's map of Dorset (1765) shows and names the Furzy Down road running north-south. It also shows on the far right the turnpike road of 1752, adopting the old Sherborne road along the ridge east of Cerne Abbas*

*'Cross-in-Hand' on Gore Hill, Dorset, possibly a boundary stone for the Cerne Abbey lands*

6 miles from the Frome valley, the Furzy Down Road now has to descend the steep northern scarp of Batcombe Hill. Although a road runs down a wooded combe from Gore Hill the older route is probably that of the well-defined bridleway down the western side of the woodland, to the edge of a spur where a deeply-hollowed track cuts steeply across open chalk grassland to Great Head (623046). From there its course to Chetnole and Yetminster is uncertain, although it may be suggested by a sequence of footpaths east of the present road, continuing along Back Lane and Harbury Lane northwards from Chetnole.

As Professor Good has pointed out, two problems are inherent in study-

*The George and Pilgrim's Hotel, Glastonbury, a fifteenth-century inn for pilgrims visiting Glastonbury Abbey in Somerset*

ing old roads. One arises from the fact that a road system is a network, without definite beginnings and endings. Travellers in the past, like those today, had a wide choice of routes by which to travel between two places not especially close to each other. Secondly, it is very probable that the medieval road network was much more dense than the present one, so that today's roads account for only part of it. Additionally, although he was writing about Dorset, his comments apply to Wessex as a whole, in that, with the exception of motorways, the total length of road constructed in the last 250 years is small when compared with the huge total road mileage in the area. It follows, then, that most of the roads in use today are medieval, in the sense that they were first used, say, between the ninth and fifteenth centuries. Among these, pilgrims' routes to the great abbeys at Glastonbury and Shaftesbury would have been established quite early. The fifteenth-century hospice and chapel at Chapel Plaister, near Bradford-on-Avon (840678) served such travellers, while the George Inn at Glastonbury, dating from about 1470, is one of the great English survivals of a famous inn for medieval pilgrims. But the roads we are mainly concerned with are those which have, for one reason or another, passed out of currency and survive only as bridleways and foot-paths.

## Salisbury – Blandford

This is a good example of such a track. After the Roman road system decayed the earlier Old Sarum to Maiden Castle route enjoyed a brief revival. But the increasing importance of Weymouth, the growth of New Sarum and the contemporary development of Blandford as a market town on a good crossing of the Stour, resulted in a realignment of routes. Wimborne retained its importance on the Salisbury-Poole axis, as well as giving access to Wareham and Corfe, while the monastery at Cranborne, together with the position of Cranborne as capital of the important hunting forest of Cranborne Chase, resulted in that town gaining a route-importance far greater than its present size would suggest.

From Salisbury the road crossed Harnham Bridge, and used the old Shaftesbury road up Harnham Hill, but at the top followed one of two possible courses. The first is by the line of the present main road, crossing the River Ebble at Coombe Bissett (108265), where a charming medieval pack-horse bridge suggests an ancient use. The present A354 continues the line to Coombe Bissett Down, where a minor road heading due south at 102240 marks its course towards Toyd Farm. An alternative from Harnham Hill is represented by the modern minor road past Wellhouse Farm (128275) to the Ebble valley at Honington, and the farm lane southwards past Down Barn (123243) to the northern corner of Great Yews. Farm tracks and field paths continue the route, by Grim's Ditch to the important junction at 090205 where ancient and modern boundary stones stand close together at the junction of grassy, hedged tracks, half a mile south of where the Coombe Bissett route joins the Honington one.

For the next mile south-westwards the road's course across Toyd Down as a rough lane between wide-set hedges in a remarkably lonely landscape

*Medieval packhorse bridge at Coombe Bissett, near Salisbury*

(below) *The Cranborne to Salisbury road on Toyd Down. The boundary stones mark the junction with the Saxon Wilton Way, which branches off to the left*

evokes a hint of what medieval travellers experienced. Without the hedges, as it would have been even when Celia Fiennes rode that way from Salisbury to Blandford in about 1690, the sense of exposure would have been greater. A milestone on the eastern side of the track indicates that this formed part of the 1755 turnpike from Poole Gate to Coombe Bissett, and there is another milestone in the hedgebank on the west side of the road's continuation, as a modern deeply-hollowed lane, through Martin Wood (063164) south of Tidpit. The road enters Cranborne from the north-west, turning eastwards into the former market-place, identified by its width.

Beyond Cranborne the route is more difficult to follow. A field path from the west end of the Market Place, heading westwards to Creech Hill Farm (041133), from where further field paths towards All Hallows Farm (023127)

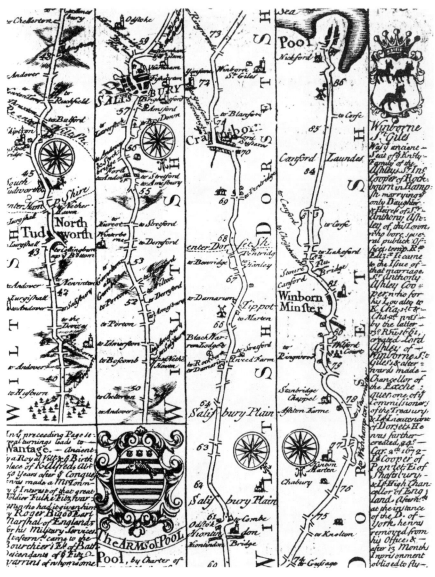

*Part of the Wiltshire and Dorset section of the Oxford to Poole road from Ogilby's map of 1675*

may be the course. West of All Hallows (where Ogilby's map of 1675 marks a church, now vanished) a length of farm lane was called Coach Road on the 1902 OS 6in map, and takes it to Tenantry Down where several ways meet (014128). The good bridleway south-west between arable fields, past woodlands on its west, and becoming a hedged lane into Gussage All Saints, probably represents the route, then following the upper Allen valley to Gussage St Michael, climbing Parsonage Hill by the present road. Its course across the ridge is lost, but some years ago when part of the east side of Horse

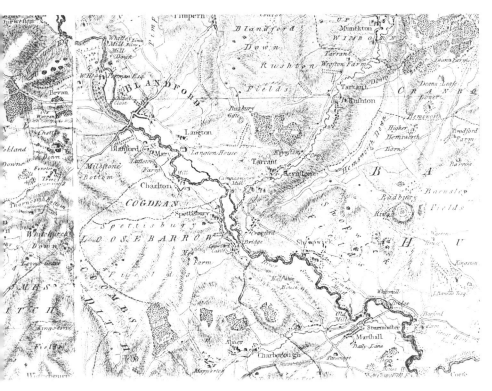

*The Blandford area, from Taylor's map of Dorset, 1765*

Down was ploughed, it revealed the track of an old road. Even today, many tracks cross Horse Down, radiating from 976093, one of these to the west becoming Turner's Lane, entering Tarrant Monkton in line with the ford and fine packhorse bridge at the northern end of the village (945091), and this may be the medieval route from Cranborne. The line continues as a hedged lane climbing Monkton Down, but at the top of the hill is diverted by Blandford Camp, and its entry into Blandford is largely that of the main access road to the camp.

Beyond Blandford the old road to Dorchester probably lay a little to the south of the present line which is largely a turnpike creation. Evidence from old maps suggest it came through Blandford St Mary, turning sharply westwards perhaps along Ward's Drove to South Lodge (874043), southwards again before running parallel to the main road, over East Down and past Whitechurch Mill Barn (855005), where there is a tumulus, to Lower Street. Although the earlier part of this route has been obscured by later enclosures, this latter part to Lower Street is a hedged lane with far more bends in it, and at Lower Street, once a much larger settlement, a series of bends takes the line from the north-west corner by West Farm, after which it is temporarily lost, although the farm road from Longmead (823983) to the main road may mark its course, joining the present road near Bladon Dairy.

From there the old line and the new one are the same, continuing across the valley of Devil's Brook and up Basan Hill. The present road running straight into Puddletown is a turnpike construction, and the medieval route continued westwards at 765959, now represented by a short length of bridleway, picking up the lane from Dewlish to cross the Piddle valley near Druce Farm on the course of the B3142. Where this bends sharply, south of the river, the old road goes ahead as a farm lane across the Puddletown ridge and into Yellowham Wood, joining the modern road to Dorchester near Yellowham Barn.

Although the medieval road network of Wessex was based on the more important centres of population, some anomalies occur. Dorchester and Shaftesbury, both important medieval towns, appear never to have had a convenient and direct road between them, while the road between Dorchester and Sherborne has changed its course significantly. It is worth considering these routes now.

## Dorchester – Sherborne

Much of the Sherborne road has long been known as the Old Sherborne Road — presumably it gained this name when the new turnpike was constructed in 1752-3 and before then as the Old Bath Road. Today, mainly through turnpiking, it falls into two distinct sections, with Middlemarsh the dividing point (672070). South of this, although turnpiking realignment in 1762 has

*Abbey Street, Cerne Abbas, which was the main approach to the abbey*

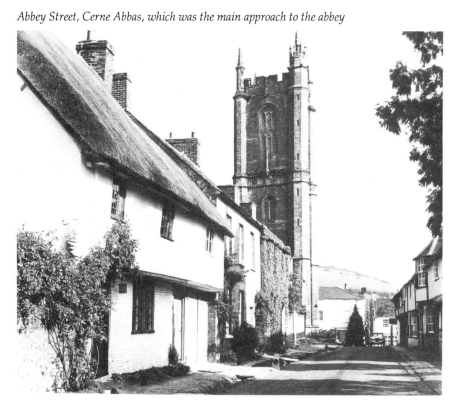

slightly changed its course, the Old Sherborne Road followed a probable prehistoric ridgeway between the Piddle and Cerne valleys, passing just above the Cerne Giant. Two link roads, each significantly hollowed by use, give access to Cerne Abbas.

North of Middlemarsh the route of the old road is completely lost for 2 miles across what, until nineteenth-century enclosures, was open country. North of Osehill Green a line of hedgerows may mark its course to Boys Hill Drove (665111) where the northern limb of a T-junction of minor roads continues its course to Hunters Bridge, then as Broke Lane to a point west of Folke (665135). There, from a triangle of waste ground, the double-hedged Green Lane evokes the nature of the old road to North Wootton Lodge, where it crosses the Bishop's Caundle road and continues through the lodge gates, descending as a pronounced holloway past the western edge of Sherborne Old Park. Gainsborough Hill takes it down a steep hill, and the line continues as a footpath and bridleway across New Road, into Gas House Hill, across the railway, entering Sherborne as South Street.

## Dorchester – Shaftesbury

Today's traveller between these places is likely to go either by Blandford or Buckland Newton and Sturminster Newton, yet there was a more direct route, long fallen into disuse, although much of it is still represented by surfaced roads — usually narrow and winding — and green lanes cutting across the quiet, secret heart of Dorset. In trying to retrace it we must

*The Puddletown Ridgeway on Waterston Ridge, looking east*

remember that the medieval landscape was open, and the traveller would have seen thousands of sheep as his route took him across the downlands which were to have their first enclosures made towards the end of Tudor times. In the 1540s Leland wrote of the countryside north of the River Frome as having 'little corn and no wood, but all about great flokkes of sheppe', while 40 years later Camden commented that these downs 'feede flocks of sheepe in great numbers.'

From Dorchester the route almost certainly crossed the Frome by one of the Mohun bridges and headed for Waterston Ridge (714945). The present 1:25,000 map shows a number of bridleways and farm tracks running northwards from the valley, converging on the ridge and crossing the Puddletown ridgeway near a number of tumuli. Before then, four tracks meet near Seager's Barn (697937), and one, coming from Dorchester by Low Burton, branching through Wolfeton Eweleaze (686933) and then working north-eastwards to Waterston Ridge, is part of a well-documented old road from Charminster to Puddletown. From the ridge, this and the other tracks descended into the Piddle valley at Muston corner, probably along or close to the present B3143, crossed the valley and continued by what is now a good, double-hedged track which climbs past Muston Copse and swings north-wards to Dole's Hill Plantation (7398).

The many tracks converging on this area suggests that it formerly formed an important focus in the local network of downland routes, and the First Edition of the Ordnance Survey maps confirms this even more forcibly although no plantation was then named. That which we are following swings east at the southern corner of the plantation, leaving the Piddletrenthide track to continue ahead along the wood's western side while the Shaftesbury track keeps to the eastern edge along a small valley. A short way beyond the northern end of the wood, our track, a narrow green lane, branches again, with one route cutting north-westwards to Thorncombe Farm and Lyscomb Hill, and the other taking a more north-easterly alignment, over a small ford, to the minor surfaced road, Drake's Lane, at 746004. There, probably as a result of enclosure realignment, one old route continues ahead to Nettle-combe and Higher Melcombe, while our route follows the lane eastwards for 200yd, regains its alignment as a hedged lane, crossing a small ridge and descending as a holloway to join the surfaced road from Cheselbourne to Ansty.

A glance at the 1:25,000 maps shows a cat's cradle of tracks around Ansty. Local topography explains why, since it is here that Blackmore Vale projects a neck southwards towards a watershed near Higher Ansty from where the Devil's Brook cuts through a narrow gap in the chalk. The Northern Ridge-way crosses the Ansty gap at Crocker's Farm; Cuckoo Lane, branching south from Bulbarrow, continues, partly as a bridleway, partly as a modern road, becoming Bramblecombe Lane to Gallows Corner (787006) and Milborne St Andrew, tunnelled between trees in its stretch each side of Gallows Corner. The old road between Sherborne and Milton Abbey crossed the gap at Ansty, so perhaps the name Ansty Cross takes on greater significance.

A very short stretch of lane, now not used, continues the old Shaftesbury

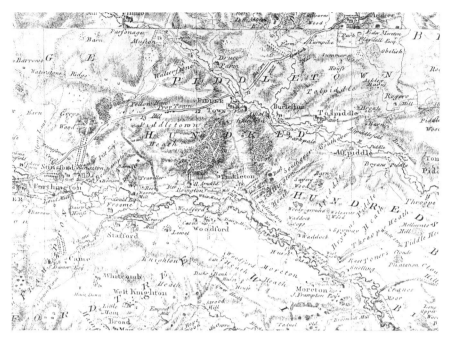

*Taylor's map of Dorset, 1765, shows 'Piddletown' and the Frome valley east of Dorchester*

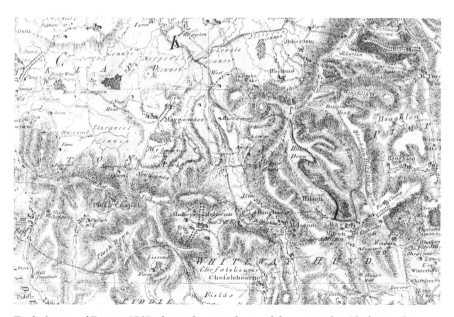

*Taylor's map of Dorset, 1765, shows the central part of the county devoid of turnpikes, indicating that the late medieval road network was still in use. Also Milton Abbey is shown, but not the new village of Milton Abbas, which was built a few years later*

road north-eastwards from Ansty Cross, soon becoming part of a modern road joining Cuckoo Lane at a slight bend (775043), and swinging north-eastwards across Bulbarrow Hill and Woolland Hill, joining the Northern Ridgeway for just over a mile before descending the downland scarp to Belchalwell Street and by the present road through Okeford Fitzpaine to New Cross Gate and Hammoon. From there the route is uncertain, although it seems likely that it may be marked by footpaths from 822152 to West Orchard and East Orchard to Hartgrove, then by Guy's Marsh and St James' Common, entering Shaftesbury from the south-west by the steep, narrow Bimport, with the sketchy earthworks remains of the fortified *burh* to its north.

## Purbeck

Its position in the only natural gap in the chalk ridge that arcs across southern Dorset from Worbarrow Bay to Ballard Point has inevitably made Corfe a nodal point for communications in Purbeck. The establishment of a Norman castle emphasised this, resulting in Corfe becoming a castle-town, a market-town, and the centre of the quarrying industry. All Purbeck roads converge on Corfe, whose main street, until the middle of last century, was always

*The Wareham and Corfe area of Dorset, from Taylor's map of 1765, showing the convergence of pre-turnpike roads on Corfe Castle, and near Stoborough, south of Wareham, in order to use the bridge there*

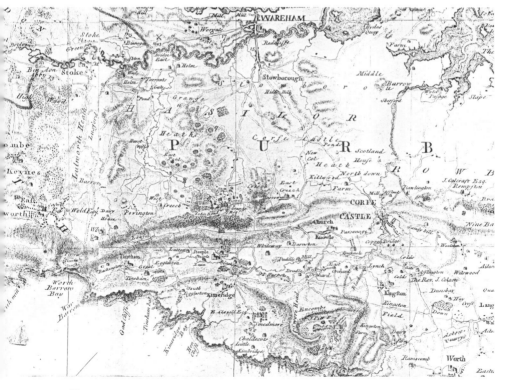

*Corfe Castle from West Street, formerly the main route into the town from the south*

West Street, now almost a calm backwater, whose southern end (958814) quietly peters out on Corfe Common. Medieval masons worked in West Street whose present surface is said to cover over 10ft of stone 'scars' or chippings. From the thirteenth-century horse-drawn sledges transported loads of stone from the limestone quarries on the ridge nearer the coast, and many of the present tracks, footpaths and farm roads fanning out from the end of West Street probably mark the old ways they took, via Blashenwell Farm, Lynch Farm, Scoles Farm, and Downshay.

Worth Matravers and Langton Matravers were the two most prominent quarry villages. Two old tracks, probably used by quarrymen since medieval times, link Worth to the workings at Winspit and Seacombe (976762 and 984767). That from Winspit in particular evokes the past, although much of the quarrying there prospered immediately after the Napoleonic Wars. Part of the quarrymen's track north of Worth is now the modern main road which joins the ridge road east of Kingston and from Afflington Barn (969793) it continues as a path across fields, down the ridge to Scoles Gate and Corfe Common.

Another track from Worth, which may have originated as a quarrymen's route, was, until 1506, used by the rector of Worth or his vicar, to serve the small chapel-of-ease at Swanage. Now known as the Priest's Way and neatly identified by well-lettered stone signs along the route, it runs eastwards from Worth across the bare plateau pockmarked by small quarries, some disused, some still working. Sometimes a corridor between limestone walls, sometimes between hedges, it spawns other tracks to north and south, but east of Belle Vue Farm its course becomes confused in a mass of old quarry workings.

Langton Cross, near Langton Herring, of medieval origin, but purpose unknown

Modern footpath/bridleway stone on the medieval Priest's Way, Purbeck

## Holloways

Our roads today have a defined width. Most are bordered by hedges, walls or fences, usually beyond a narrow verge. In some upland areas they may be unfenced, but are still defined by drainage ditches along the sides. In the days before enclosure, and before metalled roads came into being with the introduction of turnpikes, travellers often had to make wide detours to avoid deep mud or impassably boggy areas. Where land adjoining well-used routes was not cultivated, alternative tracks spread very widely, creating fan-like structures of divergent tracks. Although these are very apparent when seen from the air, good examples exist in various parts of Wessex which can be readily appreciated at ground level.

On the western side of the crest of Beacon Hill (996656), north of Devizes, the Old Bath Road shows a series of well-worn holloways where it starts to descend from the downland chalk, formerly open country, to the hedged lane approaching Turnpike Farm. Immediately to the south of Marlborough, a smaller fan of tracks descends Postern Hill to the Kennet valley, while at another Beacon Hill in Wiltshire, near Bulford (204442), a similar pattern can be seen. But by far the best-known example is near Winchester, on Twyford Down, south of the city, resulting from centuries of use by medieval traffic converging there from the south.

The present and only road over the down leaves Winchester as the A272, along Chesil Street and Bar End Road, but is interrupted by the A33 bypass. South of this, it makes for the north-eastern edge of St Catherine's Hill, taking an oblique course eastwards up the 200ft slopes, before swinging almost through a right-angle on Deacon Hill (502274) to continue southwards along the Roman alignment to Morestead. At the northern foot of Twyford Down, where the present road deviates eastwards (490277), a group of tracks fans out to its west across the rough and unenclosed slopes of the down. These tracks soon start to swing back, but are lost in arable land. However, beyond this, they can be identified again, albeit in a more 'dilute' form, where they cross a golf course midway between a bridleway to the east and a recent, enclosed track to the west. Ploughed-out lynchets running along the contours of the northern side of Twyford Down would, presumably, be of later date than the fan of holloways.

## Causeways

In contrast to the 'fan' of holloways referred to above are the causeways, or built-up roads, deliberately created to ease passage across marshy ground or land liable to flood after spells of wet weather as a result of streams and rivers overflowing their banks. One of the earliest references is in Bishop Asser's *Life of Alfred* when he stated that the king built a causeway 'of marvellous workmanship between Lyng and Athelney and fortified both places'. Although the low-lying land here in the Somerset Levels has long been drained, the raised causeway, a mile long, between these places, and carrying a minor modern road, is still prominent and easily seen from East Lyng (336291). As a whole, however, it was the great ecclesiastical landowners such as Glastonbury and Muchelney Abbeys, and the Bishops of Bath and Wells, who, especially in the thirteenth century, systematically drained and reclaimed

*A medieval bridge across the Avon near Lacock Abbey. It dates from the fifteenth-sixteenth centuries and was repaired in the seventeenth-eighteenth centuries*

To the memory
of the worthy MAUD
HEATH of Langly Bur
rell Widow.
　　Who in the year
of Grace 1474 for the
good of Travellers did in
Charity beſtow in Land
and houſes about Eight
pounds a year forever. to
be laid out on the High
ways and Cauſey lead-
ing from Wick Hill to
Chippenham Clift.

　　This Piller was
ſet up by the feoffees in
1698.

Injure me not.

Maud Heath's Causeway, near
Chippenham, showing some of
its sixty-four stone arches,
many rebuilt in the eighteenth
century. The brick wall
beyond is a later addition

(left) The monument to the
pedlar woman Maud Heath,
whose endowment enabled the
causeway to be built

huge areas of the Levels, working outwards from the fertile 'islands', and developing roads in the process.

By far the most famous medieval causeway in England is that between Chippenham and Bremhill, across the flood plain of the River Avon. Maud Heath, a pedlar woman, had to carry her country produce to Chippenham market, and frequently encountered the hazard of winter flooding. At her death in 1474 she left land and property near Bremhill to provide for the building and maintenance of a causeway from Wick Hill to Chippenham. This is still maintained as a raised path almost 5 miles long, crossing the lower-lying land on a series of low brick arches. A sundial recording the gift was erected in 1698, and in 1831 a tall column bearing a life-size but curiously-proportioned statue of Maud Heath was set up on Wick Hill.

Another medieval causeway, much shorter in length, crosses the Avon near Lacock Abbey, leading to two fifteenth-century bridges which themselves are separated by a causeway. Both bridges have pointed arches, and are about 14ft wide between parapets. Although no evidence links them with Lacock Abbey the road they carry formed part of the old London-Bath road in the eighteenth century, and was probably a well-used route long before then.

In Dorset there was a causeway 800ft long between Wareham and Stoborough and a shorter one north of the town across the Piddle marshes. One of the oldest may be that carrying the Charminster road north of Dorchester's Mohun bridges, while the Sherborne Causeway, still named on the map, was once a raised, paved road, although its former character has gone. Its title covers a 12-mile stretch of 'stone-paved Road between Shaftesbury and Sherborne' constructed under an Act of Queen Mary in 1554. The Act had not been repealed as late as 1932, although the causeway had become part of a main road.

# 4 • Maps and Travellers 1540-1800

Towards the end of the Middle Ages, and certainly by the time the Tudors reached the throne after the Wars of the Roses, there was probably some decline in the 'wayfaring' traffic using the roads. This was due in part to the waning influence of the monasteries, partly to an overall decrease in trade. The Southampton brokage books for the 1490s reveal this dwindling of internal trade through Salisbury to the Midlands, except for the carriage of wine which remained important. Trade in alum and woad for the Salisbury cloth industry also fell at that time.

It was, however, the Dissolution of the Monasteries from 1536-9 which led, not only to a social revolution that affected most existing ways of life, but, in the context of roads, eliminated that arm of English society which had done so much to maintain them. Within a few years the central government found it necessary to introduce new measures for road maintenance. Conditions had become so deplorable that in 1555 an Act of Parliament recognised the need for 'amending of highways being now very noisome and tedious to travel in and dangerous to all passengers and carriages.' The Act constituted surveyors of highways and made each parish responsible for the repair and maintenance of the highways within its own boundaries. Introducing this custom of Statute Labour the Act stipulated that each person having land with an annual value of £50 and each person 'keeping a draught of horses or plough in the parish do provide one wain or cart ... with oxen, horses or other cattle ... and also two able men'. Additionally, each household had to work 4 days a year on the parish highways — increased in 1563 to 6 days for each adult male. Each parish appointed two unpaid surveyors who had to inspect all roads, bridges, water-courses and pavements, to look after the highway, and three times a year to inspect ditches and drains by the side of it. The surveyors also had to watch the traffic using the parish roads, and the numbers of horses used to haul wagons — if many horses were drawing a wagon it was likely that the load was so heavy that it damaged the surface of the highway. Supervising all this Statute Labour were local justices, who could impose fines if work was evaded.

Although this historic Act remained in force for almost 300 years it was never very effective because, although national, its devolution through parish responsibility made its enforcement uneven. In any case it was concerned only with highways — the trunk roads of the system — and left the byway to the care of individual landowners. Many parishes failed to carry out the work or simply could not cope with the repairs needed. The Act failed particularly to specify the standard of maintenance needed, and, as so frequently happened, failed to define clear responsibilities where highways

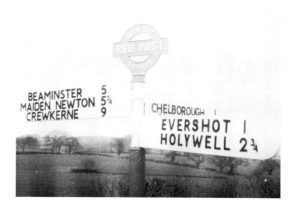

*This twentieth-century sign-post continues the old tradition of using coloured guide posts to help travellers who could not read. The top part of this is painted red. Note also the inclusion of the Grid Reference number*

formed parish boundaries. Nevertheless, some improvements in travelling conditions did ensue, resulting in an increase in travel, although this was not for a long time yet undertaken for pleasure. One outcome of this was the production in the sixteenth century, of authoritative eye-witness accounts of journeys in England: Leland's *Itinerary*, 1533-9, Harrison's *Description of Britain*, 1577, and Camden's *Britannia*, 1586. All these were surveys of the kingdom, but Camden's was by far the most complete survey of the British Isles as a whole.

# Leland

Leland's *Itinerary* is probably the best-known. He was antiquary to Henry VIII and he travelled as an explorer with antiquarian interests, but these did not include roads, which he scarcely mentioned, presumably because, travelling on horseback they were simply not relevant to his observations. He took them for granted. It is probable that he followed what were in those days the highways or main roads, having neither time nor inclination to do otherwise. With no signposts or maps to guide him it was sensible to keep to the more important routes, and it is significant that those he probably used, as deduced from the places he visited, remain today as important routes, or which can be regarded, on entirely different evidence, as roads of importance in the early sixteenth century. Even so, in fording rivers and crossing open downland, it is likely that Leland hired the services of a guide. Bridges, however, especially where they were of stone, usually merited mention, usually with the number of arches they had. This shows Leland's curiosity: merely passing over a bridge reveals little of its structure. To examine it, if only to count its arches, often necessitates stopping and viewing it from the waterside. Generally he was content to see without noticing anything more than bare facts.

*Leland in Dorset*
On one visit Leland entered the county from the west at Lyme Regis, followed the old cliff-top route to Charmouth, Stonebarrow Down to Chideock and Bridport where he turned north to Netherbury and Beaminster, possibly using the old way up the western side of the Brit valley. Turning north-eastwards he rode over Beaminster Down to Evershot and Melbury

*The corner of the Old Lyme Road, Charmouth, Dorset*

House, and southwards by Long Ash Lane (the Roman road) to Frampton, Upwey and Weymouth, carefully avoiding the county town! Eastwards, then, to East Lulworth, over the River Frome by Holme Bridge where he observed four arches (as did Hutchins at the end of the eighteenth century) to Wareham and across 'black moristical heath' to Lytchett Minster and Poole. From there he turned north again, travelling to Wimborne, Horton, and Cranborne to Salisbury.

On another occasion Leland entered Dorset from the north, travelling from Stourton to Stalbridge by way of Cale Bridge (759200) presumably following the ridge route through Cucklington, Buckhorn Weston and Kington Magna. His journey continued through Thornhill to Sturminster Newton, back to Stourton Caundle, then to Sherborne, Bradford Abbas, crossing the Melbury stream by stone bridges at Stoford and Bradford Abbas (both still in use), and Clifton Maybank to Yeovil. He returned to Stalbridge through Sherborne, along Sherborne Causeway to Shaftesbury, and along the main highway to Mere.

### Leland in Wiltshire (1539-40?)

He entered the county first from the north-east, and travelling by way of Malmesbury reached Corsham. From there his route took him by Chapel Plaister, which he referred to as 'an hermitage', traditionally a wayside chapel for pilgrims travelling from Malmesbury to Glastonbury. Passing through Monkton Farleigh he reached Bradford, where his comment on the bridge with its '9 fair arches of stone' triggers off recollections of others spanning the Avon from Malmesbury, including 'Caisway Bridge' (Kellaways — presumably on Maud Heath's Causeway), Rey Bridge at Lacock, and

Staverton Bridge, all of stone. Oddly enough he does not refer to the so-called chapel on the bridge at Bradford.

After visiting Trowbridge he rode to Farleigh Castle where he refers to the River Frome 'brekith into armelettes ... but soon meeting agayn with the principale streame, whereby there be in the causey divers smaul bridges'. He returned to Bath and continued this tour through Somerset.

His second visit to the county brought him from the south, through Damerham, 'then a 6 miles by champayn (open) ground to Honington'. He crossed the River Ebble by a bridge of three arches, and entered Salisbury over Harnham Bridge. When he visited Old Sarum he found only two surviving gates into the old town, east and west.

Again he digresses in his account to note the courses of the Rivers Avon and Wylye which meet at Salisbury, adding comments about bridges at Upavon, Amesbury, Fisherton (of stone), Crane (of stone), Harnham, Downton (of stone) and Fordingbridge (stone). Crossings of the Wylye were, presumably by fords, since no bridges are specifically mentioned.

East of Salisbury, Leland was impressed by Clarendon Park, 'a very large thyng and hath many keepers in it', but omits any reference to Milford Bridge, on the obvious route to the park, although he does mention 'Thomas Becket's Bridge of 2 stone arches, a mile al by champayn'. This must have been the old St Thomas' Bridge, 2 miles out on the London road.

Leland has left no description of either Stonehenge, which he must have seen, or of Avebury, which he apparently did not visit, although he did pass Silbury Hill. On that occasion he must have entered Wiltshire again from the north, via Lambourn, Ramsbury and Bedwyn to Marlborough, then Savernake Forest to Pewsey, passing the Manningfords and North Newton and obviously travelling up Pewsey Vale to 'The Vzes' (Devizes), a town 'most occupied by clothiars'. Westwards then to Steeple Ashton 'by champaine but frutefull grounde ... it is a praty little market toune, and hath praty buildinge. It standith much by clothiars'. He continued to Bath by Edington, Westbury and Trowbridge, and after visiting Bristol, returned to continue his explorations southwards, through Mells (Somerset) and Selwood Forest, 'a 30 miles in compace, and streatchith one way almost onto Warminstre and another way onto the quarters of Shaftesbyri', passing Witham Friary and Maiden Bradley to Stourton and Mere.

Although we do not know the exact routes which Leland took, we cannot fail to be impressed by his determination and diligence, and the observations he made, at a time when monasteries were going down and the old order was changing. Dr A.L. Rowse points out, 'He must have been obsessed by a passion, the passion for seeing the country, the love of the road, of sky, and wind and weather. He belonged to the select class that includes Celia Fiennes, Defoe, John Wesley, Cobbett, George Borrow: the first of them all'.

## Saxton

One outcome of the increase in travel was the production of more detailed maps. A Yorkshireman, Christopher Saxton, was commissioned to create the first national atlas produced by any country. Working alone Saxton completed the survey between 1573 and 1579, and it was probably intended to illustrate Holinshed's *Chronicles*. He visited viewpoints (including church towers), collected local information, travelled extensively and made copious records of countless compass bearings.

Saxton's engraved and printed maps first appeared in 1575, with the southern and south-western counties coming first. That of Dorset has a beautiful cartouche, with jewels, birds and vases of flowers, together with a splendid galleon off Swyre. As with all the others it depicts hills, rivers, towns and villages, important bridges, but no highways. Perhaps this represents the contemporary conception of roads, but it is a strange omission, as Saxton would surely have used the main highways in making his survey. Nevertheless, his Atlas is a decorative masterpiece combining clarity with information and beauty. A contemporary writer tells us that Saxton's maps 'are usual with all noblemen and gentlemen, and daily perused by them for their better instruction of the estate of this Realm.'

For the best part of 200 years no further detailed surveys were made. Saxton's maps were copied, embellished, sometimes revised by subsequent engravers and map sellers, but it was not until the 1690s that Robert Morden's edition of Saxton added any roads to most of them. Around 1610 John Speed introduced his own versions of Saxton in *Theatre of the Empire of Great Britain*, but it seems probable that the earliest maps of the Wessex counties to show roads were those brought out about 1662, based on Speed's engravings.

An explanation of the tardiness of map production between Saxton's work of the 1570s and the next maps of 90 years later may lie in the general condition of the times. The later Tudor and early Stuart reigns were periods of transition following the Reformation. Later came the decades of the Civil War and Commonwealth, and it was not until after the Restoration that a more stable situation set the stage for wide-ranging social and cultural advances which eventually led to modernisation of roads. This in turn opened the way to increased travel with a consequent need for including roads on new maps.

## Camden

William Camden was a great historian and antiquarian, and after 15 years of research he brought out his *Britannia* in 1586, the first detailed description of the British Isles. It reflected his own interests, which certainly did not include roads. Indeed, the order in which his material is presented, county by county, gives little indication of the routes by which he journeyed. His work went through six editions in its original Latin before an English translation appeared in 1610, being revised repeatedly throughout most of the seventeenth century. The 1695 edition is important because it contained county maps by Robert Morden.

## Morden

Robert Morden was a map and globe-maker at the Atlas, Cornhill, London, and worked from about 1668. In 1676 — the year is significant as we shall see — he produced a pack of playing cards, 'The 52 Counties of England and

Wales, described in a pack of cards'. Each has at the top the county name, the suit, and the number (or portrait, on court cards), with a few facts about the county, but most of the space ($2^1/_8$in x 2in) is taken up by a map of the county, including its main highways. One of the two preliminary cards contains a small map of England and Wales, and the other an 'Explanation of these Cards'. Morden includes the 'Distance from London. First the Reputed and then the Measured Miles by Esqr Ogilby — with his leave we have Incerted ... there is also the Road from London to each Citty or Towne, the great Roads are drawn with a double line, the other Roads a single line'. Thus Morden must claim credit for the first, albeit, small-scale, county maps covering the whole country to show roads. Clearly, his playing card maps were designed to instruct the young and not for serious card games. The Wessex counties appear in the 'Diamonds' suit — Hampshire as V, Wiltshire VI, Dorset VII and Somerset VIII.

On the Wiltshire map, the reputed distance from London to Salisbury is given as 70 miles, Ogilby's measured distance 83 miles, while the Dorchester distances are respectively 85 and 112, and those on the Somerset card for Bristol, 94 and 115.

Considering their representation of Wessex roads as a whole, double lines show a 'great Road' from Basingstoke running westwards through Andover and Overton, obviously continuing on the Wiltshire map to Salisbury and Shaftesbury, crossing north Dorset through Stalbridge and Sherborne to 'Evil' (Yeovil), 'Crokethorn' (Crewkerne), Chard and Axminster. The importance of this long-established great road to the west has been maintained through the centuries, although it is interesting to note that its eastern approach to Basingstoke is shown only by a single line — merely an 'other Road' — from Silchester. No other 'great Roads' are depicted in Dorset or Somerset but the route from London to Bristol via Newbury, Hungerford, Marlborough and Calne is double-lined, forking at Chippenham, with one branch going through Marshfield and the other merely reaching Bath.

What is perhaps even more revealing is the 'other Roads', particularly in Wiltshire and Dorset. The only one running north from Salisbury goes only to Amesbury, while that to Southampton is the sole southward one. No roads are depicted crossing Salisbury Plain, although one is shown running southwest from Marlborough, via East Lavington to Westbury, Frome, Shepton Mallet and Wells, almost certainly one of the main trading routes for cloth from the west Wiltshire and north Somerset wool towns.

In Dorset, Blandford seems to have been a more important focal point for radiating roads, connecting it to Shaftesbury, Wimborne, Dorchester and Sherborne. Only one other road is shown from the county town, running westwards as far as Bridport, nothing to the south, or to the north. In Somerset, roads from the coast at Minehead, Dunster and Watchet, linking it to Bridgwater, Glastonbury and Bruton, suggest a trading use, probably of coal from South Wales, and fish, while it might be expected there would be a firm link between Bristol and Wells. Obviously, roads shown on these tiny Morden maps would be neither definitive nor shown very accurately. For that we had to wait for Ogilby.

# Ogilby

John Ogilby's *Britannia* was unique in one respect, in that it gave 'a geographical and historical description of the principal roads'. Two hundred pages of text were interleaved with a hundred road maps, presented as a continuous scroll cut into strips to fit the pages of a book. Although convenient for travellers it did have the inherent disadvantage of any strip-map, namely that it could lead to distortion of direction, which Ogilby tried to minimise by having each scroll with its own compass rose to indicate direction changes. Ogilby employed surveyors to travel the roads, carefully measuring all distances by means of a perambulator wheel of known circumference, in a simple forked frame geared to a counting device, and trundled by the surveyor in front of him. Ogilby used the Statute mile of 1,760yd, introduced by Act of Parliament in 1593 but not adopted until considerably later. In 1596 the word 'road' in its modern definition was first used. Hitherto a traveller followed a 'highway' or just a 'way'.

Ogilby's scheme was approved by Charles II. Perhaps the king's recollections of his adventures on and off the road after the Battle of Worcester in 1651 quickened his interest in the new project.

Ogilby's maps show roads by solid lines where enclosed and by dotted lines where they crossed open ground. Down the centre of each road dots mark each quarter-mile. Side roads and their destinations are given, as are the names of towns, villages, rivers, castles, churches, county seats and large houses within about a mile each side of roads, as well as the more important natural features such as woods. Finally, 'Ascents are noted as the Hills in ordinary Maps, Descents, *e contra*, with their Bases upwards'!

Ogilby's *Britannia* is a remarkable body of information, not only about the principal roads he and his surveyors travelled, but in the additional, sometimes indirect, information gained. Its practical value to the historian is partly due to the accuracy of its surveying and cartography, partly because it shows roads at a time when it is unlikely that they had been altered to any marked extent since they had evolved during the previous centuries.

## The Land's End Road

The first of Ogilby's roads might be called the Great West, or Land's End Road from the capital to the far south-west, its route across northern Hampshire through Basingstoke to Andover keeping it generally north of the present B3400 and now marked by minor roads and bridleways. Beyond Andover, the present A343 Salisbury road through Middle Wallop, becoming A30 at Lopscombe Corner, follows closely the Ogilby road over St Thomas' Bridge ('Hurcote Bridge' on the Ogilby map) into Salisbury.

Near Salisbury Ogilby's surveyors made a mistake, placing Longford House and the turning to Odstock to the north of the road instead of the south. His route map clearly shows the road climbing Harnham Hill, having presumably crossed the river at Harnham Bridge, although none of these are named. Near the eighty-seventh milestone are marked 'The Race' 'The Stand' and 'Post', surely the oldest map references to an operating racecourse. Salisbury races, and the stand, came into being on a point-to-point

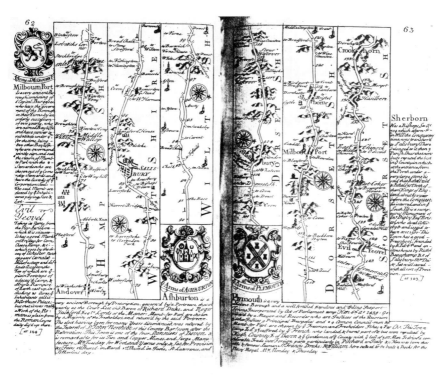

*Ogilby's map of the London to Land's End road, showing the section across Wiltshire*

---

basis in the late 1500s, and Evelyn's diary commented upon the 14-mile course and the stand in 1654. Thus, in Ogilby's time, this old 'Racecourse Way', following a prehistoric ridgeway along the downs, was still the main road from Salisbury to the west. The text to his map refers to 'One, Two, Three Mile Posts ...' and then nothing more until 'you come to Whitesheet Hill whose descent is five furlongs.' At the foot of the hill his route map glances backwards with a direction 'to Salisbury', along the valley, indicated in his notes as a 'different way'. This must have anticipated the present A30 to Wilton, but was not the old Saxon route through the villages since an additional sign on the map points to Donhead. Cochrane suggests that the preference for the difficult 'Racecourse Way' with its steep gradients at each end, instead of the easier valley 'A30' route may reflect a long-held prejudice against travelling through Wilton with its various market tolls. A century later, Andrews and Dury's Map of Wiltshire still shows the Racecourse Way with its mile-marking trees, as well as the 'A30' valley route which was to be turnpiked in 1787-8.

Beyond Salisbury Ogilby's road to Yeovil is very much the line of the modern trunk road A30, except near Milborne Port, where the present London Road enters from the south-east, and is the result of a new line worked out between 1811 and 1831, replacing the old route shown on the 1811 OS map which took the Ogilby course from Toomer Hill (703191) by what is now a farm road leading to Gospel Ash Farm, continuing westwards and descending East Hill obliquely through Crendle Hill Wood, as a bridle-way, becoming a field path across park and farmland to enter Milborne Port from the east, through a modern housing estate (680187). The 1:25,000 map significantly names part of this route 'The Old Road'. Passing along the northern part of Sherborne Ogilby's road continues to be marked closely by the A30 line through East Chinnock, goes south into Haselbury Plucknett, turning west in the village and crossing Haselbury Bridge (458110) before swinging south-westwards again into Crewkerne, named 'Crookhorn' by Ogilby. His road and the present A30 roughly coincide as far as White Down (366090), but there the old road swung southwards through Street, to adopt the Foss Way line to Axminster and hence out of our area.

## The Bath and Bristol Road

In Ogilby's day there was no road called the Bath Road. His map was produced before Bath became the most fashionable English city, and the route to the west was the Bristol Road, which ignored Bath completely, although Ogilby's map does show three side roads leading to Bath, from Marlborough westwards. Between Kintbury and Marlborough the old road took a different route from the present A4. At Avington (373684), a more northward route along Radley Bottom and then westwards in a fairly direct line is now marked by a minor road through Leverton (333700), the present A419 from Chilton Foliat to Knighton, and the minor road again through Ramsbury and down White Hill behind Ramsbury Manor. From there the route appears to be that now adopted by a lane running along Sound Bottom (225710) before descending to Mildenhall and along the north side of the Kennett into Marlborough.

Ogilby reckoned this route to Marlborough was 2 miles longer than the alternative through Hungerford, Froxfield and Savernake. Marshy ground near Hungerford, and the apparent absence of a bridge over the River Kennet, may have necessitated the northerly route as a winter one, with the 'A4' line preferred in the drier months, although even its course through Savernake Forest would rarely have been pleasant travelling. Just before entering Marlborough Ogilby's map indicates the first turning to Bath on the north side of the road. This would almost certainly be the track mentioned earlier as the 'Herepath', leading over Manton Down and dropping down into Avebury and Beckhampton (188695 to 175705 to 152716 to 135708).

Beyond Marlborough Ogilby's road was largely that now taken by the A4 to Beckhampton, Cherhill, Calne and Chippenham, albeit with a few small differences, the main one being that the old road kept to the crest of the hill westwards of Knoll Down (070695), over Cherhill Down and above the Cherhill White Horse which was not then in existence, descending to the modern line by what is now a footpath and bridleway south of Cherhill. The Bristol Road continued down Derry Hill to Chippenham and then, roughly marked by the present A420, through Marshfield to Bristol.

Ogilby's route to Bath is shown in detail on another route map as a crossroad from Chippenham to Bath and Wells. Turning off the Bristol Road at Chippenham it ran through Pickwick (present A4), swinging south-west

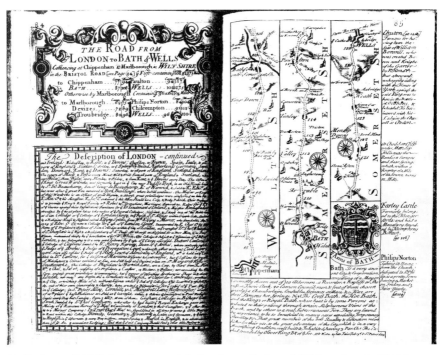

*Ogilby's map(1675) showing part of the London to Bath road (Chippenham to Wells).*
*Note the approach to Bath via Pickwick, ChapelPlaister, Kingsdown and Bathford*

and south (B3109) to Chapel Plaister (840679) and then by the narrow lane — very much a holloway — descending to and crossing the present A365 before joining the old Bath coach road westwards through Kingsdown and Bathford into Bath. It is this route which we now must consider.

The Old Bath Road, as it was called, does not appear in Ogilby's Atlas, but as there is plenty of evidence for its existence one wonders why his surveyors missed it. From Beckhampton its course must have been on or close to that of the A361 Devizes road as far as 'Three Barrows' (058674). It can be identified as a track along the edge of an arable field, running south-westwards and climbing the downs to a clump of trees marking the spot where it crosses the Saxon Wansdyke (040666). This spot is known as Old Shepherd's Shore, and the great Wiltshire antiquarian John Aubrey, a contemporary of Ogilby's, has some interesting accounts of the activities of 'Mr Ferraby, the minister of Bishop's Cannings' (the parish which includes Old Shepherd's Shore). Apparently he was also a musician with a fondness for poetry, pageantry, open-air games, and church bells. The nearness of the Old Bath Road gave him opportunities to entertain passing royalty. On 11 June 1613, Aubrey records that 'when Queen Anne (of Denmark, wife of James I) returned from Bathe', she was 'entertained at Shepherd's-shard at Wensditch, with a pastoral performed by himself and his parishioners in shepherds' weeds'. Presumably Aubrey obtained details of the great event from local records, as he did when 'King James the First was in these parts he

*Old Shepherd's Shore, above Devizes, on the Old Bath Road*

lay at Sir Edw. Baynton's at Bromham. Mr Ferraby then entertained his Majesty at the Bush in Cotefield ... .' The entertainment must have impressed the king, since 'For this entertainment his Majesty made him one of his chaplains in ordinary'.

Royal progress through the country was usually not much fun for the local inhabitants. A retinue of over a hundred people had to be lodged and fed; the royal larder had to be supplied, as well as carts and horse teams for conveying the royal baggage. Payment for these services was made, but usually below market rates, and not very promptly. In a visit to Salisbury and Bath in 1615 by King James I and Queen Anne, inhabitants of the counties through which they were to pass petitioned 'to be spared the honour in respect of the hard winter and hitherto hot and very dry summer whereby cattle are exceeding poor and like to perish everywhere'. The petition was unheeded.

From Old Shepherd's Shore the old road, now a pleasant green lane, descends westwards, crosses the Calne-Bishop's Cannings road, and continues round the southern slopes of King's Play Hill (surely a name with significance), and keeps south at the fork near Hill Cottage (008656). In the thick undergrowth on the southern hedgerow which borders the green lane here is a milestone probably erected when this route was turnpiked by the Calne Trust in 1713, and there is another similar one, also with no decipherable inscription, by the northern hedgerow, at 988659. Both are indicated on the 1773 map, given as 86 and 88 miles respectively from London.

Tracks fan out in the descent of Beacon Hill, one being a very deep-cut, steep-sided holloway. Uniting at the foot of the hill they continue as a single wide green drove towards Turnpike Farm (981664) becoming a surfaced

*The Old Bath Road with an eighteenth-century milestone, at the foot of Beacon Hill*

---

modern road past Bell Farm into Sandy Lane. Bell Farm was formerly Bell Inn where coachmen and servants were accommodated, while their employers enjoyed the greater comforts of the Bear nearby, now a large private house, but formerly an inn known to have been used by Queen Anne on one of her journeys.

The Old Bath Road turned westwards from the northern end of Sandy Lane opposite the George Inn (964683), which has the appearance of an early eighteenth-century coaching inn. At 956682 the road forks, the present route running due westwards to Bowden Hill following the line of the 1725-6 Lacock-Blue Vein Turnpike, and with a milestone at the crest of the hill. The more northward arm, now a little-used road, descends the escarpment at Naish Hill and crosses the River Avon at Reybridge (919691), half a mile north of Lacock. O.G.S. Crawford suggests that this was the medieval route, and this theory is supported by a reference in the Quarter Sessions Great Rolls, in the form of a petition 'of the inhabitants of the Towne and Parish of Lacock and of neighbouring places' against the planned demolition of Rey Bridge, in 1654. The petition 'humbly sheweth that whereas the bridge called Rey bridge, Lacock, hath bin lately by order of Quarter Sessions, broke down, and intended to be quite demolished or destroyed and by the same order anaother bridge called footebridge in the same parish is intended to be repayred for use instead of Reybridge — Now forasmuch as Reybridge lyeth directly in the roade betweene the Cittye of London and the Cittyes of Bath and Bristol and soe more convenient for Passengers and Carriages ...' and so on.

The petition further claims that 'Reybridge hath bein very usefulle for a market waye and Church waye'. All of which suggests that the old London-

*High Street, Lacock, Wiltshire, which was the main London to Bath road until the second half of the eighteenth century*

Bath road did not pass through Lacock but kept to the north, or the petitioners gave a greater importance to Reybridge than it justified in order to have it repaired. Or had something happened to the older bridge and causeway near Lacock, on the road from Bowden Hill? There is no doubt that this was the line turnpiked in 1725-6, entering Lacock from the south-east, continuing along the very wide High Street, turning north and heading north-west-wards and westwards to Corsham by what is now an unclassified road. A milestone survives at the place where this road crosses the modern A350 (913691). Although the 'Old Bath Road' was not given in detail by Ogilby, it joins at Pickwick his road indicated as having turned off at Chippenham. This third road to Bath is part of the crossroad from Chippenham to Bath and Wells, via Pickwick and Chapel Plaister (840678) where it linked up with the Beckhampton-Sandy Lane route, continuing through Kingsdown and Bathford, and entering Bath from the east along the line of the present A4. This, coming through Box, was a mid-eighteenth-century creation, a far better route for coaches than the old Shepherd's Shore-Sandy Lane route, so that from about 1755 the 'Old Bath Road' ceased to be maintained although it continued to be used by some travellers, especially those on horseback.

# London – Barnstaple

Ogilby's London-Barnstaple road passed through Wiltshire and Somerset, using the line of his 'Great West Road' as far as Andover. From there his map shows that it took a course roughly westwards and then south-westwards from the present large roundabout (336457) by the minor road now going through Monxton, and passing Amport church (he called it Apworth) on the north of the road. A short stretch of bridleway followed by a country lane south of Quarley Hill (264424) now represents its line, continuing past Cholderton Lodge and Cholderton village where it entered Wiltshire. Military training establishments now cover the landscape indicated by Ogilby's surveyors as 'pasture on both sides', and his road followed an old way into Amesbury from the east, while the present A303 bypasses the town.

West of Amesbury the Ogilby road crossed two adjacent arms of the Avon by a 'Stone bridge' and a 'Wood bridge'. The present five-arched Amesbury Bridge with a span of 87yd has the date 1775 carved on its upstream parapet marking its rebuilding by the third Duke of Queensbury. Ogilby's map shows Stonehenge clearly marked to the south of his road, so the present A344 and A360 to Shrewton represents its line. A succession of turnings on both sides of the road hint at the many routes across Salisbury Plain to Devizes and Salisbury. The course west of Shrewton apparently lay to the north of the modern road and initially is marked by a lane branching off the A360 at The Gibbet (058445), becoming a bridleway to Middle Barn 4 miles westwards. Ogilby distinctly shows turnings to Chitterne on the south of his road, and later one to Heytesbury, so it would appear that the seventeenth-century route continued westwards across the Plain towards Bowls Barrow (942468), before descending south-westwards to the Wylye valley near Boreham. Andrews and Dury's 1773 map shows tracks all over Salisbury Plain, but since most of the downland north of the A344 is now used for military training many miles of these have been 'modified' by army vehicles and are inaccessible.

The old road through Warminster was the same as that of today, and the Ogilby route beyond left by the present Sambourne road, although his map then shows so many turnings that the line of the road is difficult to associate with any present line. Shearwater is shown to the north of the road, Crockerton and the Deverills to the south, with a turning on the north to Horningsham village. That the road went to Maiden Bradley is indisputable, entering from the east, and leaving on the west by a line now followed by a footpath round the north side of Mapperton Hill. The minor road past Manor Farm and Grange Farm to Kilmington, and the bridleway across Kilmington Common, would take the Ogilby road to the Harroway (763357), then following this down Kingsettle Hill to Redlynch and Bruton, which was entered from the south along the line of the present B3081.

For almost the whole way from Andover to Warminster the road was shown as open. Beyond Maiden Bradley it was largely enclosed by hedges, and this continues. However, it is interesting to see that Ogilby shows a 'Bruton bypass', an unenclosed road south of the town, passing the dovecote of the former Bruton Priory, the route still followed today by a minor road. West of Bruton, Ogilby's road goes out of our area, through Cole north of Honeywick Hill, and by Ansford and Alford to Keinton Mandeville and King Weston (which he names as Weston Regis), then swinging north-westwards above Compton Dundon to follow the Polden ridge to Bridgwater.

# Marlborough – Devizes — Wells

Ogilby shows this as forming a branch of his road from London to Chippenham, Bath and Wells, given in the Atlas as a route from Marlborough. It keeps
along the A4 line north of the River Kennet to Beckhampton, and then as the
Old Bath Road to Old Shepherd's Shore where it crosses Wansdyke. Just
beyond 022659 it leaves the Sandy Lane route already described to swing
southwards into Devizes, probably on the line marked as a bridleway across
Roundway Down and entering Devizes from the north-east. The present
A361 west of the town probably marks the line, initially down 'Cane Hill'
(now Caen Hill), through Seend ('Sean'). West of Seend, Ogilby shows the
road making a sharp turn beyond Semington Brook, which the present road
also does, and a 'Baldane Mill' is named. A mill still exists on the same site.
The old road is probably now indicated by a lane north of the A361 running
from Littleton, through Semington, and by a bridleway and footpath to
Hilperton and Trowbridge. Near Hilperton side turnings lead southwards to
Steeple Ashton, northwards to Bradford-on-Avon (now B3105) and Whaddon, formerly far larger than it is now.

From Trowbridge Ogilby's route coincides with the present A366 across
Wingfield Common, entering Somerset by a wooden bridge over the River
Frome below Farleigh Castle, and continuing to 'Phillips Norton', where his
road map indicates a crossroads whose arms lead to Bath and Salisbury,
presumably the modern B3110. 'Phillips Norton' is described as 'a pretty
town having a Market on Friday and 3 Fairs Yearly'. At the time of Ogilby's
survey Norton St Philip continued to be an important centre of the West of

*The George Inn, Norton St Phiip, near Bath. It was built in the fifteenth century as wool
hall and inn, probably by the monks of nearby Hinton Priory. Pepys dined there in 1668
and the Duke of Monmouth during his rearguard action in 1685*

England cloth industry, although the 'golden age' of cloth manufacture, particularly of the undyed, high-quality broadcloths, was during the previous century. The road through west Wiltshire, passing through or close to Steeple Ashton, Trowbridge, Bradford-on-Avon, Westbury, Warminster, and by Frome, Bath and Norton St Philip in Somerset, must have been one of the main transport routes by which cloth was carried to London from the fulling mills of west Wiltshire.

From 'Phillips Norton' the Ogilby road continued, as its modern successor A366 does, through Faulkland to Kilmersdon, probably taking a more direct lane from the foot of Ammerdown, and past Home Farm into the village. Picking up the line of the present B3139 the old road climbed westwards over 'Old Down Heath', where his strip map shows a building, possibly the predecessor of the present Old Down Inn whose sign shows a 1640 date. Although this date has not been proved, a 1710 map of nearby Ston Easton estate shows a 'Read Lyon', while a contemporary survey describes it as 'a good house, an inn' occupied by one Edward Gould. This suggests that Ogilby's route was in use around the turn of the century.

A mile beyond Old Down he marks 'Pond'. This is almost certainly Emborough Pool, traditionally a monastic fish pond belonging either to Bruton Priory or the monks of Hinton Charterhouse, although why either of these needed a fishpond so far away (at least 12 miles) from their home is a mystery. The present B3139 takes the Ogilby line south-westwards across the Mendips, descending Horrington Hill into Wells, and his map indicates not only many side roads to east and west but that, not surprisingly, its upland course was as an open track.

## Bristol – Weymouth

Ogilby's map shows this as a principal crossroad, and even Gough's map of three centuries earlier hints at it south of Bristol. Today's traveller would probably journey by Shepton Mallet, Castle Cary or Wincanton, Sherborne and Dorchester, a 70-mile trip. Ogilby's course followed a different route which, by his measurements, was 74 miles, almost exactly the same as a modern map measurer records when used to trace his route which generally kept west of the modern line.

The Ogilby road left Bristol through Bedminster, climbed past Dundry and descended to the Chew valley near Chew Stoke, continuing southwards to ascend the Mendips by what is now called Gibbet's Brow near Compton Martin. Crossing the Mendips on or near the line of the present minor road past the Castle of Comfort Inn and Hunters Lodge, the route dropped down into Wells by what is still called the Old Bristol Road. Running south-west his route is shown as passing through Polsham where 'an Elm' is indicated. A stone bridge is shown where the road crosses the little River Sheppey, and another across the Hartlake just before his road enters Glastonbury and continues through the centre of the town, and makes the right-angled turn at the bottom of High Street as it does today.

Southwards, then, through Street and Compton Dundon into Somerton, and the line of the B3165 to Long Sutton, Long Load and Martock, where the present alignment precisely marks the Ogilby route, continuing across the Foss Way on the B3165, but passing the edge of Chiselborough, through West Chinnock and into Crewkerne ('Crookhorn'). Where Ogilby's route crossed the Foss Way his map gave no indication of its being an important road, but merely showed directions to Ilchester and Petherton Bridge. Sixty years later the Wiltshire antiquarian, Stukeley, similarly indicates the Foss as being of no importance, although he did note its intact Roman stone paving for a short distance.

There seems no doubt that from Crewkerne the A356 closely adopts the Ogilby road through Misterton and South Perrott, ascending the chalk escarpment at Winyard's Gap (492062), though not by the modern line which came later, but by the minor route looping round to the north-east. For almost the whole way from Crewkerne to Weymouth the Ogilby road is shown as unenclosed, and travellers using it must have experienced an even greater feeling of exposure than do those of today, along its open, villageless stretch of 9 miles at over 600ft across the downland between Winyard's Gap and Maiden Newton. Ogilby indicates certain landmarks — 'the Long Ash on the left' and 'the Three Sisters certain trees so called'. Directions accompany side turnings to valley villages, while 'Horston' doubtless refers to the Hore Stones, of prehistoric origin, now enclosed by fences but still visible in a triangle of grassland at the junction of the Beaminster Down road (517035). Nearby to the south-east the Fair Field on Toller Down was the site of an annual sheep fair which seems to have come into prominence during Charles II's time, and would thus have been contemporary with Ogilby's survey.

His road, now represented approximately by A356 through Maiden Newton, crossed the River Frome at Frampton, possibly by a ford since no bridge is mentioned, continuing through Frampton Park and climbing southwards to join Muckleford Lane at Hampton Lodge (633921). From there the Ogilby line is not clear. Professor Good has it running south-eastwards over Bradford Down, across the present A35 into Martinstown. Ogilby shows it distinctly entering (Winterborne) Steepleton from the north, and at the other end of the village turning south-eastwards and winding over downland to Friar Waddon passing on the west a turning 'ye upper way to Waddon'. A church is also shown here, together with an alternative route southwards for a mile. The old road could be one of a number of tracks crossing the Dorset Ridgeway on Ridge Hill, including the minor road along Waddon Hill, but what does appear certain is that the Ogilby road dropped down into the Wey valley at Upwey, continued through Broadwey, and into Weymouth.

Ogilby described the Bristol to Weymouth road as 'indifferent, well-frequented', which in his terminology meant average. Although there was no suggestion that it carried much trade, it was sufficiently important to merit special treatment in his Atlas, and it is probable that it fulfilled some maritime need. In medieval times Weymouth was a wool-exporting port, but in the middle of the fourteenth century, the twin towns of Weymouth and Melcombe Regis — where the plague started its English devastation — suffered badly. In 1571 they were united by a charter, and by the end of Tudor times

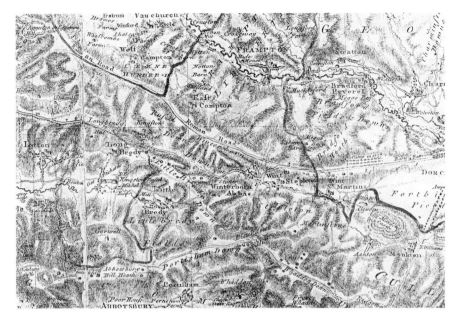

*The area west of Dorchester, from Taylor's map of Dorset, 1765. This shows 'Longbredy Hut' — a toll house and refreshment stop for coach traffic — near the eighth milepost from Dorchester, and the'Ogilby' road over Blackdown and Waddon Down*

were enjoying a revival of fortunes as a trading port, and perhaps the overland route to Bristol may have been thought safer for the carriage of imported Spanish and Portuguese wines. Or did the monarch drop a hint to his official cosmographer that a map of the road from Bristol to Weymouth could be a useful inclusion in his road-book, bearing in mind his hazardous journey to the south coast following his defeat at the Battle of Worcester in 1651?

## The Civil War

During the period of the Civil War, particularly the incidents and drama between 1642 and 1647, many parts of Wessex experienced the movements of armies large and small, with important battles at Lansdown near Bath and Roundway Down above Devizes. There is little doubting Joan Parkes' assertion that 'the Civil War had been for the roads an unmitigated evil. They were subjected to hard usage and had received less than the modicum of attention previously bestowed. Parishes had neglected to appoint surveyors; parishioners had refused to perform statute duty ... However, following the Restoration and stable government ... a rapid extension of the stage-coach services took place; trade and commerce made sudden growth, the population prospered, causing a vast increase in road traffic.'

One interesting reference throws light on the Civil War's effect on local trade. Like other western wool towns Marlborough was predominantly Puritan and therefore supported Parliament. Through it passed a huge amount of Wiltshire cloth bound for the London market at Blackwell Hall, a trade which Parliament needed to continue financing the war. But in December 1642 it fell to Royalist troops and remained in their hands for some time, and so long as Royalist forces held it they could control movement of cloth to London. It was not only Parliamentary finances that suffered. Wiltshire merchants, clothiers and carriers not only saw their livelihoods threatened but recognised the hazards of transporting goods to London. On one occasion they assembled in a large group at Marlborough, where they negotiated with the Royalist governor of Donnington Castle near Newbury that 'on payment of £3 for each waggon, they should continue on their journey, unmolested by Royalist troops.'

## Charles II's Route Through Wessex, 1651

After his defeat at the Battle of Worcester on 3 September 1651 the 21-year-old Charles II realised that to survive he must flee the country, preferably by one of the Channel ports. By 12 September he and a small group of friends had reached Bristol, but it was not until 15 October that he finally succeeded in leaving our shores, at Shoreham harbour, not to return until the spring of 1660. After staying with friends near Bristol, Charles and his friends journeyed secretly through Wessex, mainly on horseback, often in disguise. Their exact route is not known, but can only be conjectured from the known facts about where they stayed.

Trent, near Sherborne, was his chief base, where plans were laid for an escape via Charmouth. A room at the Queen's Arms (named after Catherine of Aragon who stayed there in 1501) had been booked, but the escape plan had to be aborted. The journey was made via Monkton Wyld (336964), but after the change of plans the small party made their way to Bridport where they had a meal at the George Inn (now, Beach's shop with a fine late eighteenth-century façade). To avoid capture Charles' group were forced to head northwards, probably along Lea Lane towards Bradpole, Mangerton and Nethbury to Broadwindsor where they had to ask where they were. Under false names they stayed at the Castle Inn (burned down in 1856 and rebuilt as two cottages) where a plaque records their visit on 23 September. From there they returned to Trent where they stayed another two weeks while new plans were worked out.

On 6 October they left for Heale House near Amesbury, home of a loyal lady, Mrs Hyde. Travelling by Sandford Orcas, Wincanton and Mere, where they stopped at the George Inn for a drink, their route then took them through Hindon, Chilmark and Teffont to Wilton, crossing over to the Avon valley and along the west bank to Heale House (128364). During his few days there Charles even managed a sight-seeing visit to Stonehenge, where, as he subsequently told Pepys, 'We stood looking upon the stones for some time'.

Eventually, Charles, with his friend Colonel Phellips of Montacute, left Heale House, on 13 October, and rode eastwards past Old Sarum and Clarendon Park corner, across the downland dome of eastern Wiltshire to Tytherley and the Test valley at Mottisfont. They subsequently made their way, via Hambledon and across Hampshire into Sussex, past Arundel,

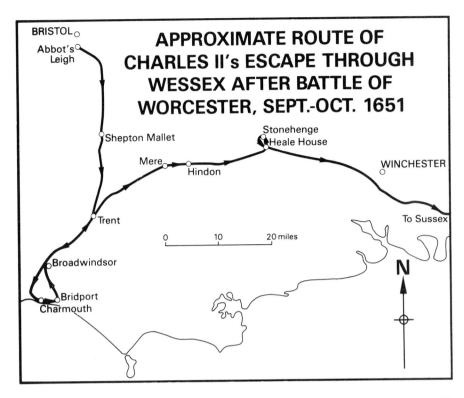

**APPROXIMATE ROUTE OF CHARLES II's ESCAPE THROUGH WESSEX AFTER BATTLE OF WORCESTER, SEPT.-OCT. 1651**

BRISTOL

Abbot's Leigh

Shepton Mallet

Mere

Hindon

Stonehenge
Heale House

WINCHESTER

Trent

To Sussex

0    10    20 miles

Broadwindsor

Bridport
Charmouth

N

*The former George Inn, Bridport, Dorset, where Charles II stayed during his flight from Worcester in 1651*

across the Arun at Houghton Bridge and the Adur at Bramber Bridge. On the morning of 15 October Charles left England for exile that was to last 8 years.

*A former inn in Broadwindsor, where Charles II slept in September 1651, during his escape following the battle of Worcester*

## Duke of Monmouth

Charles II's illegitimate son, James, by his mistress Lucy Walter, was born in Rotterdam in 1649 during the king's previous exile, and brought to England by his father at the Restoration, to be created Duke of Monmouth in 1663. Charles had no legitimate sons, so at his death in February 1685, his brother the Catholic Duke of York succeeded to the throne as James II. But the Duke of Monmouth, then living in Holland, was persuaded to lead an invasion and attempt to usurp the throne. With three ships, eighty-two men, but short of everything else, he landed on 11 June 1685 at Lyme, the nearest port to Taunton where he planned to establish his base.

He built up a small army numbering 1,000 men and 150 horses, moved northwards to Axminster, Chard and Ilminster to Taunton, reaching there on 18 June. More supporters joined him and he was proclaimed king at the town's market cross. Meanwhile, the Royal Navy had arrived at Lyme, occupied the town and thus cut off Monmouth's retreat, while James II's troops had reached east Somerset, heading for Bristol, intending to secure its safety.

Monmouth advanced northwards to Bridgwater, across rain-sodden Somerset Levels to Glastonbury and Shepton Mallet, gradually raising their number to over 6,000 men with whom he planned to march on Bristol. Bad weather forced him to change plans, so from Keynsham he had to retreat eastwards towards Bath, which refused entry, so Monmouth's army moved southwards to Norton St Philip. The first real contest occurred near there on 27 June, where regular troops forced Monmouth's men to retreat to Frome.

He decided to return to Shepton Mallet and Wells, eventually reaching Bridgwater on 3 July.

Lord Feversham's troops, hurrying to Glastonbury and Somerton to prevent Monmouth escaping south-west to Devon and Cornwall, encamped at Weston Zoyland, and it was near there that the inevitable, conclusive battle occurred, on the night of 5-6 July. The Battle of Sedgmoor, was fought among watery rhines and low-lying moors about half a mile north-west of Weston Zoyland (352355). The rebels were no match for well-trained Royalist forces, 400 were killed and 200 prisoners taken and temporarily locked in Weston Zoyland church.

Monmouth and Lord Grey escaped to Dorset, aiming for Poole, travelling — as Monmouth's father had done 34 years earlier — in secret, and probably by way of Shaftesbury and Berwick St John, using the Ox Drove to Woodyates (029194), where they abandoned their exhausted horses and Monmouth disguised himself as a shepherd. The fugitives tramped south-eastwards, crossing the Allen probably at Stanbridge, and moved to Woodlands, and it was near there that the would-be king, now alone, was captured, hiding in a ditch by a hedge where grew a prominent ash. The 1:25,000 map marks the place as 'Monmouth's Ash' (062073). A few days later, on 15 July he was executed at the Tower of London.

# Other Seventeenth-Century Travellers

In the two decades after the Civil War more settled conditions gradually brought about increased travel for the sake of satisfying curiosity about one's own country. The diarists John Evelyn and Samuel Pepys made long journeys, usually by four- or six-horse coach throughout southern England, and obviously without harm. Although they rarely, if ever, commented about the roads it may well be that they were enjoying the best of the pre-turnpike network before too many wheels destroyed it. They both liked civilised pleasures, enjoying places such as Oxford and Bath, and Pepys records that on his return journey from Bath to London he 'took coach and away ... and rode all day with some trouble for fear of being out of our way over the Downs, where the life of the shepherds is, in fair weather, only pretty'. He visited, and was much impressed by, Avebury, after which he, 'took coach again, but about a mile off it was prodigious to see how full the Downs are of great stones'. He obviously travelled by the Old Bath Road, continuing over Manton Down to Marlborough, where he 'lay at the Hart, a good house, and a pretty fair town ... houses on one side having their pent-houses supported with pillars, which makes it a good walk. My wife pleased with all.'

## Celia Fiennes

One of the most intrepid travellers of late Stuart times was a Wiltshire lady, Celia Fiennes, born in 1662 at Newton Tony, a few miles east of Salisbury. From 1687 until 1703 she made a series of journeys, mainly in England, and recorded in clear, direct, unemotional prose her observations. The full, large octavo version of her account was not transcribed and published until 1888, when it was called *Through England on a Side Saddle in the time of William and Mary*. The version edited and introduced by Christopher Morris and published in 1947, simplified this to *The Journeys of Celia Fiennes*, and presents a startlingly alive account of this remarkable lady's adventures three centuries ago.

Unfortunately, as with so many other writers since, she says little about roads, except when there was some particular characteristic meriting special comment. It was natural for her to visit Salisbury frequently, and she noted 'pretty large town streetes broad but through the midst of them runs a little rivulet of water which makes the streetes not so clean or so easye to passe in, they have steppes to cross it and many open places for horses and carriages to cross it'. Even today Wells has streams of water running along the gutters of the High Street, and Cheap Street, Frome, has a runnel down the centre of its paved surface.

As part of a longer journey, probably in 1685, she visited Wilton House and then rode to Blandford '18 miles through a haire waring (hare warren) and a forest of the Kings (Cranborne Chase) — Blandford — thence to Merly (House 1 mile south of Wimborne), by Wimborn over a great river called the Stoure (a large arched bridge) — thence to Poole a little seaport town 4 miles off ....' Initially her route was probably by the old Wilton Way, but we do not know how she crossed Cranborne Chase, or reached Wimborne from Blandford, although we could surmise that it may have been by the old road by Tarrant Crawford and Shapwick. Her bridge over the Stour must have been Julian's Bridge, built 50 years earlier, whose eight stone arches would have impressed her. It was widened on the south side in 1844.

Philip Lea's edition of Saxton's map of Dorset, published in 1690, shows a road from Wareham through Lytchett Minster to Wimborne, the southern part of which is now the modern main road, but the northern section from Beacon Hill (970946) may be marked by the minor road through Hill View and Lambs Green to the river crossing. Celia would have followed this southwest from the bridge to Lambs Green and then taken a lane to Merley House.

From Merley she rode to Wareham where 'we passed over a bridge where the sea flowed in', into the Isle of Purbeck, where — as usual in her travels she stayed with a relation (of which she seems to possess plenty) — at Quarr (988797) 2 miles south-east of Corfe Castle. She refers to the many stone quarries in the area although she probably did not know that marble from Quarr went to Winchester Cathedral and Corfe Castle in earlier times. She subsequently left Purbeck near Tyneham where 'we ascend a high hill of great length' heading for Piddletrenthide, passing what she called 'a Castle called Bindon', by which she must have meant the meagre ruins of Bindon Abbey. Later, at Bridport, 'the ways are stony and very narrow, the town has a steep hill to descend through the whole place.'

Of the roads above Lyme she noted '... the wayes are also difficult by reason of the very steep hills up and down, and that so successively as little or no plaine even ground, and full of large smooth pebbles that make the strange horses slip and uneasye to go; the horses of the country are accustomed to it and travell well in the rodes; in the opener wayes they use a sort

*Julian Bridge, Wimborne, dated 1636*

of waine or carriage made narrower than our southern waggon but longer, and so load them high'. She returned from this trip by way of Bridport, Dorchester and Blandford, and since, in the later stage of this journey she records going 'over Woodbery Hill eminent for a great Faire that is kept there of all things' one can only speculate the exact course of her route.

One surmise is that, from Dorchester, she took the old road (now A35) to Yellowham Hill and joined the Ridge Way to enter Puddletown from the west, continuing either through Burleston and Tolpuddle, then following a route leaving the A35 at 800945, and now represented by a succession of field paths, bridleway and farm lanes along the north side of the Piddle to Turner's Puddle (830935) or by the old road, now a bridleway and minor road from Athelhampton along the south side of the river, through Affpuddle and Throop, to the old ford at Turner's Puddle. From there a double-hedged holloway runs north-west over the heathy landscape of Black Hill past an old boundary stone (838942) into Bere Regis. An alternative way from Dorchester would have taken Celia south of the River Frome, through West Stafford and across Woodsford Heath to Moreton where the river is crossed by an old ford, at least 60yd wide, where there is now a footbridge (805895). From Moreton a direct route led north-eastwards to Turner's Puddle, and a less direct one slightly to the east, now a footpath passing east of Clouds Hill, to Chamberlayne's Heath (840917). This joins the Wool-Bere Regis road for a short distance before swinging eastwards near Bowcroft Hill, fording the Bere stream to Dodding's Farm and then climbing Woodbury Hill by a track now lost. Bere Regis was not mentioned.

To work out the route from Woodbury Hill would involve even more speculation. We know from her writing that she passed Charborough Park, probably towards its western side, though on a more direct route than the present A31, an 1841 re-routing of an older road. Charborough was built for Sir Thomas Earle before 1661, and he was a cousin of Celia's, and her

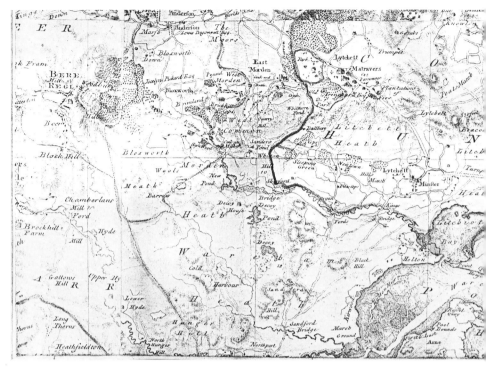

*Bere Regis and the eastern heaths, from Taylor's map of Dorset, 1765. Note the absence of roads across the heath and the consequent isolation of Bere Regis*

description of the house suggests she stayed there, but apparently not on this occasion, for she rode 'thence 6 miles to Blandford, thence 18 to Salesbury and 8 mile to Newtontony....'

On another visit to the west Celia Fiennes comments on the country of west Dorset '... an enclosed country and narrow lanes you cannot see a bow shott before you, and such up and down steep hills....' Near Forde Abbey she refers to 'narrow stony lanes up hills and down, which steeps causes the water on raines to trill down on the low ground that for a few hours or a day there will be noe passing in the bottom ....' On one occasion one night's rain caused the water to be so deep that she could not go to church as 'the water would have come over the windows of the Coach'. From Lyme, on this visit, she went through Maiden Newton to Dorchester, 'all a fine hard gravel way and much on the downs, this is good ground much for sheep'. She continued through Puddletown, Milborne and Winterborne Whitchurch to Blandford, and home via Salisbury.

In 1687 she rode through Wiltshire into Somerset: extracts from her account throw some light on travelling conditions:

'... from thence [Mere] to Wincanton which is on a steep hill and very stony; you go through the town all the way down as it were a steep precipice, all rocks; thence to Castle Cary ... as we returned from thence we came to Bruton a very neat stone built town, from it we ascended a very steep high hill all in a narrow lane cut out of the rocks, and the way is all like stone steps: the sides are rocks on which grow trees thick, their roots run amongst the rocks, and in many places fine clear springs bubble out, and run a long way out of the rocks, it smells just like the sea: we were full an hour passing that hill, though with four horse and a chariot, my Sister, self and maid; thence to Wylye which is a place of much water, so to Newtontony in all 30 miles'.

The 'very steep high hill' can only have been Kingsettle Hill on the Harroway, which she rode along eastwards towards Wylye. Celia Fiennes' way through Wincanton, incidentally, would have been by the steep road north of the present church road, descending to a small stream and the Castle Cary road. In her time Wincanton was far from the main London road which was the Harroway to the north, crossing the Wincanton-Castle Cary road (now A371) at the junction with the Bruton-Sparkford road at A359.

There is little doubt that in Ogilby's time the Kingsettle Hill road was a busy and important one. Just over a century later the first large-scale map of Somerset (1782, by Day and Masters), showing the maturing turnpike road network, delineates it clearly. The old road is shown crossing the Brewham brook close to where the Bull Inn now stands, at the hamlet named in 1782 as Hardway. With its unusual outside stone stairway, the Bull Inn may well be a seventeenth-century structure existing when Ogilby's surveyors worked along that road.

Another interesting sidelight on travelling conditions in pre-turnpike days comes from an account of a journey through Wiltshire in 1712 by John Saunders, a manservant accompanying Mrs Sarah Hickes during a visit from Buckinghamshire to London, and thence to Bath. Their journey brought them to Marlborough and then by the old coach road over Manton and Fyfield Down, across the Ridgeway, and down the Herepath into Avebury. They travelled with Mrs Hickes' friends, Sir Richard and Lady Holford who lived at Avebury, and they obviously visited the great stone circle. On 22 August they rode (presumably by the old road to Old Shepherd's Shore) to

'Alcannons that is 5 miles from Avebury [he may have meant Bishop's Cannings] and through the Vicese Green [Devizes — by Southbroom] which is 1 mile from Alcannons, through Potterne it is 1 mile from Vicese Tuft. [His distances are way out!] We rod to the 5 lanes [still named at a meeting of bridleways at 982586] in the next lane that turned towards Worton we came to a great deep myer across the lane we had no way to ride by so we were forced to pass through it. My Mrs got safe through it by God's great mercy though with great difficulty to the horse and dainger to herself. I rid through after her but my horse floundered so very much that his tackel broke and down came ye portmantow and I had a very dangerous fall but God preserved me that I had no hurt'.

They continued through Worton, Marston, Coulston and Tinhead where they stayed at the Court. On the Sunday they travelled in their host's coach to service at Imber, and visited the Priory church at Edington. On Friday 26 September 'we went from Tinhead with ye Salisbury coach to Bath', arriving about 9 o'clock that evening. The coach, one surmises, came across Salisbury Plain by the old Bath road by Yarnbury and Chitterne Down, descending the northern scarp of the Plain by Coulston Hill to Tinhead, a route which was

*The old Salisbury to Bath road at Coulston Hill, near Tinhead in Wiltshire*

later turnpiked, and whose milestones still survive, although they would not have been there in Mr Saunders' time.

# Eighteenth-Century Travellers

### Defoe

In the 1720s Daniel Defoe travelled across the downlands of Wessex during his great journey from London to Land's End. His comments highlight some of the difficulties encountered by travellers at that time, and for centuries previously:

> 'Shaftesbury is fourteen miles from Salisbury over that fine down or carpet ground, which they call particularly, or properly, Salisbury Plain. It has neither house or town in view all the way, and the road which often lyes very broad, and branches off insensibly, might easily cause a traveller to loose his way'.

Roads were inadequately surfaced and unenclosed, so they became progressively wider as successive travellers sought routes which were free from mud, potholes, and large loose boulders. They were usually without signposts, and it was not uncommon for people to become lost. Defoe found his way because 'there is a certain never failing assistance upon all these downs for telling a stranger his way, and that is the number of shepherds feeding, or keeping their vast flocks of sheep, which are everywhere in the way, and who, with a very little pains, a traveller may always speak with....' However, he may not always have been the wiser, the West Country dialect being what it was. Defoe's route in this instance was, of course, that Salisbury-Shaftesbury road already mentioned, the so-called 'Race-course road'. Another 40 years were to elapse before it became turnpiked.

Defoe was a reporter and less interested in antiquities and scenery than were earlier travellers, although he did spend a day visiting Stonehenge during his western tour. He also diverted from Salisbury to see something of the New Forest and Lymington, travelling down the east bank of the Avon, and visiting Clarendon Park on the way. His preference was for lush countryside and 'modern' houses, but above all else his interests lay in social and economic matters. Hence his detailed observations on downland sheep farming and in the clothing towns, listing these by counties:

| | |
|---|---|
| Somersetshire | Frome, Pensford, Philip's Norton, Bruton, Shepton Mallet, Castle Carey and Wincanton |
| Wiltshire | Malmesbury, Castlecomb, Chippenham, Calne, Devizes, Bradford, Trowbridge, Westbury, Warminster, Meer |
| Dorset | Gillingham, Shaftesbury, Bemister, and Bere, Sturminster, Shireborn |

'which are interspersed with ... innumerable villages, hamlets and scattered houses ....' But of roads Defoe has little or nothing to say.

## James Woodforde

Most of his *Diary of a Country Parson 1758-92* refers to his last 25 years in Nor folk, but the period 1758-75 covers the years in Somerset, where his father was Rector of Ansford, near Castle Cary, and he himself held curacies. During his Oxford years 1759-63 he travelled frequently between his home and the university, by various routes.

*The old Marlborough road from Salisbury, north of Everleigh*

*Old Down Inn on the Mendips, where Parson Woodforde changed coaches on some journeys from Ansford to Bath in the 1770s*

In September 1759, riding with his father's man, he crossed Wiltshire, by Bruton and the Harroway to Hindon, Deptford, Yarnbury Castle, Madding-ton (Shrewton) and Netheravon to Everleigh, where he stayed at the Rose and Crown (now the Crown, which William Cobbett used and greatly liked in 1826), before continuing the next day through Shalbourne to Hungerford. His usual way, by stage-coach, was by Bath and Cirencester, with an overnight stop in Bath, but he recorded the first occasion, in 1774, when he travelled all the way by post-chaise, taking $14^1/_2$ hours to cover the 100 miles from Oxford to Ansford, and sharing the vehicle with Coleridge's brother, the two men paying £7 14s 6d each. A curate's pay then was little more than £30 a year, a labourer's wage a shilling a day. A contemporary writer reckoned that on an average journey, using turnpike roads, travellers paid at a toll-gate about every 7 miles. Travel was definitely for the better-off.

More locally, Woodforde lived a busy social life, outside his church duties, attending race meetings at Wincanton, Sherborne and Bruton, boxing at Cannard's Grave near Shepton Mallet, and playing fives against the church wall at Babcary near Ansford. When he visited Bath, via Old Down, he travelled by post-chaise, paying half a guinea for each half of his journey.

### John Wesley

John Wesley was undoubtedly the most prolific of eighteenth-century travellers, both in the number of places he visited, the journeys he made over about 50 years, and the volume of words he noted in his journal, which, in its revised and edited form covers eight bulky books. This mighty traveller was not seeking the 'remarkable and curious', but to bring instruction and light to those in darkness. From the late 1730s right through to within a few months of his death in 1791 he covered 250,000 miles, mainly on horseback, but in his later years by post-chaise. Based in Bristol for most of the time he made extensive and repeated journeys through Wessex and the West Country, in all kinds of weather, and, unusually, reading while riding, with the reins loose on the horse's neck, which implies that the roads he used were such that his horse could make its way without stumbling.

He was frequently at Chippenham, Shaftesbury, Wincanton, Salisbury and Winchester — Sarum and Winton to him. He regularly did the round of the clothing towns of west Wiltshire and east Somerset, occasionally reached Dorchester and Corfe Castle, but Marlborough only rarely. Four days from his 1774 diary shows a typical Wesley itinerary:

Oct 10    Salisbury
Oct 11    Corfe Castle
Oct 12    Langton Matravers and Swanage
Oct 13    Portsmouth

Other brief entries offer mere outlines:

1790    Sept 27    I left Bristol: about eleven I preached in Devizes, and in the evening at Sarum
                 29  About noon I preached at Wilton
1787    Feb   26  Together, Sarum, tea, coach, Dorchester, dinner, mail-coach 10 Exon, supper, prayer 12

Unfortunately, roads are rarely mentioned. However, an incident recorded for 28 February 1748, on a journey from Fisherton (near Salisbury) to Longbridge Deverill (beyond Hindon, Wilts), throws a little light:

'About ten o'clock we were met by a loaded wagon, in a deep, hollow way. There was a narrow path between the road and the bank ... when the wagon came near, my horse began to rear and to attempt climbing the bank ... [Wesley was thrown from his horse] ... I fell on the path between the wagon and the bank ... but was unhurt.'

He rode on to preach at Deverill at 12 noon, and in the evening at Bradford-on-Avon.

## Arthur Young

Arthur Young published the account of *Six Weeks' Tour through the Southern Counties of England and Wales* in 1768. Although he was much interested in agriculture he did not ignore local industries, frequently commented on towns he passed through, and the quality of accommodation at the inns where he stayed. He occasionally praised the roads along which he travelled, which were the new turnpikes wherever possible. For the first time we have a useful survey of their condition, although his comments are terse — 'very good', 'very bad', or 'middling'. However, in what was for him almost a rush of blood to the head, he bestows on one main road unusually fulsome praise:

'...I chiefly travelled upon turnpikes: of all of which that from Salisbury to four miles the other side of Romsey, towards Winchester, is, without exception, the finest I ever saw. The trustees of that road highly deserve all the praise than can be given...'

He goes on to describe its construction:

'They first lay a foundation of large stones, which they level with smaller ones, then make a layer of chalk on that gravel, and lastly, another of sifted gravel exceeding fine, and in some places tending towards a sand ... and yet the traffic on it is very great by waggons ... but scarcely the print of a wheel is to be seen on it for miles ... and I really believe there was not a loose stone to make a horse stumble, nineteen miles from Salisbury'.

The road described was the Salisbury and Southampton Trust road, turn-piked in 1753. Of 'The Lyons' at Salisbury he wrote 'Good, but very dear' 'The Bell' at Romsey was merely 'good', while he found 'The Bear' at Devizes 'Exceedingly good, and remarkably civil'.

## Hon John Byng (later Lord Torrington)

During the 1780s and 1790s another horse-back traveller kept a record of his many journeys undertaken mainly for pleasure and curiosity. Byng was rather old-fashioned in his habits, looked back nostalgically to the roads and inns of his youth, and disliked intensely the new turnpikes, considering them flat, straight and ugly — an interesting comparison with present-day atti-tudes to motorways. He peevishly complained how they brought a sameness of speech and manners into every district.

On his summer tours, taken leisurely on 'a sufficient horse', he carried a small portmanteau behind him, while a servant usually rode ahead with most of the luggage, and also to see that appropriate accommodation was ready at an inn where they would spend the night. He obviously had a poor opinion of most inns, so carried his own sheets in the luggage. Unlike most of today's travellers he liked to make an early start, travelling 10 miles before breakfast, thus making the most of what he thought were the finest hours of the day. In this he has a lesson for most of us! From his 1782 diary, we read:

August 26 (from Ringwood)
'By seven o'clock I was on horseback, and crossed much bleak, heathy country till near Longham where I passed an handsome river (Stour) over a long stone bridge' [presumably that referred to by Hutchins as having been 'new built' in 1728, and widened ten years after Byng's visit].

He continued through Poole to Wareham and 'its neat bridge built lately over the River Froom' (since replaced by a concrete structure). From there he went to Corfe Castle, though not presumably by the new turnpike road of 1765-6, for he refers to 'a noble view ... on the left hand of the ruins of Corfe Castle', so he may have come by the old road by Cotness, East Creech and along the ridgeway. Subsequently, after returning to Wareham, he headed westwards for Dorchester.

'... I rode forward ten miles without either fatigue or any dull thought ... and in a busy employ of opening gates which presented themselves every quarter of a mile... [So he was not using a turnpike] ... After two hours riding I quitted the Dorchester road and the gravel, for I was not encumbered by hills and stoney paths from which I had views of the sea, at two or three miles distance; the road was like a broken-up pavement ... I rode but at a foot's pace. The fields are of pasture to the hill-tops, with many stone walls, and I saw two or more old, deserted mansions; in short, a very detestable country; but it soon changed for the better, with the roads, near the village of Preston ... I descended to the sea-beach, and in two miles entered the town of Melcombe Regis, joined by a short bridge to that of Weymouth'.

It seems likely that the later part of his route took him along the Coastal Ridgeway through Winfrith and Poxwell, but we cannot be sure.

# Larger Scale Maps

Undoubtedly the most important advance in eighteenth-century cartography occurred in 1759 when the Royal Society of Arts offered a prize of £100 for new and accurate county maps drawn at a scale of at least one inch to the mile. This provided a stimulus for surveyors and cartographers. Isaac Taylor, a professional surveyor much employed by landowners in Hampshire and Dorset to survey their estates produced the first large-scale map of Hampshire in 1759 and of Dorset in 1765. Not only was it the first Dorset map on the 1-inch scale but it was the first to show all the roads rather than a selection of the main ones.

Andrews and Dury's great map of Wiltshire, produced in 1773, was on the even larger scale of about 2in to the mile, engraved by Andrews on copper plate, and comprising eighteen numbered sheets each measuring about 25in x 18in, which, when mounted together form a map measuring roughly 9ft x 6ft 3in. These eighteenth-century county surveys were financed almost wholly by subscriptions raised within the county, and the cost was high, probably £2,000 or more, representing 400 subscriptions of five guineas each. Day and Masters' large-scale map of Somerset was published in 1782, and like the others referred to, paid careful attention to the gardens and parks associated with the larger houses. Churches and houses are usually drawn in perspective, while roads are indicated by double lines, with turnpike gates marked, but little distinction is made between different types of highway. Milestones are shown on the Wiltshire map, with distances (but not place-names); relief is represented by vertical shading, woods by compact groups of roughly-drawn tree-tops, while the most prominent feature on most maps is the marking of Hundred boundaries by broad, usually coloured, lines.

It would be too much to expect maps of that date to be perfect. Surveying techniques were far less accurate than those of today, particularly in the field of compass bearings, so that directions cannot wholly be relied on. In addition, the amount of travelling, on horseback, needed to cover a county was enormous, so it is probable that, in the remoter areas, local information may have been a substitute for personal inspection and survey. Thus, although they cannot completely be relied upon, within their limitations these eighteenth-century maps give a fairly complete picture of the contemporary road system of the Wessex counties.

In 1787 new small-scale maps were produced by the great engraver John Cary, contained in his *New and Correct British Atlas: being a new set of County Maps from Actual Surveys*. The atlas is folio size and the maps measure 9³/₄in

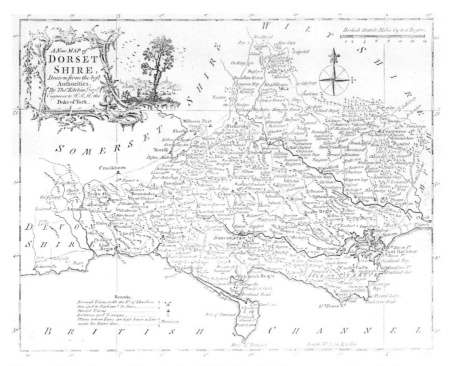

*Thomas Kitchen's map of Dorset, about 1750. Note that there are no main roads shown north of Shaftsbury, and no direct link between Shaftesbury and Cranborne, Blandford or Dorchester, nor Blandford and Wimborne*

x 7³/₄in, showing towns, villages, rivers, canals, bridges, and roads with distances marked alongside. The Dorset one is on a scale of approximately 6¹/₂ miles to the inch, and is a model of clarity. It forms a fascinating comparison with one of about 1750, by 'Thomas Kitchin, Geogr, Engraver to HRH the Duke of York'. According to its inscription: 'A New Map of Dorsetshire, Drawn from the best Authorities', it was copied from earlier surveys. Only a handful of main roads are shown, mainly those of Ogilby's day, plus one running north-westwards from Wareham, through Bere Regis, Abbeymilton and Sturminster to just west of Shaftesbury, joining the main Sherborne road near Stour Provost. No road runs north from Shaftesbury, and no roads are shown in Purbeck.

In 1789 Cary engraved new county maps for Gough's translation of Camden's *Britannia*, on a larger scale, with each map about 20in x 16in. Recognising how the new turnpikes were bringing about an increase in travel, he moved into the Ogilby tradition by publishing, also in 1789, a little gem of a book, his *Traveller's Companion*, which, although measuring only 6¹/₂in x 4¹/₂in, consisted of clearly drawn maps of each county, showing the main roads exceptionally well.

Haywood and Harrison's map of Dorset, produced in 1789, shows interesting differences from Cary's of the same year, presumably since it was 'Engraved from an Actual Survey' (with improvements), rather than a new

*John Cary's map of Dorset, 1787. Note that compared with Kitchen's map the road network has been filled in by the new turnpikes, but there is no direct link between Shaftesbury and Dorchester*

survey. On a slightly larger scale (about 4 miles to the inch) it shows towns, villages, rivers and roads clearly, but the retention of Hundred boundaries adds unnecessary complication. Cary correctly shows Cerne Abbas as lying NNW of Dorchester, while Haywood has it due north; Cary has Charmouth due west of Bridport, Haywood puts it south-west, with a resultant distortion of road orientation in that area. However, both maps agree on the apparent importance of the road from Weymouth, via Upwey and running northwards to Frampton, then north-westwards via Maiden Newton to Crewkerne — clearly the Ogilby route to Bristol. Haywood has obviously misplaced 'Piddleton', which is completely ignored by the Dorchester-Blandford road and although Cary got it right, both maps also show a direct route through Dewlish, Milton Abbey and Winterbourne Stickland. Taylor, incidentally, clearly marks the turnpike through Milborne St Andrew, complete with milestones. The difference between the maps of Haywood and Cary is very marked in Marshwood Vale, where Haywood, probably copying an older map, shows few roads, but Cary's much more thorough survey depicts what is virtually the present-day network. With such differences between contemporary maps eighteenth-century travellers must surely have experienced no small degree of confusion, and it is not, therefore, surprising that more detailed itineraries started to appear, offering much more guidance.

*Haywood's map of Dorset, 1789 is interesting for its apparent errors: 'Piddleton' is neglected by through roads and Lyme Regis is shown south-west of Bridport*

*(opposite) Two sections from Cary's* Traveller's Companion *(1806). Note the reference (p47) to the continuing use from Harnham Hill of the Old Racecourse road to Shaftesbury, and Alfred's Tower and the Hardway (p118)*

---

# Itineraries

Travellers in the late eighteenth century needed detailed instructions about available routes. The county maps already described were not really suitable, being too large and bulky. Strip maps or written lists offered better alternatives, and in 1783 Thomas Kitchin produced his *Travellers Guide*. Two years later Daniel Paterson's *British Itinerary*, set an approach which was to become the standard against which all others could be judged for the next 60 or 70 years. Very much in the Ogilby mould it included strip maps as well as a good set of written instructions. The style is clear and uncluttered, and its success is evident from the number of editions it went through, as the illustrations from the eighteenth edition of 1822, revised by E. Mogg, show.

In 1798 John Cary republished in extended form, but without the maps, his *Traveller's Companion*. Its title explains its purpose: 'Cary's New Itinerary, or an Accurate Delineation of the Great Roads, both Direct and Cross, throughout England and Wales: with many of the Principal Roads in Scotland, from an actual admeasurement made by command of His Majesty's Postmaster-General for Official Purposes' ... by John Cary, Surveyor of Roads to the General Post Office.

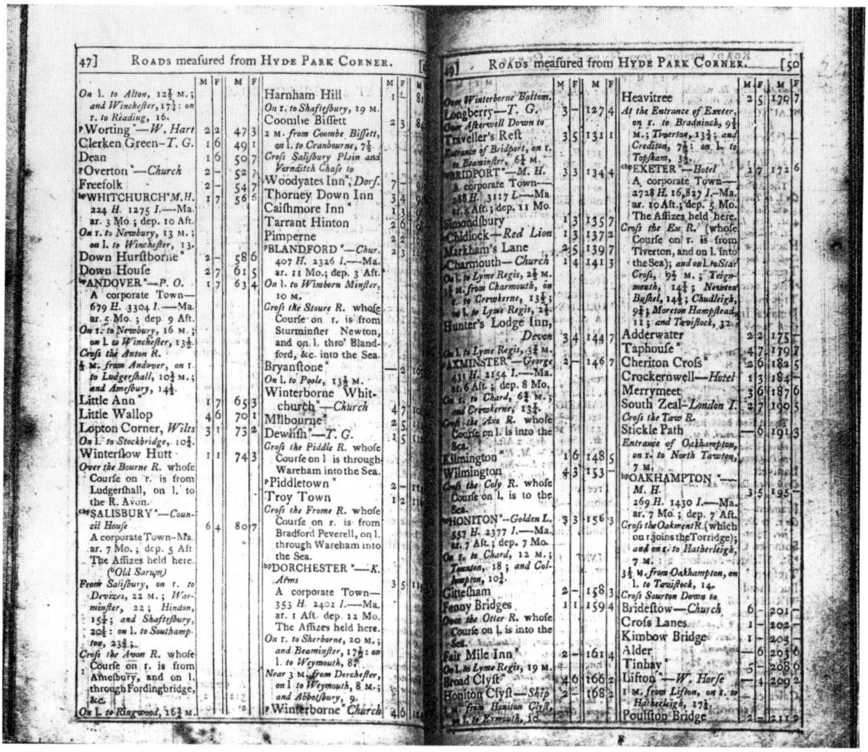

47] ROADS measured from HYDE PARK CORNER.

On l. to Alton, 12½ M.; and Winchester, 17¾: on r. to Reading, 16.
Worting — W. Hart 2 2 47 3
Clerken Green—T. G. 1 6 49 1
Dean 1 6 50 7
Overton — Church 2 – 52 7
Freefolk 2 – 54 7
WHITCHURCH M.H. 1 7 56 6
224 H. 1275 I.—Ma. ar. 3 Mo; dep. 10 Aft.
On r. to Newbury, 13 M.; on l. to Winchester, 13.
Down Hurstborne 2 – 58 6
Down House 2 7 61 5
ANDOVER — P. O. 1 7 63 4
A corporate Town—679 H. 3304 I.—Ma. ar. 5 Mo. ar; dep 9 Aft.
On r. to Newbury, 16 M.; on l. to Winchester, 13½.
Cross the Anton R.
½ M. from Andover, on r. to Ludgershall, 10½ M.; and Amesbury, 14½.
Little Ann 1 7 65 3
Little Wallop 4 6 70 1
Lopton Corner, Wilts 3 1 73 2
On l. to Stockbridge, 10½.
Winterslow Hutt 1 1 74 3
Over the Bourne R. whose Course on r. is from Ludgershall, on l. to the R. Avon.
SALISBURY — Council House 6 4 80 7
A corporate Town—Ma. ar. 7 Mo.; dep. 5 Aft. The Assizes held here. (Old Sarum)
From Salisbury, on r. to Devizes, 22 M.; Warminster, 22; Hindon, 15½; and Shaftesbury, 20½: on l. to Southampton, 23½.
Cross the Avon R. whose Course on r. is from Amesbury, and on l. through Fordingbridge, &c.
On l. to Ringwood, 16½ M.

Harnham Hill 1 –
On r. to Shaftesbury, 19 M.
Coombe Bissett 2 3
2 M. from Coombe Bissett, on l. to Cranbourne, 7½.
Cross Salisbury Plain and Vernditch Chase to
Woodyates Inn, Dorf. 7 –
Thorney Down Inn 3 4
Caishmore Inn 1 3
Tarrant Hinton 2 6
Pimperne 2 2
BLANDFORD — Chur. 2 3
407 H. 2326 I.—Ma. ar. 11 Mo.; dep. 3 Aft.
On l. to Wimborn Minster, 10 M.
Cross the Stoure R. whose Course on r. is from Sturminster Newton, and on l. thro' Blandford, &c. into the Sea.
Bryanstone – 2
On l. to Poole, 13½ M.
Winterborne Whitchurch — Church 4 7
Milbourne 2 5
Dewlish — T. G. 1 5
Cross the Piddle R. whose Course on l is through Wareham into the Sea.
Piddletown 2 –
Troy Town 1 2
Cross the Frome R. whose Course on r. is from Bradford Peverell, on l. through Wareham into the Sea.
DORCHESTER — K. Arms 3 5
A corporate Town—353 H. 2402 I.—Ma. ar. 1 Aft. dep. 12 Mo. The Assizes held here.
On r. to Sherborne, 20 M.; and Beaminster, 17½: on l. to Weymouth, 8⅛.
Near 3 M. from Dorchester, on l. to Weymouth, 8 M.; and Abbotsbury, 9.
Winterborne Church 4 6

49] ROADS measured from HYDE PARK CORNER. [50

Over Winterborne Bottom.
Longberry — T. G. 3 – 127 4
Over Askerwell Down to
Traveller's Rest 3 5 131 1
Entrance of Bridport, on r. to Beaminster, 6½ M.
BRIDPORT — M. H. 3 3 134 4
A corporate Town—288 H. 3117 I.—Ma. ar. 10 Aft.; dep. 11 Mo.
Simondsbury 1 3 135 7
Chidiock — Red Lion 1 3 137 2
Markham's Lane 2 5 139 7
Charmouth — Church 1 4 141 3
On l. to Lyme Regis, 2½ M.
1½ M. from Charmouth, on r. to Crewkerne, 13½; on l. to Lyme Regis, 2½.
Hunter's Lodge Inn, Devon 3 4 144 7
On l. to Lyme Regis, 3½ M.
AXMINSTER — George 2 – 146 7
431 H. 2154 I.—Ma. ar. 6 Aft.; dep. 8 Mo.
On r. to Chard, 6½ M.; and Crewkerne, 13½.
Cross the Axe R. whose Course on l. is into the Sea.
Kilmington 1 6 148 5
Wilmington 4 3 153 –
Cross the Coly R. whose Course on l. is to the Sea.
HONITON — Golden L. 3 3 156 3
557 H. 2377 I.—Ma. ar. 7 Aft.; dep. 7 Mo.
On r. to Chard, 12 M.; Taunton, 18; and Colhampton, 10½.
Gittesham 2 – 158 3
Fenny Bridges 1 1 159 4
Over the Otter R. whose Course on l. is into the Sea.
Fair Mile Inn 2 – 161 4
On l. to Lyme Regis, 19 M.
Broad Clyst 4 6 166 2
Honiton Clyst — Ship 2 – 168 2
1 M. from Honiton Clyst, on l. to Exmouth, 10.

Heavitree 2 5 170 7
At the Entrance of Exeter, on r. to Bradninch, 9½ M.; Tiverton, 13½; and Crediton, 7½: on l. to Topsham, 3½.
EXETER — Hotel 1 7 172 6
A corporate Town—2728 H. 16,817 I.—Ma. ar. 10 Aft.; dep. 5 Mo. The Assizes held here.
Cross the Ex R. (whose Course on r. is from Tiverton, and on l. into the Sea); and on l. to Star Cross, 9½ M.; Teignmouth, 14½; Newton Bushel, 14½; Chudleigh, 9½; Moreton Hampstead, 11; and Tavistock, 32.
Adderwater 2 2 175 –
Taphouse 4 7 179 7
Cheriton Cross 2 6 182 5
Crockernwell — Hotel 1 3 184 –
Merrymeet 3 6 187 6
South Zeal — London I. 2 7 190 5
Cross the Taw R.
Stickle Path – 6 191 3
Entrance of Oakhampton, on r. to North Tawton, 7 M.
OAKHAMPTON — M. H. 3 5 195 –
269 H. 1430 I.—Ma. ar. 7 Mo.; dep. 7 Aft.
Cross the Oakment R. (which on r. joins the Torridge); and on r. to Hatherleigh, 7 M.
3½ M. from Oakhampton, on l. to Tavistock, 14.
Cross Sourton Down to
Bridestow — Church 6 – 201 –
Cross Lanes 1 – 202 –
Kimbow Bridge 1 – 203 –
Alder – 6 203 6
Tinhay 5 – 208 6
Lifton — W. Horse – 4 209 2
1 M. from Lifton, on r. to Hatherleigh, 17½.
Poulston Bridge 2 – 211 2

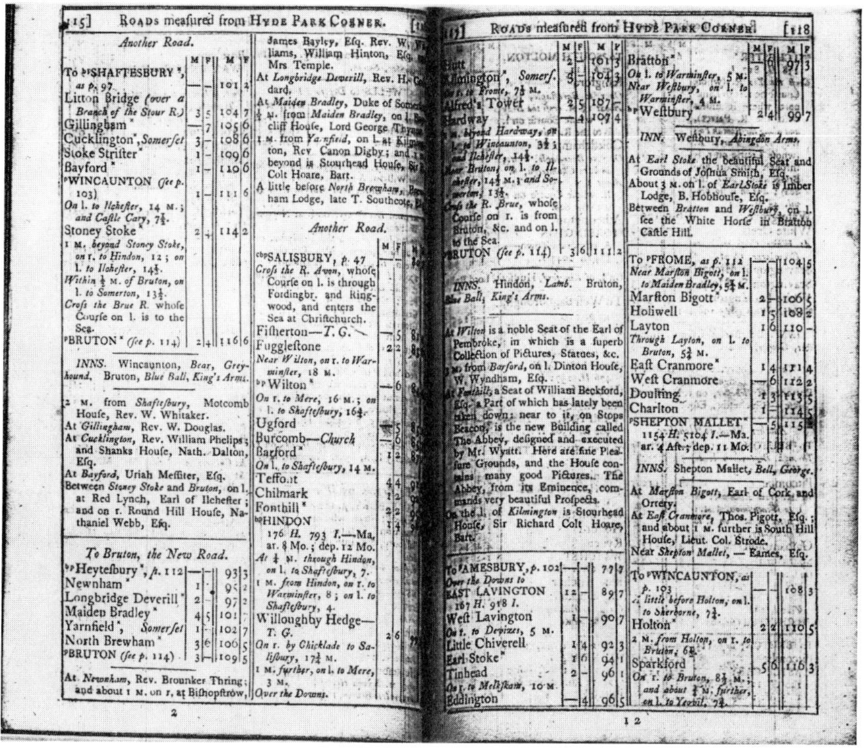

115] ROADS measured from HYDE PARK CORNER.

Another Road.

To SHAFTESBURY, as p. 97 – – 101 2
Litton Bridge (over a Branch of the Stour R.) 3 5 104 7
Gillingham – 7 105 6
Cucklington, Somerset 3 – 108 6
Stoke Strister 1 – 109 6
Bayford 1 – 110 6
WINCAUNTON (see p. 103) 1 – 111 6
On l. to Ilchester, 14 M.; and Castle Cary, 7½.
Stoney Stoke 2 4 114 2
1 M. beyond Stoney Stoke, on r. to Hindon, 12; on l. to Ilchester, 14½.
Within ½ M. of Bruton, on l. to Somerton, 13½.
Cross the Brue R. whose Course on l. is to the Sea.
BRUTON (see p. 114) 2 4 116 6

INNS. Wincaunton, Bear, Greyhound. Bruton, Blue Ball, King's Arms.

2 M. from Shaftesbury, Motcomb House, Rev. W. Whitaker.
At Gillingham, Rev. W. Douglas.
At Cucklington, Rev. William Phelips; and Shanks House, Nath. Dalton, Esq.
At Bayford, Uriah Messiter, Esq.
Between Stoney Stoke and Bruton, on l. at Red Lynch, Earl of Ilchester; and on r. Round Hill House, Nathaniel Webb, Esq.

To Bruton, the New Road.

Heytesbury, p. 112 – – 93 3
Newnham 1 – 95 2
Longbridge Deverill 2 – 97 2
Maiden Bradley 4 5 101 7
Yarnfield, Somerset 1 – 102 7
North Brewham 3 6 106 5
BRUTON (see p. 114) 3 – 109 5

At Newnham, Rev. Brounker Thring; and about 1 M. on r. at Bishopstrow,

James Bayley, Esq. Rev. William Williams, William Hinton, Esq. and Mrs Temple.
At Longbridge Deverill, Rev. H. Goddard.
At Maiden Bradley, Duke of Somerset.
¼ M. from Maiden Bradley, on l. Bradley House, Lord George Thynne.
1 M. from Yarnfield, on l. at Kilmington, Rev Canon Digby; and beyond is Stourhead House, Sir Richard Colt Hoare, Bart.
A little before North Brewham, Brewham Lodge, late T. Southcote, Esq.

Another Road.

SALISBURY, p. 47
Cross the R. Avon, whose Course on l. is through Fordingbr. and Ringwood, and enters the Sea at Christchurch.
Fisherton — T. G.
Fugglestone
Near Wilton, on r. to Warminster, 18 M.
Wilton
On r. to Mere, 16 M.; on l. to Shaftesbury, 16½.
Ugford
Burcomb — Church
Barford
On l. to Shaftesbury, 14 M.
Teffont
Chilmark
Fonthill
HINDON
176 H. 793 I.—Ma. ar. 8 Mo.; dep. 12 Mo.
At ¼ M. through Hindon, on l. to Shaftesbury, 7.
1 M. from Hindon, on r. to Warminster, 8; on l. to Shaftesbury, 4.
Willoughby Hedge — T. G.
On r. by Chicklade to Salisbury, 17½ M.
1 M. further, on l. to Mere, 3 M.
Over the Downs.

2

[117] ROADS measured from HYDE PARK CORNER. [118

Stott 2 – 101 3
Kilmington, Somerf. 3 – 104 3
On r. to Frome, 7½ M.
Alfred's Tower 2 5 107 –
Hardway – 4 107 4
½ M. beyond Hardway, on r. to Wincaunton, 3½; and Ilchester, 14½.
Near Bruton, on l. to Ilchester, 14½ M.; and Somerton, 13½.
Cross the R. Brue, whose Course on r. is from Bruton, &c. and on l. to the Sea.
BRUTON (see p. 114) 3 6 111 2

INNS. Hindon, Lamb. Bruton, Blue Ball, King's Arms.

At Wilton is a noble Seat of the Earl of Pembroke, in which is a superb Collection of Pictures, Statues, &c.
½ M. from Barford, on l. Dinton House, W. Wyndham, Esq.
At Fonthill, a Seat of William Beckford, Esq. a Part of which has lately been taken down; near to it, on Stops Beacon, is the new Building called The Abbey, designed and executed by Mr. Wyatt. Here are fine Pleasure Grounds, and the House contains many good Pictures. The Abbey, from its Eminence, commands very beautiful Prospects.
On the l. of Kilmington is Stourhead House, Sir Richard Colt Hoare, Bart.

To AMESBURY, p. 102 – – 77 –
Over the Downs to
EAST LAVINGTON 12 – 89 7
167 H. 918 I.
West Lavington 1 – 90 7
On r. to Devizes, 5 M.
Little Chiverell 1 4 92 3
Earl Stoke 1 6 94 1
Tinhead 2 – 96 1
On r. to Melksham, 10 M.
Eddington – 4 96 5

Bratton – 6 97 3
On l. to Warminster, 5 M.
Near Westbury, on l. to Warminster, 4 M.
Westbury 2 4 99 7

INN. Westbury, Abingdon Arms.

At Earl Stoke the beautiful Seat and Grounds of Joshua Smith, Esq.
About 3 M. on l. of Earl Stoke is Imber Lodge, B. Hobhouse, Esq.
Between Bratton and Westbury, on l. see the White Horse in Bratton Castle Hill.

To FROME, as p. 112 – – 104 5
Near Marston Bigott, on l. to Maiden Bradley, 5½ M.
Marston Bigott 2 – 106 5
Holiwell 1 5 108 2
Layton 1 6 110 –
Through Layton, on l. to Bruton, 5½ M.
East Cranmore 1 4 111 4
West Cranmore – 6 112 2
Doulting 1 3 113 5
Charlton 1 – 114 5
SHEPTON MALLET – 5 115 2
1154 H. 5104 I.—Ma. ar. 4 Aft.; dep. 11 Mo.

INNS. Shepton Mallet, Bell, George.

At Marston Bigott, Earl of Cork and Orrery.
At East Cranmore, Thos. Pigott, Esq.; and about 1 M. further is South Hill House, Lieut. Col. Strode.
Near Shepton Mallet, — Eames, Esq.

To WINCAUNTON, as p. 103 – – 108 3
A little before Holton, on l. to Sherborne, 7½.
Holton 2 2 110 5
2 M. from Holton, on r. to Bruton, 6½.
Sparkford 5 6 116 3
On r. to Bruton, 8½ M.; and about ¾ M. further, on l. to Yeovil, 7½.

12

# 5 • Trade Routes

## Drove Roads

Although we do not know for certain when droving began we can surmise that in prehistoric times herds of livestock were moved from one grazing area to another. It is likely that 'British trackways' marked on Ordnance Survey maps, sometimes called 'ox droves' or 'drift ways', were ancient drovers' routes, and, as we have seen in Chapter 1, they could be regarded as among the earliest roads, preserved for us through continued usage by herds of oxen and sheep, and successive generations of drovers and traders.

Droving became important during the Middle Ages, reaching its peak early last century, before the building of railways resulted in the quicker and more convenient movement of cattle over long distances. By the sixteenth century, when towns and cities were becoming too large for their meat supplies to be met by the products of their immediate countryside, and the meat demands of the Navy were also increasing, droving increased in importance. Drove roads were an integral part of the road network of the country, and cattle often shared them with other trade traffic such as wagons and packhorses. In the reigns of Mary and Elizabeth I drovers had become so numerous that the authorities decided to control them through statutes licensing 'badgers of corn and drovers of cattle', specifying that a drover must be at least 30 years old and a married householder, and that his licence was to be renewed annually. Anyone contravening this was liable to be fined £5. One outcome of this statute was that it gave status to the true drover whose profession became recognised as an honourable one to such an extent that drovers not only controlled large-scale movements of livestock but carried important  messages, and, more significantly, became travelling bankers.

It was quite usual for a drover to have over £1,000 worth of cattle in his charge, and it was quickly realised that this 'money on the hoof' was far less vulnerable to highway robbers than its equivalent in guineas carried in saddlebags. Hence, a merchant who may need to pay a bill in some other town or city on a drover's route would pay him, and the drover would keep the money at home and settle the account at the end of his journey from the proceeds of the sale of his beasts. Drovers and the men they dealt with often used promissory notes or bills of exchange, which constituted a system of credit. These notes often remained in circulation for some time before encashment, being used in the same way as bank-notes later. It was a Welsh drover, David Jones, having married into wealth, who established the Black Ox Bank at Llandovery, its promissory notes carrying an engraving of a black ox. These were only accepted by the bank from sound customers and were useless to thieves. London agents were appointed to cash them; the business grew, more branches were opened, and the bank was taken over by Lloyds in 1909.

A law passed in Queen Anne's reign forbade any drover from declaring himself bankrupt as a means of escaping financial obligations. An earlier law of Charles I's time prohibited him from Sunday droving, presumably for the good of his soul rather than out of any consideration for his beasts, which, in any event, were rarely driven more than a dozen miles a day. With herds of up to 200 cattle or 2,000 sheep, progress would inevitably be slow and laborious. Herds would be split so that one drover would have up to fifty cattle or 500 sheep, and would be helped by dogs. Early last century drovers were paid 3 or 4s a day — about twice as much as a farm labourer — out of which they had to pay their own lodging expenses, up to 9d a night in winter, half this in summer; they were also allowed 10s for the return journey.

The profits from droving are hard to evaluate. Costs and returns varied with the time of the year and the conditions of the beasts. On an average drove of 200 cattle they could be between 2s 6d and 5s a head early last century. It was obviously in a drover's interest to do his best to ensure that his beasts were in good condition by the time they reached the big markets, and since large distances had to be covered the animals' feet were shod. Cattle have cloven hoofs, involving eight small shoes for a complete shoeing, which, by the middle of last century, cost 1s per beast. Sheep were not shod, and geese had to walk through a mixture of sand, sawdust and tar. Geese-driving was, of course, a shorter-distance affair.

Although drovers and the drove-roads along which they travelled with their herds and flocks played an important part in the economic life of Wessex for so long, very little documentary evidence survives either about the men or their routes. Accounts of financial transactions are rare, and it seems that drovers were so regular a part of the everyday agricultural scene that, unless they were involved in disputes or court-cases, their activities are largely un-recorded. The drove roads survive, either as little-changed and little-used downland tracks following the ancient ridgeways, as green lanes and bridleways, or with modern surfaces and wide carriageways, as today's motor roads.

The import of cattle and sheep from South Wales and from Ireland formed a significant part of the seventeenth-century trade of Somerset ports, particularly Minehead. Later the Old Passage crossing of the River Severn between Beachley and Aust, beneath the site of the Severn Bridge, was used increasingly, with stock then driven to the market at Bristol, or, if London-bound, by way of Bath and Calne on to the Ridgeway north of Avebury, following this eastwards to the Thames at Goring. In Owen's *New Book of Roads* of 1792 the ferry charges for the Old Passage were quoted as 8d for a horse, 4d for a beast, 2s a score for sheep, and 4d for a man, woman or child.

Although usually the droving was in the charge of Welsh drovers surviving seventeenth-century accounts show that some Wessex farmers bought beasts at Welsh fairs and brought them back to their own farms. Account-books of Lord Poulett of Hinton St George, near Chard, the Strode and Strangway families of west Dorset, and Lord Shaftesbury of Wimborne St Giles, all show that they bought cattle in Wales for fattening on their own lands. In a 1623 court action, William Brounker, a yeoman grazier of Whaddon near Bradford-on-Avon, stated that for 30 years he was accustomed 'to repayre to certen Fayres in Shropshire and the County of Radnor to buy Rother beasts (cattle) there to stocke his grounds....' This incidentally illustrates the speed of his droving journey — fifty cattle were driven from Kington to Bradford-on-Avon (around 90 miles) in 5 days. In that same year Thomas Gerard of Trent, near Sherborne, wrote of the importance of the fat cattle trade between Dorset and London, and of the busy cattle market at Somerton, probably one of the 'clearing-house markets' for beasts imported through Minehead and Bridgwater.

A century later Defoe commented on the area of the Somerset Levels where 'farmers were wholly employed in breeding and feeding of cattle'. He also noted a great trade in Dorset Horn ewes and lambs, adding that they were sold in large numbers to farmers in the south-eastern counties to be fattened for the Christmas market. In his *General View of the Agriculture of the County of Dorset*, 1793 Claridge was interested in the breed's ability to lamb twice a year, and that during the mid-September lambing, coming a fortnight after Weyhill Fair, dropped their lambs on the road, from where some might even be brought up in farmhouses to be ready for the Christmas market.

But to return to the drovers' routes. It must be emphasised that today, when the downlands of Wessex are networked with tracks, duplicating and

*Ox Drove at Win Green*

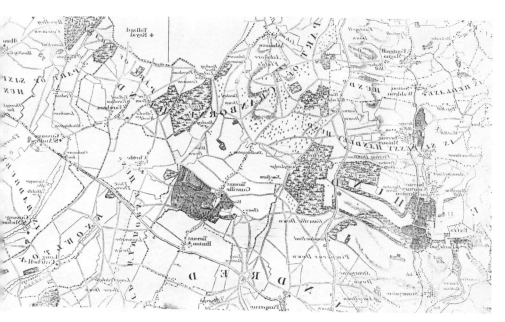

*Greenwood's map of Dorset (1826), showing tracks on Cranborne Chase*

crossing one another, some prehistoric in origin, some Roman, and many now motorised, it is almost impossible to state with certainty that any particular one was a drove-road. Place names and field name evidence are significant pointers; the words 'drove', 'drift', 'ox' and 'sheep' in the names of lanes are good clues, as are the names of inns. Lanes running between banks or hedgerows well to the side of a present track or surface, indicating wide verges for grazing left at the time of field enclosures, are often but not always useful guides to droving use. Finally there is the evidence of small clumps of trees, usually Scots pines, which were used a lot in Wales to indicate drove routes. In Wessex, such tree-clumps may have been planted in conspicuous places as landmarks, or at junctions of tracks.

Two long stretches of downland tracks in Wiltshire are named on OS maps as 'Ox Drove', the longer is that, probably of prehistoric origin, running eastwards from near Win Green (926206) for 12 miles almost to Toyd Clump (090229). Except for two short lengths of surfaced road, this is a green lane following the ridge above the Ebble valley. At its western end it joins the Great Ridgeway, while from its eastern end numerous downland tracks fan out, leading to various Avon crossings between Britford and Breamore, and no single course can be positively identified. What is indisputable is the evocative nature of the track.

From Win Green it follows the scarp, and on Monk's Down becomes a metalled road for a mile. South of the Iron Age fort of Winkelbury Hill the Ox Drove becomes a wide green lane over Trow Down and South Down, passing tracks leading southwards to the woods of Cranborne Chase. Grassy verges are summer-bright with harebells and scabious and meadow cranesbill. At 992216 a lane comes north from Handley, crosses the Ox Drove, and runs

*Drover's Inn, Gussage All Saints, Dorset*

*The Drover's House, Stockbridge, formerly used by cattle drovers. The Welsh inscription survives, painted on the wall*

down to Ebbesbourne Wake in the valley, and for a mile on Woodminton Down the drove is again metalled before continuing as a green lane over Cow Down Hill, on a course slightly north of east. Before passing Hutt Farm the Ox Drove encounters another crossroads (038223) where the lane from Martin, crossing the Salisbury-Blandford road at Martin Drove End, heads north-westwards for Broad Chalke in the Ebble valley. In another 3 miles the Ox Drove itself meets the busy trunk road and loses its quietness. A few miles to the south, at Gussage All Saints, The Drovers' Inn is one of the few Wessex pubs whose name points to an earlier use.

'Ox Drove' is also the name given on the recent l:25,000 map to part of the road previously described, between Hindon and Wilton. Much of this is a wide green lane with the usual drove-road characteristics, although — apart from its name — it lacks appropriate documentation. Like its namesake, it avoids villages, but whether it was merely part of a longer-distance route can

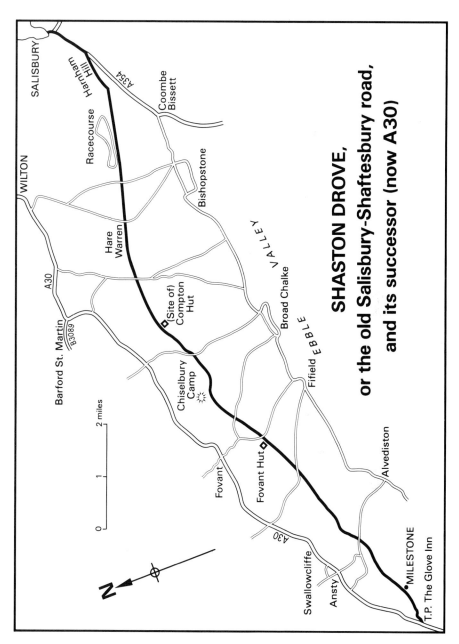

**SHASTON DROVE,
or the old Salisbury-Shaftesbury road,
and its successor (now A30)**

merely be surmised. However, both 'Ox Droves' have a distinctive east-wards orientation, and may have been used by Welsh drovers heading for Stockbridge, in Hampshire, an ancient crossing-point of the River Test on which many droves converged (352352). A remarkable piece of evidence for its association with Welsh drovers comes from an inscription on a seven-teenth-century house on the west bank of the river, just south of the main road. Still known as The Drover's House, its front wall bears the well-maintained notice, in Welsh, '*Gwair tymherus porfa flasus cwrw da a gwal*

131

*The Salisbury to Shaftesbury road, which was an 'Ogilby' road, coach road and turnpike, at the top of White Sheet Hill, looking west*

*cysurus'*. Roughly translated this means, 'Fine hay, sweet pasture, good ale and a comfortable bed.'

The old Salisbury to Shaftesbury road already described, following the chalk ridge between the Nadder and Ebble valleys, was used by drovers. Local folk-memory refers to it as 'Shaston Drove', particularly in its section from White Sheet Hill to Harnham Hill. 'Shaston' was, of course, the old name for Shaftesbury.

In the Somerset Levels around Langport, in parts of Dorset near Evershot, Sherborne and Leigh, mainly in the north and west of the county, and along the Vale of Pewsey in Wiltshire, many short stretches of lane, road or track include the word 'drove' in their name. Some carry people's names, others farm names, in their identities. Some seem merely to have been cartways ending in fields, especially in Pewsey Vale. Others may be bits of old roads no longer needed after other parts were surfaced, and have been long abandoned to greenness. Generally speaking, however, these droves are old green ways along which cattle and sheep were taken to and from pastures, markets and fairs. Their names survive in local memory and sometimes in local records. Within their context of field, farm, village and market they were as important as the long-distance droves whose names have vanished.

## Fairs

In *Far from the Madding Crowd* Hardy paints a word-picture of Woodbury Hill Fair as he must have experienced it in 1873, a year before his novel was published.

*Woodbury Hill above Bere Regis, the site of an important Wessex fair from medieval times*

---

[Above...]'the decayed old town of Kingsbere (Bere Regis)...Greenhill (Woodbury) was the Niji Novgorod of South Wessex; and the busiest, noisiest, merriest day of the whole statute number was the day of the sheep fair. This yearly gathering was upon the summit of a hill which retained in good preservation the remains of an ancient earthwork... To each of the two chief openings on opposite sides a winding road ascended, and the level green space of ten to fifteen acres enclosed by the bank was the site of the fair.'

To it, in slow processions, came the sheep,

'multitude after multitude, horned and hornless...' Shepherds who attended with their flocks from long distances started from home two or three days, or even a week, before the fair, driving their charges a few miles each day — not more than ten or twelve — and resting them at night in hired fields by the wayside at previously chosen points, where they fed, having fasted since morning.'

Woodbury Hill Fair, established in the thirteenth century, was the most important in Dorset, and in Wessex as a whole was second only to the great St Giles' Fair outside Winchester. It was a 5-day event starting on 18 September each year, and its local significance is illustrated by the use in manorial and other documents of the term 'Woodbury Day', instead of a date, in the common field grazing regulations. Quarter Sessions records contain frequent references to the Fair, and its importance extended as far west as Dorchester, since in September 1648 a public thanksgiving in the town was postponed because 'it falls out to be on Woodbury Fair eve, at which time most of the Towne will be from home.'

Two roads up opposite sides of Woodbury Hill are now bridleways, the western one steep and much overgrown, and the eastern one a hedged lane running along a spur of downland, through Bere Wood and into Bloxworth

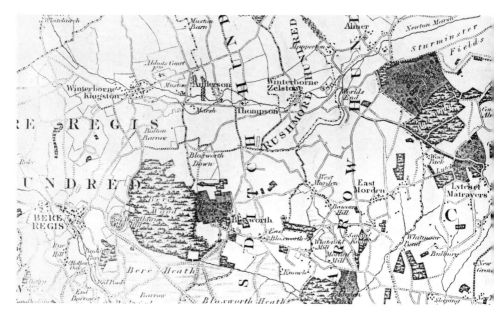

where its surfaced continuation eastwards follows the old road to Lytchett Minster. In late Norman times Bloxworth was a chapelry of Cerne Abbas, so the Woodbury Hill track may have experienced monastic traffic in addition to its six centuries of fair-bound livestock. When Surtees visited Bloxworth in 1835 he referred to the small heaps of gravel of white chalk by the heathy track, acting as early 'waymarks' but commonly described as 'Dorset milestones'.

Although fairs were important occasions, they were not well documented, nor are the roads by which visitors, shepherds, farmers, tradesmen, circus performers, pedlars and packmen travelled. However, Francis Ashley, the Recorder of Dorchester and one of the county justices, kept notes of the people who were tried before him between 1614 and 1635. Each occasion of Woodbury Fair brought its crop of thieves and tricksters, and what is particularly relevant, the home-towns of both them and any witnesses. From London, Bristol and Exeter, Southampton, Winchester and Newbury they came, as well as folk from Dorset and its neighbours. Michael Farringdon, a linen-draper from Coventry, had standings at the fair; in 1620 a cook and baker from London, one Robert Watkins, set up a stall selling refreshments, and his fire one evening frightened the night-watchman into thinking other booths were seriously threatened. A pedlar from St Albans gave evidence. Other traders mentioned included a Honiton mercer, Coventry chapmen, a Devon weaver who came to sell cloth and buy cheese; a shoemaker and pack-saddle maker from Wells, and bonelace sellers from Berkshire and Oxfordshire. Few of these traders would have had carts; packhorses carried their goods, and they themselves would have walked, or if they were fortunate, ridden on their own horses.

When Hardy saw Woodbury Fair it was still thriving. Forty years later, by the beginning of World War I, it had dwindled into insignificance. The hilltop

(above) *The Weyhill Fair Inn, near Andover in Hampshire*

(left) *Geenwood's map of Dorset (1826), shows the pre-turnpike network east of Bere Regis, but Woodbury Hill Fair was still important*

is quiet now, and the solitary farm (which was probably an inn) seems to emphasise the melancholy silence. So, too, at Yarnbury in Wiltshire, where part of the great Iron Age fort near the busy A303 (035403) was the site for a sheep fair held annually on 5 October. In *A Shepherd's Life* W.H. Hudson, describes it by the name Wiltshire folk used,

> 'Yarnborough Castle ... was formerly one of the most important sheep fairs in the county, but for the last two or three decades [ie from about 1880] it has been falling off and is now of little account ... One farming family has sold their sheep there for 88 years [since about 1820] without missing a year, and always at the same spot.'

In the same book Hudson refers to a sheep fair at Britford, in the Avon valley just below Salisbury, and describes a scene around the middle of last century when, as a boy, the shepherd Caleb Bawcombe and his smaller brother

> 'were in charge of the flock on the downs and were on the side where it dips down to the turnpike road about a mile-and-a-half from the village [Martin: 069196] , when a large flock driven by two men and two dogs, came by. They were going to the Britford sheep fair and were behind time. Isaac [Caleb's father] had started at daylight that morning for the same fair'.

Tan Hill is named on modern maps (082646) above the Vale of Pewsey, and the second highest point in Wiltshire, 958ft. The First Edition Ordnance Survey names it St Ann's Hill, as does the author's 1913 Fourth Edition, so 'Tan' is a relatively recent corruption. Its annual fair for sheep and horses was on 6 August, but these ceased in 1932. A writer at the beginning of this century states that in previous years shepherds were guided to it through the night by beacons lit for that purpose. The 1773 map shows at least eight tracks converging on St Ann's Hill, including three from the north and three from the south.

The greatest of all the sheep fairs was probably that at Weyhill (317466)

west of Andover, on the geographically important site by the great London-Land's End road. Elizabeth granted a fair charter about 1600 but the fair probably pre-dates that by two centuries. Celia Fiennes refers to its taking place at Michaelmas, while Defoe, writing about 1720, calls it 'the Greatest sheep fair in England', quoting a local grazier 'who believed there were five hundred thousand sheep sold there in one fair', a wild exaggeration. One-tenth of that would be more realistic. Defoe adds that the sheep sold were 'not for immediate killing but are generally ewes for store sheep for the farmers'. A century later Cobbett quotes a figure more likely to refer to a year's sales, for he later adds that the sales on the year of his visit (1826) must have amounted to £120,000 less than the previous year which, at 16s a ewe, produces a total of at least 150,000 ewes. Nevertheless, it all adds up to enormous numbers of stock being driven along the roads and tracks of downland. For the most part graziers and shepherds would steer clear of the new turnpike roads in order to avoid paying tolls, so the old green lanes, droves, and ridgeway routes would be followed.

On the same great road to the west (now largely the A30), but at the western end of our part of Wessex, another famous fair exerted a wide trading influence. Whitedown Fair was an annual event for Whit week, from 1361 for at least five centuries. It is hard to imagine a more obvious place for such an occasion, with the great west road through Shaftesbury, Sherborne, Yeovil and Crewkerne swinging south-westwards from the end of Windwhistle Hill to follow the Foss Way to Axminster, with a continuation to Exeter and the rest of Devon. Nearby was the Foss itself running northwards to Ilchester, with a link to Chard. Thus, on open downland just below the 700ft contour, many important roads met (366089), with access to south Somerset, west Dorset, east Devon and, of course, London. By the late fifteenth century the fair had been extended to 4 days, and an unusual record survives which shows its trading influence between 1637 and 1649, half of that period, of course, being during the Civil War unrest. While most of the regular dealers and traders at Whitedown came from villages and towns within a 12-mile radius, quite a number came from much farther afield, including cattle-dealers from Glamorgan and other parts of South Wales. Contemporary records of Taunton Fair also include many references to cattle sold by Welsh drovers to Somerset farmers for fattening on the lush grasslands, from where they were driven eastwards, across Wiltshire and Dorset to the demanding markets of the south and east: London, Farnham and Southampton.

One of the great wool fairs, established in medieval times and continuing until the late seventeenth century, was at Norton St Philip, in north Somerset. Like many others in the West Country, it coincided with the church's patronal festival, and lasted for several days around the feast of Sts Philip and James, 1 May. On those occasions the 'great house or inn called the George' was emptied of most of its furniture, and filled with packs and bales of wool of the merchants. There was still sufficient accommodation for traders and customers, and rooms for lodging and entertainment, so that inns like the George played an important role in the marketing process. Pepys and his wife dined there during a visit to Somerset in 1668, while only 17 years later the ill-fated Duke of Monmouth made it a temporary headquarters.

# Markets

The importance of markets in medieval times has been referred to in an earlier chapter. Such markets reached their peak of importance during the seventeenth century, but, as roads began to improve the influence of many, small, local markets gradually declined. Some had already done so, through being engulfed by those of their larger neighbours — Frampton, for example, succumbed to Dorchester, Glastonbury to Somerton, and Steeple Ashton to Market Lavington. At Bere Regis and Beaminster, Blandford Forum and Bridport, fire or plague accelerated a decline. But where the corngrowing chalklands met the dairy-farming, cloth manufacturing claylands, markets flourished. These included Bruton and Wincanton in Somerset, Salisbury, Wilton and Warminster in Wiltshire, and Shaftesbury in Dorset. In the mid-seventeenth century Aubrey described Warminster as 'held to be the greatest corn-market by much in the West of England.' Two hundred and seventy years later, in the 1820s, Cobbett repeated the assertion, 'It is a great corn-market, one of the greatest in this part of England.' He also approved the way the market at Warminster was operated.

> '...here things are still conducted in the good old honest fashion. The corn is brought and pitched in the market before it is sold; and when it is sold it is paid for

*The Pitchmarket, Cerne Abbas, at the junction of Abbey Street and Long Street, where the main medieval market was held*

on the nail.... Almost everywhere else the corn is sold by sample; it is sold by juggling in the corner ... there is no fair and open market....'

At Cerne Abbas the southernmost house of a rare surviving row of timber-fronted buildings in Abbey Street is 'The Pitchmarket', so named because the pavement fronting it was the place where farmers formerly showed or pitched their samples of grain on market day. Cerne's market charter had been granted by King John in 1214 to the Abbot, passing after the Dissolution to a Thomas Emerson, and the building may well date from the sixteenth century. In 1773 Hutchins could still refer to Cerne's 'well-frequented market', but a century later the Post Office Directory admitted 'the market has been discontinued for some years.' Undoubtedly the railways, which never came to Cerne, killed it off by about 1860. Long Street, dating in its present form from about 1910, was originally Market Street, its roadway undoubtedly wider in times past. Even then it would have been closed on market days, when through traffic had to use Back Lane.

Successful markets imply good communications. Yet again, documentary evidence about roads is meagre in the extreme. Disputes over market rights provides incidental evidence, for example, about the importance of Shaftesbury as a market centre, and a 1632 report stated that 'there is a greater store of corn vented in that towne ...than in any three townes in this county [Dorset]...for it standeth midway between the hill and the vale.' On market days and fairs the confusion in its streets must have been incredible, and right through to the turnpike days of the eighteenth century obstructions caused

*Gold Hill, Shaftesbury, the medieval way into the town from the south, by the eastern side of the abbey precincts*

by market standings resulted in arguments between traders and travellers. Shaftesbury lay not only on the road from London to Exeter but also on that from Bristol to Poole. More roads still radiate from it than from any other Dorset town. There were twenty-four licensed inns and alehouses for the entertainment and accommodation of stall-holders and travellers: to a permanent corn-market could be added a butter-cross, as well as poultry, fish and cheese crosses erected in the sixteenth century. Cattle and swine were sold on Gold Hill; agricultural products and a great range of wares were regularly offered for sale, most of it, as well as corn and livestock, brought along the busy converging roads, probably the same routes used by today's traffic. The picture would have been the same at Salisbury, Devizes, Marlborough, Dorchester, Warminster, Yeovil and Blandford, whose market-places, even on present market-days, are probably pale echoes of their noisy, distinctive liveliness of earlier centuries. Marlborough's handsome High Street, one of the widest in England, is still the site on two Saturdays each October of the Small and Large Mop Fairs, formerly hiring fairs where farm workers and servants found jobs for the following year. Professor Hoskins believes that the immense width of High Street originated, perhaps, in late Saxon times as a huge open-air sheep market at an important focal point at the heart of Wiltshire's downland.

In market towns and villages, Market Street, High Street and Portway are sure clues to the sites of former or continuing markets. No such clear guidance helps to point out the ways by which traders came, and it seems unlikely that any roads and tracks in Wessex were made specifically to meet

*Milton Abbas, Dorset, rebuilt on a new site in 1771-86*

the needs of such markets. Throughout the area communications evolved to meet the needs of the time. From the seventeenth century to the arrival of the railways there is an increasing amount of information about the people and traffic using roads rather than of the routes themselves. Some of this incidental evidence will be considered later, in the chapter devoted to turnpikes.

Among the very few Wessex roads whose names give an indication of the trade they carried is a Coal Road near Milton Abbas. This name applies only to a short section of an old track, now an indistinct and little-used field-path running north from the A354 near Deverel Down (823987) to Hoggen Down (813018) above Milton Abbas. The section forms part of a route by which it is thought coal was transported from the coast at Wareham, through Bere Regis, and by what are now field-paths and bridleways by Roke Farm and Longmead to the main road east of Milborne St Andrew.

Also associated with Milton Abbas is the Ice Drove, a track following the ridge northwards between Delcombe Bottom and Hilton Bottom, but stopping abruptly on Bulbarrow Hill. Its name excites but fails to satisfy the imagination, and one can merely surmise that it was related to the transport of fish. Among the still-visible streets and house sites of the former market town of Milton Abbas, which in medieval times had a market and fairs, is one named on an old estate map as Fishway Street, about 500yd south-south-east of the abbey church today. Further north, a few miles from Shaftesbury, a short stretch of track (830158), its southern end obviously realigned, and called Fishey Lane, suggests a possible continuation of a route running from Bulbarrow and Belchalwell Street towards Shaftesbury.

Little doubt exists as to the extent of the fish trade which operated from the Dorset coast. Walter Yonge, a Justice of the Peace and MP for Honiton, Devon, who lived at Axminster, left a diary covering the years 1604-28 in which he refers to strings of packhorses, tied head to tail, being loaded by fish jobbers with fresh fish on the beach at Lyme Regis preparatory to their long journey to London. On the return trip they sometimes brought luxury goods including silk, haberdashery and even books from the capital. Writing about 1675 John Aubrey refers to the market at Devizes where 'they bring fish from Poole hither which is sent hence to Oxford.' This overland packhorse trade in fish was only one of innumerable packhorse and carrier services throughout Wessex in the seventeenth and eighteenth centuries, but much local research is needed to fill out its details.

## Smugglers' Roads

If the roads so far mentioned were concerned primarily with legitimate trade, it is likely that on occasions they witnessed the carriage of goods of a more illicit nature. During the period when smuggling activity was at its greatest, roughly from 1720-1830, scarcely a place along the Dorset coast between Poole and Lyme was not used for the bringing ashore of large quantities of brandy, rum and wine, cocoa beans, tea, coffee, vinegar, pepper and salt, silk and cloth. Lulworth Cove was one of the most notorious landing places, from where loads were carried away by vast numbers of country folk, inland to Puddletown and Dorchester, Sherborne, Castle Cary, Bruton, Shepton Mallet and beyond to Bristol.

Cerne Abbas, the Piddle valley villages, Corfe Mullen were all places which played a significant role in the contraband, while villages in Blackmore

*Wool Bridge (dating from the sixteenth century or earlier) and Woolbridge Manor, Dorset*

Vale were said to be 'abounding with great numbers of dangerous rogues.' The Ship Inn at Wool and the World's End at Almer were favourite refreshment stops, and Cranborne Chase provided excellent cover for secret routes northwards into Wiltshire until its disafforestation in 1830, and the Blandford-Salisbury road was one of their favourites. The most famous Wiltshire ringleader, Isaac Gulliver, who in the second half of the eighteenth century employed about fifty men in the business, took over the Blacksmith's Arms on Thorney Down, changed its name to the King's Arms, and used it as his headquarters. Legends are more common than facts about routes used by smugglers, and the area can throw up only one known 'Smugglers' Lane', already referred to as part of the Great Ridgeway, climbing eastwards for a couple of miles from the Iwerne valley (865110) north of Blandford. However, Woolbridge Lane near Wool is known to have been the scene of a clash between smugglers and a party of revenue men and dragoons in 1779.

# 6 • Turnpike Roads

Wessex roads, like those elsewhere throughout the country, were revolutionised through the introduction of the turnpike system during the eighteenth century. Within the area covered by this book, by about 1840 — before the coming of the railways — various turnpike trusts were responsible for at least 1,000 miles of road, about half of this mileage being in Dorset. Professor Good sums up their effect on the county:

> 'The effects of the turnpike trusts on local road communications was profound. Until they came the road system was one which had grown up, almost casually over many centuries, and which could not therefore be expected to mould itself quickly to changing circumstances. On this old pattern the turnpikes impressed a new outline, designed more to meet the requirements of the times.
>
> They went far towards providing the basic road network appropriate to the contemporary needs of the population, and so it is today, that though there are many main roads that were never turnpikes, there is scarcely an old turnpike which is still not an important traffic artery and likely long to remain so'.

With a few notable exceptions, which will be discussed later, the same may be said of the Wiltshire turnpikes, which, incidentally, have a longer history than those of Dorset.

Nationally, the first turnpike act had been passed in 1663, allowing tolls to be levied to provide money to repair a section of the Great North Road in the counties of Hertford and Huntingdon. This established the important principle that those who used the roads should contribute towards the cost of their maintenance. In 1706 an Act of Parliament created a turnpike trust in which a body of private persons were appointed as trustees to manage the highway between Fornhill in Bedfordshire and Stony Stratford in Buckingham. This marked the real beginning of the turnpike system which, over the next 140 years resulted in the creation and management of 23,000 miles of English roads.

Turnpikes were planned by local landowners, traders, merchants, manufacturers, councils — anybody with an interest in improving local roads and thus promoting increased trade and travel — and prepared to invest some capital towards that end. Being generally small in scale, rarely involving more than 30 miles of road, usually much less, they suffered from lack of capital, central organisation, and sometimes from any real control. Adjacent turnpike trusts rarely seem to have co-operated, and inevitably there was opposition from farmers, drovers and carriers. Some traders opposed turnpikes because they believed new roads, by possibly changing market patterns, would harm their interests, as well as raising their costs through the imposition of tolls collected at turnpike gates.

The word 'turnpike' was used in 1477 in the Paston Letters in the context of a gate in a walled town. In its newer use it referred to the spiked tollgate at the entrance to a stretch of road controlled by a turnpike trust authorised by Parliament, where tolls could be collected from travellers and others using that road. The tolls were usually mortgaged in advance to provide the necessary capital for road improvements. Initially, turnpike trusts were intended merely to be temporary bodies to be dissolved when road improvements were concluded, after which it was hoped that the old Statute Labour system would keep them in good repair, and the original creditors repaid. Early Turnpike Acts were therefore usually limited to 21 years, after which time Parliament hoped that the tollgates would be removed with resultant free travel. This did not happen, and turnpike acts were almost automatically renewed. If a trust maintained its roads and kept out of debt it must have been well managed, thus justifying encouragement. In any case, experience showed that maintenance was as expensive as the initial improvement, so that tolls were constantly needed.

In most cases turnpike trusts did not at first make any new roads but generally took over existing ones, concentrating on improving worst sections. Most of the routes were already in existence but in a number of cases new roads avoiding the steepest hills were created. A multiplicity of routes was reduced to a single, usually more direct, line, consequently concentrating traffic using it, and establishing the basis of the main roads of today.

Turnpike roads were not popular. The ordinary countryman was content with his old road, rough though it may be, but free from tolls. Packmen, carriers and drovers resented the tolls which, increasing the costs of their journeys, reduced their profits. The new roads may have made for quicker movement but the delay at tollgates slowed it down, particularly on a drove where stock were allowed to pass only singly so that they could be counted.

The system of tolls, with its tollbars, tollfarmers and turnpikemen, was obviously the chief source of revenue for the trustees, but it was difficult to manage and was open to fraud. A number of trusts tried initially employing their own servants to collect the tolls, paying turnpikemen, perhaps, £10 a year for being on duty each day from 4am or 5am until late at night. It is hardly surprising that this system was short-lived in favour of the arrangement, gradually adopted throughout the country, of 'letting' the tolls. In this the right of toll collection was put up for auction, sold to the highest bidder who became the 'farmer' of the tolls at one or more tollgates. For such a person this often became profitable, for after paying the trustees and the toll collectors, any balance left over from the tolls he could keep for himself.

For the toll collectors old buildings were converted into toll houses or new ones were specially constructed, each rarely costing more than £50. Erected close to the gate itself and near the edge of the road, they provided rent-free accommodation. Generally, their architecture can be described as vernacular. They are built of local materials, simple and functional in design, although later additions adapting them to modern needs invariably spoil their proportions. Some are single-storied, some two-storeyed, sometimes flush with the road, sometimes with an angled bay window to allow a view

(above) *A typical eighteenth-century toll house, near Castle Cary, Somerset*

(right) *Shane's Castle toll house, Devizes, a later toll house in early Victorian castellated style about 1830-40. Notice the space above the porch for the list of tolls*

of approaching traffic, and sometimes with a small porch or deeply-over-hanging eaves to give some protection to the gatekeepers. Eventually, after their toll collecting days had ceased, they were sold, and many still survive, often in use as highly individual if rather small private houses.

Every toll house was supposed to display a list of tolls charged. So far as the author knows, no Wessex toll-boards survive *in situ*, although a few have found their way into local museums and local history collections. The toll schedule for the Bradford-on-Avon trust is probably typical of the quite complicated scale of charges for around 1750:

| | |
|---|---:|
| Coach with 4 or more horses | 1s 0d |
| Coach with 2 horses | 6d |
| Carriage with 1 horse | 3d |
| Wagon or cart, with 5 or more horses | 1s 0d |
| Wagon or cart, with 4 horses | 8d |
| Wagon or cart, with 3 horses | 6d |
| Wagon or cart, with 2 horses | 3d |
| Wagon or cart, with 1 horse | 2d |
| Horse, laden or unladen, not drawing | 1d |
| Cattle, per score | 10d |
| Sheep, pigs, etc, per score | 5d |

(above) *A boundary stone marking the end of a trust's jurisdiction*

(left) *A boundary stone where a turnpike passed from one parish to another*

Various categories of traffic were usually exempt from tolls: churchgoers, electors, soldiers, mail coaches, agricultural vehicles.

Tolls were assessed in various ways by different trusts at different times, and took into account such factors as number of horses drawing, number and breadth of wheels of wagons and coaches, and the weight. A few trusts, especially those on busy roads, had weighbridges at some turnpike gates — the Shepton Mallet Trust had two (Cannard's Grave and Downside), and the Bath Trust had five.

The introduction of turnpikes did not affect a parish's former duty to maintain its roads by statute labour, and trust surveyors could continue to demand up to 6 days' annual labour from each adult parishioner. Parish surveyors had to supply the names of eligible persons, and a turnpike trust could levy a fine of 1s 6d on defaulters, and this money payment in lieu of labour tended to be increasingly favoured by both parishes and trusts, not least because the labour was frequently so unskilled as to be useless, or it was drunk, or it was women or children . A more common practice was to leave it to the 'undertakers', partnerships of men who supplied tenders to contract at an agreed price of 5s to 7s 6d a rood (5½yd).

Specifications for road construction varied from one trust to another, according to the amount of traffic expected, the type of terrain, and the money available. Turnpike roads were commonly 6yd wide, rarely less than 5yd nor more than 8yd, between drainage trenches along each side. Quite often not the whole width was metalled, although by the golden days of stagecoach travel a far more professional class of surveyors had entered the scene, introducing much better methods of road constructions.

Although final responsibility for any turnpike trust lay with its trustees it was the surveyor whose expertise or otherwise determined the quality of the roads, and in this context the great McAdam family played an important role in the building of many roads in Wessex and the West Country from 1816 to

1861. John Loudon McAdam, born at Ayr in 1756, was appointed Surveyor of the Bristol Roads in 1816 — the Bristol Turnpike Trust had the biggest road mileage (179) of any English trust — a position he held for 10 years, when he was succeeded in the post by his son Loudon who held the post until 1857. Meanwhile J.L. McAdam became Surveyor of the Bath Roads, 1826-36, and one or the other of his three sons (William, James and Loudon) were surveyors of four other Somerset trusts, Frome, Shepton Mallet, Wells and Yeovil; and William also served as surveyor for seven Wiltshire trusts — Black Dog, Devizes, Market Lavington, Melksham, Salisbury, Westbury and part of Warminster, together with a 2-year spell, 1824-6, with the very local Cerne Abbas Turnpike Trust in Dorset. William and James also held survey-orships for a number of Hampshire trusts, including those centred on Winchester.

J.L. McAdam's observations on the effect of traffic on the surfaces of existing roads led to his 'instructions for repairing a road' given in a Report from the Select Committee on Highways and Turnpike Roads, 1810-11. These suggested how the stone should be broken, the tools to be used — preferably from a sitting position — with an insistence on broken stone only, without earth or other matter, laid to a depth of 10in. 'Such a road … will be smooth, hard and durable, and cannot be affected by the wet, or by frost, and will therefore be good at all seasons of the year.'

This was a counsel of perfection, and some trusts, heeding the advice, produced good roads while others, perhaps with less demanding surveyors, or less capital, or both, continued to produce poor roads. Present-day motorists ruefully recognise the problem is still with us. Half a century before McAdam's ideas were being introduced, Arthur Young's travels through southern England, mainly by post-chaise, and already referred to, included the comment about the Salisbury to Romsey road, 'by rendering the surface so immovably firm, that carriages make no holes for (water) to settle in; and having everywhere a gentle fall, it runs immediately off … it is everywhere broad enough for three carriages to pass each other, and lying in straight lines … it has more the appearance of an elegant gravel walk, than of a high road'.

# The Bath Road

In 1706-7 an Act was passed placing the responsibility for repairing all roads leading into the city in the hands of local Justices of the Peace. The preamble claimed that Bath was 'a place of very great resort from all parts of the Kingdom of Great Britain and from foreign parts, for the use and benefit of the baths, and drinking the mineral waters there'. Of the roads listed the most important was the main road from London, entering the city via Kingsdown (819670) and Batheaston, involving the long descent of Kingsdown Hill.

At the same time the Wiltshire justices were authorised by an Act to improve the road from Cherhill Hill through Calne to Studley Bridge on the Bristol road, a distance of 3 miles, much of it across marshy ground on both sides of Calne, invariably damaged by wagons laden with woollen cloth, being conveyed from Calne and nearby wool towns eastwards to London.

But this was not yet the main road into Bath. That followed a route from

*Turnpike Cottage (left) and the Old Bath Road (right), north of Beacon Hill*

Marlborough, over Manton Down to Avebury, thence to Beckhampton, and across the downs to Old Shepherd's Shore (040666), westwards over Beacon Hill and the steep descent to Horsley Upright Gate (981664). This section from Old Shepherd's Shore was turnpiked in 1713, while the next bit, from Horsley Upright Gate through Sandy Lane, down Bowden Hill, through Lacock, Corsham and past Chapel Plaister was turnpiked in 1725, thus completing one route from Marlborough to Bath. Renewal Acts were passed at intervals until 1783, by when a more northerly route was preferred.

This road via Chippenham took longer, and the piecemeal approach of tackling even an important road is well illustrated in the following list, with places arranged topographically, and the appropriate Turnpike Acts given:

| | |
|---|---|
| Newbury (Speenhamland to Marlborough) | 1726 |
| Marlborough to Cherhill | 1743 |
| Cherhill to Studley Bridge | 1707 |
| Studley Bridge to Chippenham | 1727 |
| Chippenham to Corsham | 1743 |
| Corsham via Box to Bath | 1756 |

This is the route of the present A4, and following its completion the line of the Old Bath Road over the downs, through Sandy Lane and Kingsdown, became less used, and is now a delightful downland track, described in an earlier chapter. In 1726 petitions were sent from Marlborough and the area around complaining that the road from Speenhamland was so bad that passengers and droves from London to Bristol were 'obliged to follow bye-ways and trespass on corn and commons, and by thus avoiding Marlborough, to occasion considerable loss to that place'.

The new turnpikes may have been great improvements on earlier roads

*Toll house at Kingsdown near Bath, on the Blue Vein Road, an early turnpike into Bath from London*

but they were far from satisfactory. A critic, in a letter to the *Gentleman's Magazine*, September 1754, commented on the Bath Road,

> 'It is the worst public road in Europe, considering what vast sums have been collected from it ... it errs and blunders in all the forms; its strata of materials were never worth a straw; its surface was never made cycloidal; it had neither good side ditches, nor footpaths for walkers; no outlets were made for water that stagnates in the middle of the road; it was never sufficiently widened, nor were the hedges ever cleared...'

He was obviously not very impressed.

Most turnpike trusts had come to realise that a moderately-convex cross-section was best, its surface built up with small pebbles and gravel. Narrow and winding sections of road were being widened and straightened, a few roadside trees were being felled, and even occasional humble cottages removed.

A particularly observant traveller, during a journey in post-chaise from London to Marlborough in 1767, made copious notes of what he saw, and in a long letter to the *Reading Mercury* suggested that the steep descent from Savernake Forest to Marlborough could be made safer by 'removing some of the ground at the top of the hill and laying it at the bottom'; that in some places the surface was too rounded for safety, and if the road were widened a little this convexity could be reduced. He made a particularly pertinent observation about milestones:

> 'I further took notice, that those mile-stones which were placed on the North-side

*A late eighteenth-century milestone in Savernake Forest, near Marlborough, giving very precise distances*

of the road, and were thereby exposed to the heat of the sun all day [sic!], were generally more free from moss, and more plain and legible than those which stood on the South-side. And I should think, that if the numbers on them were to be in Arabic figures, instead of the Roman letters, they would be more easily read by the passengers as the post-chaises pass by them very fast: thus for instance, 48 is more easily read than XLVIII.'

He also suggested, incidentally, that when coaches travelling in opposite directions met, they should pass 'on the right hand of the road, as it would prevent any disputes who should give way to the other.' Clearly, there was no rule of the road in the eighteenth century.

Present-day travellers using the A4 are constantly reminded of its turnpike origins, not only through the road itself, but by the many milestones which survive, most of them on the north side. From about the 1740s, most turnpike acts included clauses stipulating that distances were to be measured and stones erected recording these. Each trust chose its own size and style of milestone, either of rectangular, triangular or rounded section, designed to show the traveller the distance from the last town passed through, the next one along the road, and — frequently — the distance from London, measured from Hyde Park Corner. By looking at the milestones on the way it is easy to tell when one passes from the roads of one trust to those of another. Some are barely legible, some half-obscured, some have been moved or lost through road-widening, and some have been well restored. Those erected by the Speenhamland to Marlborough Trust are vastly different from those west of Marlborough of the Beckhampton Trust dating from 1742-3 which in turn contrast with those of the Calne Trust, 1785, of which a good example is seen on the west side of Cherhill Hill. Milestones of the Bath Roads are appropriately elegant and consist of a cast-iron plate fixed to a stone, and having a black-painted hand on a white ground, with the distance only to the Guildhall, Bath given in miles and furlongs. Many of these excellent stones survive around Bath as do the Trust's triangular cast-iron plaques marking parish boundaries, with dates. A few milestones survive on the course of the Old Bath Road over Beacon Hill, but their inscriptions are illegible, and these must date from before 1783 when the last Renewal Act for this route was passed.

A milestone on one of the Bath roads (the Foss Way near Radstock) about 1820, showing an elegant design and exact distance

A milestone of 1750 on the old Salisbury road on Mere Down, Wiltshire. Note the use of 'Sarum' and that the stone has been vandalised by having 'WA' added to the correct 'C' from London

Costs of milestones varied slightly according to different charges for materials and labour. Made by local stonemasons to a trust's specification, those east of Marlborough cost £1 each in 1746. It is worth noting, however, that milestones two centuries ago were subjected to vandalism. Local farmers doubtless found that tall rectangular ones made good gateposts, and although turnpike acts made it an offence to pull up or deface them, it was found necessary to recut or even replace them, every 30 years or so. Trusts were also responsible for lamps at turnpike gates, graduated posts where road flooding was liable to occur, direction posts at crossways, and pumps for road watering.

The line of today's A4 reflects the many improvements and alterations made to the original turnpike route, especially from 1743 onwards. The Chippenham Trust turnpiked the stretch from Studley Bridge to Pickwick, on the western side of Corsham where it joined the Lacock Trust's road from Sandy Lane. But even when this was done in 1745, coaches for Bath still continued to use the Chapel Plaister-Kingsdown approach into the city, until 1756 when the more direct route through Box and Batheaston was introduced. Slightly changed in 1826 west of Box to take a more northerly and less steep gradient down Ashley Hill, this western section is that of today's A4. The most exposed stretch of the entire route from London was the downland section between Beckhampton and Cherhill, which regularly posed hazards in bad winter weather, when snow often made it impassable, in spite of high

*Salisbury Plain from Andrews and Dury's map of Wiltshire, 1773. Note the large number of tracks crossing the plain. The hachuring at the top indicates the steep northern escarpment of the limestone plateau. The prominent double lines are not roads but boundaries of the hundreds*

earthen banks built alongside the road. An account in the *Bath Journal* of 12 February 1770 records such an incident, when

'...some Gentlemen and 2 Ladies, passengers belonging to two of the Bath Machines on their way to London, had undergone great distress in going over

Cherhill Down ... in the Hurricane one of the Coachmen was blown off from his Box, this increased the fears of the Ladies and Gentlemen not a little!'

Apparently they then opened the coach windows to try to alleviate the pressure of the wind on the side of the coach, but they soon felt so cold they decided to get out and try to walk to the inn at Beckhampton (presumably the present Wagon and Horses). Immediately they left their coach it blew over; one of the Gentlemen 'lost his hold and was blown from his companions upwards of 150 yards, where he lay till assistance came to him ....'

The road by which they had travelled can still be traced, more easily in a westwards direction, from the 82nd milestone from London, beyond the Beckhampton crossroads. Identified now by a useful layby, the old road continued straight up the slopes of Knoll Down to a prominent beech clump on the crest, through this wood, and from its western end is now recognised as a green holloway between banks with stunted bushes. It keeps above the Cherhill White Horse, passes the Lansdown Column (erected in 1845), but on the western descent from the downs becomes lost in arable land. However, a lane formerly known as Green Lane, probably marks its line, about half a mile south of the present main road opposite Cherhill village. In 1787 the Beckhampton Trust, after consulting with the Calne Trust, constructed a new road about 2 miles long across the lower northern slopes of the hill, and this section, opened in 1792, continues in use today.

Reference has been made to milestones. These are usually considered as good evidence of turnpike roads. However, the highway boards who assumed responsibility for the roads after the demise of turnpike trusts continued to erect milestones, as did the local highway authorities which followed. Some milestones, however, antedate the turnpike trusts, particularly on roads which were in regular use, as well as on roads which never became turnpiked such as the Old Marlborough Road, the so-called Western Drove Road, and the Bath-Salisbury Road across Salisbury Plain. Thus, the presence of a milestone is not necessarily proof that a particular road was turnpiked; the presence of a tollhouse is conclusive, however.

On the old road from Salisbury to Shaftesbury conveniently described as the 'Racecourse Way', Andrews and Dury show a 'Mile Tree' soon after leaving Salisbury, then a '2 Mile Tree' and '3 Mile Tree', and so on to an '8 Mile Tree' near the 'Salisbury Plain Turnpike' by Chiselbury Camp. In 1723 William Stukeley wrote:

'...the road from Wilton to Shaftesbury, called the Ten Mile Course ... a traveller is indebted to Lord Pembroke for reviving the Roman method of placing a numbered stone at every mile, and the living index of a tree to make it more observable.'

By Stukeley's time the lime trees must have grown to a reasonable size, so probably they had been planted, and the milestones erected, about 1700, a very early date. Neither trees nor milestones survive today, although at the top of White Sheet Hill a milestone dated apparently 1739 or 1789 still indicates XCVII miles from Hyde Park Corner and XIV miles from Salisbury. The much easier valley route was turnpiked in 1787-8, superseding the old road across the chalk uplands, and has been the main road ever since.

*Fovant Hut, a refreshment place for coach travellers on the old Salisbury-Shaftesbury road west of Salisbury. This was for centuries one of the main roads from London to the west*

An Act of 1744 made milestones compulsory on most roads, so any erected before then could be regarded as early by national standards. Another Act of 1766 extended the use of milestones to all roads, an undertaking probably more honoured in the breach than the observance. As has been remarked, dating milestones is an uncertain business, and in the absence of good documentary evidence the style of lettering can provide a clue — the cruder and more uneven this is, the earlier is the milestone likely to be. One feature of Wessex milestones is their use of abbreviations: Salisbury was much more conveniently carved as Sarum, while Shaston, Hardy's name for Shaftesbury, was occasionally preferred to the much longer word.

## Around Sherborne

Apart from the London-Bristol/Bath road, all but a handful of the Turnpike

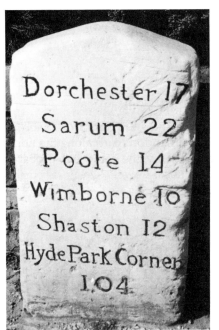

Trust Acts for the area of Wessex within this survey were passed between 1750 and 1790. It may be that the resilient nature of the old chalk ridgeways across southern Wiltshire and much of Dorset caused the turnpike movement to introduce its roads a little later here than elsewhere, and it may be that when they were created their chalky matrix compacted so well that it impressed Young.

Acts of Parliament setting up trusts usually gave powers for 21 years, and these were subsequently renewed by continuing Acts, mainly local in nature. Scores of such Acts still exist, mainly in the Public Records Office, but relatively few in County Record Offices. These tend to

*Milestone at Blandford Forum, Dorset*

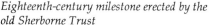

*Eighteenth-century milestone erected by the old Sherborne Trust*

*A ninetenth-century milestone erected by the Sherborne Trust, on the same road*

go into administrative detail but rarely do they give more than an outline of the routes. In the late eighteenth century map references were vague, and where landmarks were referred to, these were often private dwelling houses, identifiable only by the name of the contemporary occupier. Thus, an addition to the Shaftesbury and Sherborne Trust Act of 1755-6, referred to a road 'From Samuel Wise's new house in Sherborne to Mary Hathway's house in Bishop Caundle'. This commenced in Sherborne as South Street, climbed Gainsborough Hill along the old great road to Dorchester, and turned eastwards at 647148 as the present main road (A3030) to Bishop's Caundle.

At the same time a shorter stretch of road 'From East Corner by Castle Town road into Sherborne road' was brought into the Trust, presumably as an alternative for Pinford Lane (the original London road) along the north side of Sherborne Park, which was stopped by the same Act probably because passage along there would have enabled travellers to evade paying a toll at the turnpike in Oborne Road, where the cottage still stands (649175) near Blackmarsh Farm. This is one of only a few of the twenty-five gates in use by the Sherborne Division of the Trust in 1854. White Post Gate (640194) at the crossroads on the Wincanton road (B3135), and Farthing Gate (662086) on the Dorchester road (A352) also survive, the latter a probable late replacement for that at Revels Inn (about 2 miles south), where two gates belonging to different trusts stood close to each other. Nearby (675056) a stone by the roadside marks the northern limit of the Weymouth and Dorchester Turnpike. Taylor's map shows the turnpike gate near this point,

*White Post Toll House on the Wincanton Road north of Sherborne*

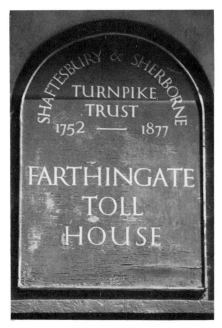

*Signboard of a Dorset toll house near Sherborne*

*Milestone of about 1840 near Dorchester on the 'New Road' of the Maiden Newton Trust*

but the toll house has long since vanished. Sherborne's other surviving toll house is at Westhill (643145) by the junction of the Bishop's Caundle road with the Dorchester road at the top of Sherborne Hill. This is Hardy's

*The Wylye and Nadder valleys from Andrews and Dury's Wiltshire map of 1773. The wavy black lines represent simple contouring*

'Sherton turnpike on the Bath road where Bathsheba Everdene's employees caught up with her on her flight'. This road and its gradient-easing cutting was built in 1848 as a replacement for the steeper Watery Lane, now a bridleway joining the Thornford road near Limekiln Farm.

If not at first, then over the years turnpikes frequently improved upon the

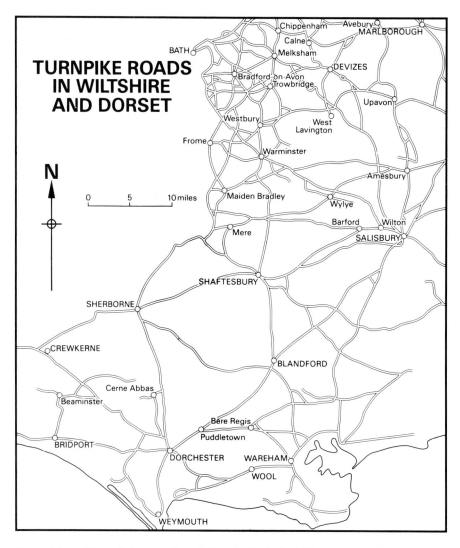

**TURNPIKE ROADS
IN WILTSHIRE
AND DORSET**

N

0    5    10 miles

line of the old road they replaced. Particularly in hilly areas gradients were eased through the building of sweeping curves to allow teams of coach horses to negotiate more gradual ascents. Traces of the old roads can still be found, either as little-used lanes or bridleways. Thus, the Maiden Newton Trust built an easier route up the escarpment at Winyard's Gap (492063) on the main road (A356) from Crewkerne, probably early last century, leaving the old road as a steep, deep-cut holloway to its north, still a surfaced lane with a side-road leading to Halstock.

The same Trust was responsible for what may be described as an early bypass, in a continuing Act of 1840 which authorised the building of a completely new road into Dorchester from the west side of Charminster (674927). This New Road, or Lower Charminster Road, ran in a wide sweep over Wolfeton Meadows, entering Dorchester as it does today by the Grove. Thus, it cut out a mile of road belonging to the Cerne Abbas Trust which ran

*West Ward toll house at
Wolfeton Meadows near
Dorchester*

*Distance indicator, in High
West Street, Dorchester*

HYDE PARK CORNER 120
BLANDFORD ............ 16
BRIDPORT ............ 15

through Charminster before continuing up the Cerne valley, although it was
linked to this by what is now a short stretch of the A352. More importantly
it avoided the narrow, winding main street of Charminster itself. A neat,
contemporary toll house still stands at the western end of Wolfeton Meadows, and a tall, elegant milestone, also of 1840, graces the northern embank-
ment of this road, identifying it by name (673928)

## Turnpike Roads around Salisbury

In Stuart times Salisbury was one of the most important road centres in
southern England, linked even then to London and Southampton, Oxford
and Marlborough, Exeter and Poole, with lesser highways to Bristol, Winchester and Blandford. Although by 1750 roads in the Devizes, Warminster,
Marlborough and Chippenham areas of Wiltshire had been turnpiked, it was
not until 1753 that an Act authorised repairs of roads leading out of Salisbury.
A flurry of turnpiking activity resulted in improved roads to Southampton,
Basingstoke (and therefore London), Blandford , Shaftesbury, Wimborne,
Warminster and Devizes. The success of most, the failure of a few — these are
the legacy of the 1750s and early 1760s to the present-day traveller.

Road improvements west of the city were the work of the Fisherton (or
Wilton) Trust which regularly met at the Deptford Inn (099385) in the Wylye
valley. They assumed responsibility for the new road to Heytesbury (now

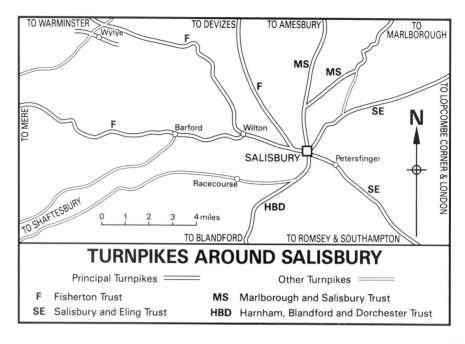

## TURNPIKES AROUND SALISBURY

| Principal Turnpikes ═══ | | Other Turnpikes ═══ |
|---|---|---|

| **F** | Fisherton Trust | **MS** | Marlborough and Salisbury Trust |
|---|---|---|---|
| **SE** | Salisbury and Eling Trust | **HBD** | Harnham, Blandford and Dorchester Trust |

Labels on map: TO WARMINSTER, Wylye, TO DEVIZES, TO AMESBURY, TO MARLBOROUGH, MS, MS, F, F, SE, TO MERE, F, Barford, Wilton, SALISBURY, Petersfinger, TO LOPCOMBE CORNER & LONDON, Racecourse, SE, N, TO SHAFTESBURY, 0 1 2 3 4 miles, HBD, TO BLANDFORD, TO ROMSEY & SOUTHAMPTON

A36), the Mere road as far as Willoughby Hedge (A303 and B3089) and the ridgeway route towards Devizes (mainly A360). Generally, new roads favoured the valleys, with the result that the old Salisbury-Bath road across the Plain fell into disuse. Military occupation today renders the middle part of this impassable, but it is still pleasantly evocative to follow the old road, largely a wide green lane, from Stapleford (067370), past Yarnbury Castle (036405) to Chitterne Down (021434) and Breach Hill (006463). The road can

be picked up again farther north as a farm track from Littleton Down (975510) to Coulston Hill and Tinhead near Edington. Many undated milestones survive, giving distances to Bath and Sarum.

The former main road from Salisbury to Warminster along the south side of the Wylye valley lost its importance, although a short section each side of Wylye village was turnpiked by the Amesbury Trust in 1761-2, presumably to cover access from neighbouring villages to the Trust's most important turnpike from Mullen's Pond near Thruxton (296458)

*Milestone at Yarnbury Castle, Salisbury Plain (may have been moved to its present position)*

*Toll house of 1833 on Tarrant Hinton Down, above Blandford*

through Amesbury, across the Wylye valley at Deptford, to Willoughby Hedge (870335) — the line of the A303 today.

South-westwards from Salisbury the modern A354 originated in 1755 as the Great Western Turnpike, or more specifically the only road of the Harnham, Blandford and Dorchester Trust, probably the most important in Dorset, and the simplest, as it had no branches. Much of it was new construction, the biggest road undertaking of the day in Wessex, perhaps comparable then with a motorway today. The new road adopted a more northerly course than its predecessor of Ogilby's time, tended to disregard

*Taylor's map of Dorset, 1765, showing part of Cranborne Chase*

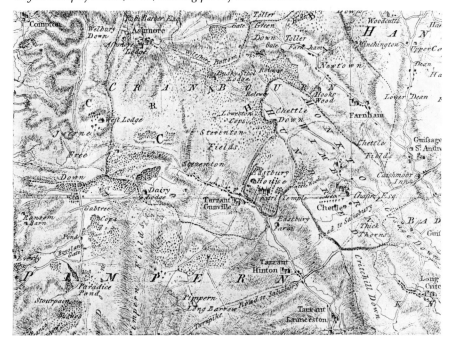

Blandford

5

Sarum

17

local villages, and, more significantly, missed Cranborne completely. In so doing it probably followed a drier course near the valley-heads of the Gussage, Tarrant and Crichel streams, thus obviating the need for much bridge-building, although a new bridge across the Ebble at Coombe Bissett superseded the medieval pack-horse structure a few yards away. Ignoring Sixpenny Handley and Pentridge the new road took advantage of a section of the Roman road south of Woodyates (028194).

Initially there were only two toll-gates between Salisbury and Blandford, at Coombe Bissett and Cashmoor, but in 1833 another was added at Tarrant Hinton, surviving and inhabited today, its design identifying its former function. Nearby is one of a series of good milestones to be seen along the road, their lettering suggesting they may be the eighteenth-century originals. Inns at Cashmoor, Thickthorn and Woodyates existed in 1791, and it was at Woodyates that George III liked to break his journeys from London to Weymouth. In the middle of last century Woodyates Inn was still a posting-house with four available pairs of post-horses. All parcels and packets for Lord Shaftesbury at nearby St Giles' House, and throughout the neighbourhood, were cleared at Woodyates Inn which operated as a post-office when the mail coaches called.

Taylor's map (1765) appeared a few years after this road and identifies it clearly. Between Cashmoor Inn and Tarrant Hinton he also marks, just to its north, 'Road to Salisbury', suggesting that there the turnpike followed a new line. On the modern OS map the old road is marked by a bridleway and parish boundary running north-east from Tarrant Hinton. West of Blandford also the turnpike took a new line, bypassing Milton Abbas well to the south. This may have damaged Milton's trade and thus have contributed to the ease with which Lord Milton, from 1771-86, was able to destroy the village and realign it nearby. Cary, in 1787, and Haywood two years later, show the new turnpike and the old road through Milton Abbas, via Winterborne Stickland, Houghton and Cheselborne to Puddletown, now largely a series of lanes.

## Puddletown and Wimborne

Established by an Act in 1840 this last major Dorset trust was particularly significant in that it radically changed road communications in east Dorset. Until then these had been predominantly north-south, based on the twin focal points of Blandford and Wareham. Afterwards they became mainly east-west, based on Poole and Dorchester. Their present-day legacies are the important trunk roads eastwards from Puddletown (and hence from Dor-

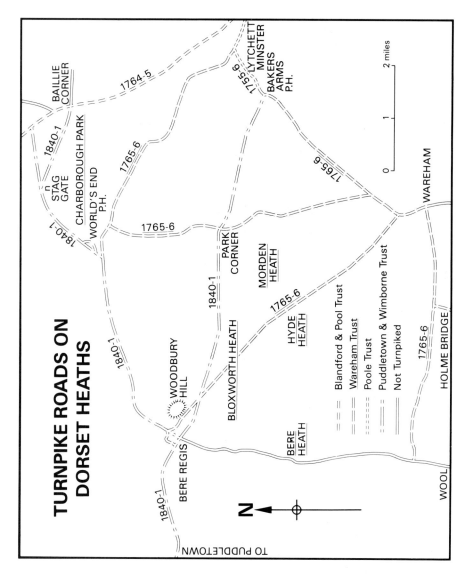

TURNPIKE ROADS ON
DORSET HEATHS

chester): starting as the A35 and branching at Bere Regis, with the A35 continuing to Poole, Bournemouth and Southampton, while the A31 takes a more northerly course through Wimborne and Ringwood. Effectively, the trust's 24 miles of largely new roads radiated from Bere Regis, to Puddletown, Wimborne and Lytchett Minster. Although it opened up communications in east Dorset the new trust was never a financial success, because it came too late, for within 7 years of its completion the railway line from Wimborne to Dorchester, through Wareham, provided too strong an opposition.

One of the roads was described as running from the Royal Oak inn at Bere Regis (848948) to the Poole and Wareham turnpike near the St Clement's inn, now the Baker's Arms, at Lytchett Minster (955926). This was a completely

Poole Trust milestone, probably of 1798, near Cranborne

Nineteenth-century milestone near Cranborne

Milestone on the Wareham to Bere Regis road (1765)

new construction as far as Park Corner (914937) and then followed an older line, and its course is a good example of a late turnpike, in three straight alignments, across the southern slopes of Woodbury Hill and then through the Bloxworth woodlands to Park Corner. The first section rendered redundant the northern mile of an earlier (1765) turnpike of the Wareham trust leading into Bere Regis and entering the village, unexpectedly at its northern end, presumably so that it could serve the Woodbury Hill fairground as well. From the A35 crossroads at 863942 this is now a quiet, minor road, and in spite of new building developments at Town End, an eighteenth-century milestone survives at 852952, with better ones along the Wareham road.

The Puddletown road into Bere Regis used old roads but included new constructions, especially from Tolpuddle Ball (808946), and created a new entry into Bere Regis from the west, which hitherto had been through Sitterton village along a line now marked by a track and hedgerow. The toll house at Athelhampton (772943), cunningly disguised as the entrance-lodge to Athelhampton House, still stands. But, apart from the roads themselves, the most prominent memorials to the Puddletown and Wimborne Trust are the massive brick walls and three great gates of Charborough Park built 1843-4. The north side of the arch of the East Almer Gate has an inscription marking the new turnpike: 'This road from Wimborne to Dorchester was projected and completed through the instrumentality of J.S.W. Sawbridge Erle Drax Esqre, MP in the years 1841 and 1842'. The road actually went only to Puddletown where it met the Harnham, Blandford and Dorchester turnpike.

This road from the north-east end of Bere Regis to Stag Gate and Newton Marsh (943997) initially followed an older road as far as the White Lane corner on Bloxworth Down (873965), was then a new construction to Red Post (884971), adopted an older line to the junction west of the World's End (906977), and bypassed Mapperton and Almer before swinging eastwards on a straight alignment past Stag Gate (925994). One effect of this turnpike was to reduce traffic along the Winterborne valley road so that the string of villages — Winterborne Kingston, Winterborne Muston, Winterborne Anderson, Winterborne Tomson and Winterborne Zelston, as well as Mapperton and Almer — are spared the throng of vehicles travelling along the A31. A series of footpaths and lanes link them along the northern side of the river.

## Enclosure Roads

Throughout Wessex as a whole thousands of acres of forest, woodland, marsh and waste, as well as much of the chalk downland, were divided, portioned out and enclosed by their individual owners from the seventeenth century onwards. Occurring initially by private agreements, later under Acts of Parliament, the process continued until late last century. In Wiltshire the common arable fields at Charlton near Donhead St Mary were enclosed in 1867, while at Grimstone, a few miles north-west of Dorchester, this did not take place until 1907.

Except in Portland and the Purbeck area of Dorset, enclosure was by hedges. Early seventeenth-century records provide abundant evidence of the effect they had, and many parishes reported problems in the traditional activity of 'beating the bounds', because hedges blocked the way. In 1630 Dorset justices received complaints that various roads were in a dangerous condition 'by reason of certaine Inclosures lately made by various persons by which they have streightened [narrowed] the way.' Several hundred miles of Wessex roads and tracks had already evolved before this enclosure process developed, and the subsequent planting of hedges to define their boundaries, and to prevent travellers and driven livestock from encroaching on the newly-enclosed fields, merely confirmed the routes of such tracks.

The 'rule of thumb' method of dating a hedge from the number of shrub

species growing in a sample length, evolved a few years ago by Dr Max Hooper, helps to substantiate the likely age of many Wessex tracks. The formula is, that in a 30yd sample of hedge, one species of shrub represents roughly 100 years since planting. Admittedly there are marked regional variations, and the greater the age of a hedge, the wider are the tolerances of date.

To be strictly accurate, the date of a hedge does not specifically date the track it borders, but merely suggests that, at the time of its planting, the track was already there. The magnificent double hedge along the Wilton Way on Throope Hill (092253) is, at least, a four-species one, as is that along parts of the Furzy Down road, dating them about 1600. At the

*Boundary Stone on Wilton Way, Toyd Down*

other end of the spectrum, single-species hedges represent post-turnpike dates, while those of two species, indicative of late eighteenth-century planting, are commonly seen bordering many turnpikes of that date.

When a one- or two-species hedge borders a straight stretch of road, and the adjoining fields and field tracks are similarly straight and hedged, the explanation is that the associated fields were enclosed by Act of Parliament. Such landscapes were formally planned by professional surveyors who drew straight lines on maps, which were translated into similar lines in the countryside. These were bordered by single shrub species, usually haw-thorn, and the new stretches of road accompanying them were created usually with a standard width between hedges, 30 or 40ft, and often having a wide grass verge on one or both sides. Main, or turnpike roads already existing at the time of the Parliamentary enclosures were usually left unal-tered, but a number of lesser roads were made anew.

Straightness is not the only clue to enclosure roads. Right-angled bends, more apparent on large-scale maps than on the ground, where road improve-ments have ironed out many of these, are significant of the surveyors' work, particularly where these occur at parish boundaries. Enclosure was often a piecemeal process, with even neighbouring parishes enclosing their arable fields or surviving common land at different times. Thus, one area to be enclosed may have a straight road to a point on the parish boundary where it met an existing road. An adjoining parish, being enclosed at a different time, might plan for its road to meet the parish boundary at the same point, but in practice it may not be carefully aligned, so that a small kink occurred. But if the alighment was a lot out, the resultant larger kink would produce two right-angled bends in the road.

Enclosure roads showing the features mentioned can be seen around Leigh, south of Sherborne, where the common was enclosed in 1803, while part of Holwell parish, in Blackmore Vale, was enclosed a few years earlier, in 1797. There, the road running eastwards from the village towards King's Stag shows all the characteristics — a series of short, straight alignments, with a wide grass verge along one side, together with roadside farms and cottages all dating from the early nineteenth century. But the most impres-sive of the later enclosure roads are those on the Dorset heathlands, where fine lengths of long straight roads frequently represent the realignment last century of older tracks. Roads running northwards from Wareham — to Bere Regis, Wimborne, and Lytchett Minster — are good examples of such realignments. Modern road improvements in south and east Dorset add further emphasis to the 'no-nonsense' directness of such roads.

# Carriers

In the early seventeenth century a Shaftesbury resident stated that 'there is usually brought into the market-place sometimes forty carts of corn, some-times more, sometimes less, besides divers horse-loads of corn ... also to be sold.' Four-wheeled carriers' wagons were probably being used a century earlier, but details of common carriers' services are first recorded about 1770. Salisbury guides of that time refer to thirty carriers bringing goods to the city's Tuesday market, half of them managing to get there and back to their home village within the day, the others needing to stop overnight. By then, it seems there were three types of carriers: long-distance stage wagons travelling between West Country towns and London; local carriers from villages up to about a dozen miles away, and the 'overnighters' from farther away, such as Andover, Poole, Marlborough and Winchester.

Carriers' lists of 1774 and 1825 show little difference between these dates. Long-distance wagons were declining slightly, probably as a result of the competing stage-coach services, but the local network had widened and increased. Forty years later these local services had trebled, but the emergent railways had all but killed off the long-distance operators, except for those on routes not served by the railways. Indication of carriers' charges comes from Quarter Sessions for Somerset in 1756: '...for the carriage of every hundredweight of goods (about 50 kilos) from the City of London to the City of Bath, or town of Frome, five shillings, and for every twenty miles beyond these places, one shilling...'. From London to Wincanton the rate was 6s, and to Milborne Port, 5s 6d. One shilling per hundredweight for 20 miles seemed to be the average rate.

Early directories provide good examples of carriers' services. From the late 1830s come these illustrations:

*From Blandford*

| To London: | Russell & Co's waggons, to the Bell, Friday Street, Cheapside: every | Sun at 2pm |
| | | Tues at 8pm |
| | | Thurs at 12 midnight |
| | through Salisbury, Andover, Basingstoke | |
| | Russell & Co's van at 5am except Mon | |
| To Exeter: | Russell & Co's waggons from their Warehouse, East Street, | |
| | every Mon at 5am | |
| | Wed at 12 noon | |
| | Fri at 10pm | |
| | through Dorchester, Bridport, Axminster and Honiton | |
| | to their Warehouse, Southgate St. | |
| | Russell & Co's van at 5pm each day except Mon. | |

Similar thrice-weekly services operated from Dorchester to London and Exeter, while there was a weekly service from Weymouth to Bath and Bristol. From Sherborne, Brown and Brice's wagon ran to London on Wednesdays and Saturdays, with their van operating on Tuesdays, Thursdays and Saturdays, all from the George Inn. Much more detail is given for a service to Bristol and Bath:

'Beale's waggons leave Sherborne early on Monday mornings and arrive at Bristol about 6 o'clock on Tuesday morning, and return at 10 the same night, reaching Sherborne early on Thursday morning. They arrive at Weymouth the same evening and return the following afternoon to Sherborne.'

But it was the local carrier who formed the first and vital link in the chain which brought even the most isolated hamlet in touch with the outside world as represented by the early Victorian market town. It was his cart and

An advertisement sheet, about 1840, for coaches from the Crown Hotel, Blandford, Dorset. (By courtesy of Sir Joseph Weld and the Dorset Record Office)

subsequently his wagon that was also the local taxi, even though the exposure during a journey, particularly in severe weather, may often have caused serious illness. Relating to Blandford again, the Post Office Directory 1848 shows the extent of carriers' services locally, but also introduces a link with the new railway line at Wimborne:

*From Blandford*

TO LONDON: Ford & Co's waggons leave their office, West Street, every morning at 10 for Wimborne, thence proceed, via South Western Railway to Southampton, Romsey, Winchester & London; also every evening at 8 for Salisbury & London.

Wm Gould's waggons leave his office, East Street, every morning for Wimborne, thence proceed, per railway, to London.

TO BATH: James Coward, every Tues from the 'Three Choughs', and Henry Dodimead, Wed & Sat from the 'Three Choughs'.

TO BERE REGIS: George Bevin, Sat from the 'Crown and Anchor'.

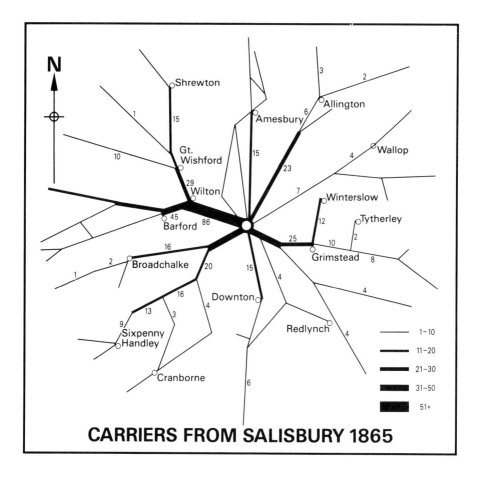

N

Shrewton

1

15

10

Gt.
Wishford

Amesbury

3

2

Allington

6

15

23

Wallop

4

Wilton

29

45

Barford

86

7

Winterslow

Tytherley

12

2

10

Grimstead

8

16

Broadchalke

2

20

15

25

4

1

16

Downton

13

3

4

4

4

9

Sixpenny
Handley

Redlynch

4

Cranborne

6

| | 1–10 |
| ▬ | 11–20 |
| ▬▬ | 21–30 |
| ▬▬▬ | 31–50 |
| ▬▬▬▬ | 51+ |

# CARRIERS FROM SALISBURY 1865

The figures show the number of common carriers' journeys into Salisbury per week (after J. Chandler)

| TO BRISTOL: | James Coward, Tues, and Henry Dodimead, Wed & Sat from the 'Three Choughs', and John Ings, Wed, from the 'Red Lion'. |
|---|---|
| TO CHILD OAKFORD: | James Roberts, Wed & Sat from the 'Half Moon'. |
| TO GUSSAGE: | William Kent, Sat from the 'Crown & Anchor'. |
| TO HANDLEY: | James White, Sat from the 'Portman's Arms' and William Wyatt, Sat from the 'King's Arms'. |
| TO IWERNE MINSTER: | John Hunt, Tues, Thurs, Sat from the 'King's Arms'. |
| TO POOLE: | John Ings, Tues, from the 'Red Lion'. |
| TO SALISBURY: | John Matthews, Wed & Sat from the 'Bell'. |
| TO SHAFTESBURY: | Wm Barnes, Sat, from the 'Three Choughs' |
| TO STURMINSTER NEWTON: | James Stickland, Thurs & Sat from the 'Bell' and Wm Goodfellow, Sat from the 'Crown & Anchor'. |
| TO WHITCHAMPTON: | John Kent, Sat from the 'Star'. |
| TO WIMBORNE: | George Fry, Sat from the 'Star' and Joseph Orman, Mon, Wed, Fri from the 'Black Bear'. |
| TO YEOVIL: | John Ryall, Tues from the 'Three Choughs'. |

If the number of carriers indicated a market's importance, no Wessex town could rival Salisbury, where over a hundred might have been counted in the Market Place on a Tuesday morning in the 1860s, most of whom attended the Saturday market as well. Devizes and Dorchester could manage only about forty, Blandford half that number.

A different picture comes from Swanage in the busy days of the Purbeck quarrying trade early last century where one writer recalls,

'I have seen over fifty waggons, each loaded with three or four tons of Swanage stone, dragged down through the streets in one day, the wheels spanned without a shoe. It was nothing unusual to find ruts nine and ten inches deep in the narrow road ... During the hot weather of summer the almost ceaseless grinding of these heavy vehicles would crush the roads to powder, and when the wind rose the dust would be almost suffocating.'

In *A Shepherd's Life*, written just after the turn of the century (1910) W.H. Hudson records that

'about 1840 it was customery [*sic*] to burn peat in the cottages [at Martin, in South Wiltshire], the first cost of which was about four-and-sixpence the wagon-load — as much as I should require to keep me warm for a month in winter; but the cost of its conveyance to the villages on the Plain was about five to six shillings a load, as it came from a considerable distance, mostly from the New Forest ... coal at that time was only used by the blacksmiths in the villages, and was conveyed in sacks on ponies or donkeys — one of the coal carriers had eight donkeys, with jingling bells on their headstalls, and their burdens of two sacks of small coal on each.'

He, too, comments on Salisbury's importance

'...as the capital of the Plain, the head and heart of all those villages, too many to count, scattered far and wide over the surrounding country ... with the carriers' carts drawn up in rows on rows — carriers from a hundred little villages on the Bourne, the Avon, the Wylye, the Nadder, the Ebble, and from all over the Plain.'

## Stage Coaches and Mail Coaches

In 1657 the office of Postmaster-General was established, with the 'exclusive right of carrying letters and the furnishing of post-horses' at a charge which, in the following year became 3d a mile, a service initially restricted to places on the main, or post-roads. In 1670 it was extended to places on bye-roads — Ogilby's 'crossroads'. Thomas Gardiner's survey of 1677 confirms that the great road to the west, through Salisbury, Shaftesbury, Sherborne and Crewkerne to Exeter was used by the post-horses, with by-posts from Shaftesbury southwards to Blandford, Dorchester, Weymouth and Poole, and from Crewkerne to Axminster and Lyme.

Also from 1657 comes the earliest record of a stage coach service between London and Bath, advertised in a London weekly newspaper of 19-26 May to run every Monday and Thursday. This pioneering service soon faced competition from another operator, also advertising a coach and four horses to carry pasengers 'from London to Redding, Nubery, Marlborough, Bath or Bristol ... from the Red Lyon in Fleet Street, upon any Thursday.' Within a few years many more proprietors increased the competition, while in Dorset the first regular stage-coach service from London had been announced in

April 1658, leaving the George Inn, Aldgate, every Monday, Wednesday and Friday:

'To Salisbury in two days for XXs
To Blandford and Dorchester in two days and a half for XXXs
To Exeter in four days for XLs'.

During the eighteenth century coach design, springing and construction made great advances. In 1776 a duty was imposed on them, and following the General Turnpike Act of 1773 stage-coaches became the main carriers of mail, superseding the 'Post Boys' on horseback. In 1784 Palmer's first mail coach ran from London to Bath and Bristol: 'in sixteen hours, with a Guard for its protection … and constructed so as to accommodate four Inside passengers in the most convenient manner … at £1 8s 0d per passenger … No outsides allowed.'

Cary's *New Itinerary* for 1806 and 1817 includes a passenger timetable which illustrates the gradual speeding-up of the service originated by the famous mail coach *Diligence*.

dep.   Bath 5.30pm
       Chippenham 7.05pm
       Calne 8.00pm
       Marlborough 9.30pm
       Hungerford 10.40pm
       Newbury 11.35pm and reaching London about 7.0am.

Only severe weather or an accident upset these times. The most famous snow-storm in coaching history occurred during Christmas 1836 when, over the Wiltshire downs there were snowdrifts 12-16ft deep between Marlborough and Devizes. The Bath and Bristol mails were abandoned 80 miles from London, and two guards eventually brought them by post-chaise drawn by four horses, completing the journey in 36 hours, and for 17 miles they had driven across fields. That same Christmas three outside passengers on a coach had died of cold by the time it had reached Chippenham.

Bad weather was not the only hazard faced by travellers. Although it was the mail coaches which are usually associated with highwaymen, robbers and footpads were working their nefarious activities centuries earlier. References in Justices' accounts from all over Wessex, from the mid-seventeenth century onwards are obviously concerned with the robbers who were caught, usually to end their days on the gallows at Salisbury or Dorchester.

There seems little doubt that lawlessness had 'peak periods', at the close of the Civil War, at the end of the seventeenth century, and again during the French wars of the late eighteenth century. People were accustomed to highwaymen, and a tradition appeared to have grown that such characters were no ordinary criminals. Riding good horses and carrying expensive weapons they were the 'gentlemen of the road'. Many, indeed, came from good families. One, called Biss, hanged at Salisbury in 1695, was believed to have been the son of Sir Walter Biss, parson of Bishopstrow near Warminster. A contemporary, William Davis, ostensibly a farmer and inn-keeper, spent the best part of 40 years, riding around the lonely roads of Salisbury Plain as a highway robber.

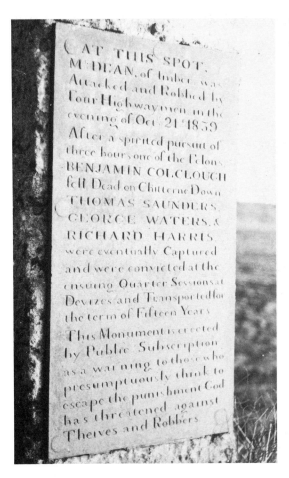

AT THIS SPOT,
M. DEAN, of Imber was
Attacked and Robbed by
Four Highwaymen in the
evening of Oct. 21. 1839
After a spirited pursuit of
three hours one of the Felons
BENJAMIN COLCLOUGH
fell Dead on Chitterne Down
THOMAS SAUNDERS,
GEORGE WATERS, &
RICHARD HARRIS
were eventually Captured
and were convicted at the
ensuing Quarter Sessions at
Devizes and Transported for
the term of Fifteen Years
This Monument is erected
by Public Subscription
as a warning to those who
presumptuously think to
escape the punishment God
has threatened against
Theives and Robbers

Throughout most of the eighteenth century a famous gang of highwaymen was based at Cherhill, lying just off the Bath road at the western foot of the chalk downs. Mr Plenderleath, rector of Cherhill from 1860 to 1892, noted that, even in the middle of last century, his own uncle, born in 1776, 'when he heard of my having accepted a living in Wiltshire, solemnly exhorted me never to think of driving across the downs without my servant and myself being provided with firearms.' The Cherhill gang had just ended its activities when Plenderleath moved to the village so that it was through local gossip that he heard that

'one of the men is reported to have sometimes gone out upon his marauding expeditions in the summertime without a stitch of clothing, as he said that not only did such an apparition frighten people upon a dark night, but also that a naked man was less easily recognised than one who appeared in ordinary costume.'

Although travellers, either on horseback or in a coach or chaise, usually yielded quickly to even the most amateur highwayman, Wessex farmers were often made of sterner stuff. The Imber church register records burials of two such robbers in 1716, each shot on the same day, but at different places, by farmers they had attacked. Undoubtedly the most famous account of a

# DORSET

ANY PERSON WILFULLY INJURING ANY PART OF THIS COUNTY BRIDGE • WILL BE GUILTY OF FELONY AND • UPON CONVICTION LIABLE TO BE TRANSPORTED FOR LIFE BY THE COURT

7&8 GEO 4 C30 S13   T FOOKS

*One of a number of well-known notices, dated 1827, found on Dorset bridges. This example is at Sturminster Marshall*

Salisbury Plain highway robbery is that commemorated on a large stone by the side of the A360 Salisbury-Devizes road above West Lavington. The Robbers' Stone (008514) records the event:

'At this spot Mr Dean of Imber was attacked and robbed by four highwaymen in the evening of October 21, 1839. After a spirited pursuit of three hours, one of the Felons, Benjamin Colclough, fell dead on Chitterne Down. Thos. Saunders, George Waters, and Richard Harris were eventually captured, and were convicted at the ensuing Quarter Sessions at Devizes, and transported for a term of fifteen years. This monument is erected by public subscription as a warning to those who presumptuously think to escape the punishment God has threatened against Thieves and Robbers.'

Warnings of a different kind appear on a number of Dorset's bridges. These date from 1827-8, following an Act passed in an endeavour to prevent vandals from damaging these important structures. One wonders whether the authorities then were any more successful than those of today in stopping vandalism. Equally, one is curious as to how (or why) one would wish wilfully to injure a bridge.

Cary's *Itineraries* and the many editions of Paterson's *Roads* — more fully entitled the *New and Accurate Descriptions of all the Direct and Principal Cross-Roads in Great Britain* — which had superseded Ogilby's *Britannia* in 1771, were the standard works on roads until the detailed, large-scale Ordnance Survey maps of the later part of last century. From them we gain confirmation of the more important routes being used by coach travellers in those three decades of coaching's 'high noon' from about 1810 to 1840.

We find for example, that in his road from London to Barnstaple Paterson takes the southern fork at Stonehenge (A303 today) by 'Willey' and Chicklade to Willoughby Hedge, continuing along the Harroway to Kilmington,

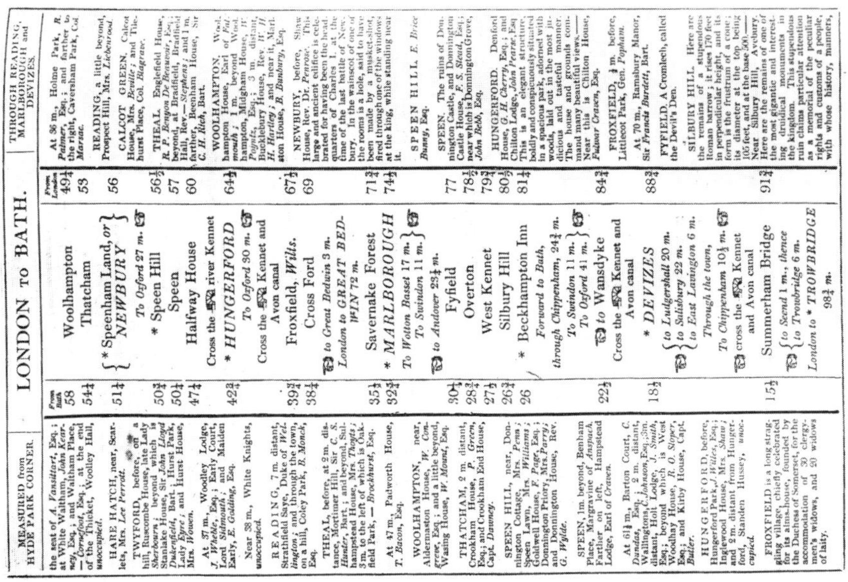

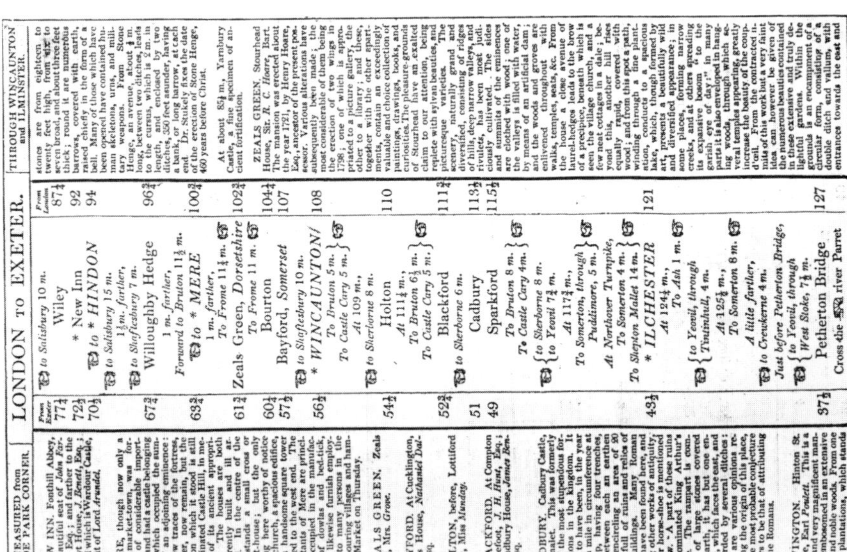

Four tables from Mogg's 1822 edition of Paterson's Roads, printed sideways across the top and bottom of the page.

## Top table

**LONDON TO BATH.**

| From Bath | MEASURED from HYDE PARK CORNER | From London | |
|---|---|---|---|
| 49¾ | Woolhampton | 58 | |
| 53 | Thatcham | 54¾ | |
| 56 | { Speenham Land, or NEWBURY } | 51¼ | |
| | To Oxford 27 m. | | |
| 56½ | *Speen Hill | 50½ | |
| 57 | Speen | 50¼ | |
| 60 | Halfway House | 47¾ | |
| | Cross the river Kennet | | |
| 64¾ | *HUNGERFORD | 42¾ | |
| | Cross the Kennet and Avon canal | | |
| 67¾ | Froxfield, Wilts. | 39½ | |
| 69 | Cross Ford | 38¼ | |
| | London to GREAT BEDWIN 72 m. | | |
| 71¼ | Savernake Forest | 35¼ | |
| 74½ | *MARLBOROUGH | 32¼ | |
| | To Wotton Basset 17 m. | | |
| | To Swindon 23 m. | | |
| | To Andover 24½ m. | | |
| 77 | Fyfield | 30¾ | |
| 79¼ | Overton | 29¼ | |
| 80½ | West Kennet | 27¼ | |
| 81¼ | Silbury Hill | 26¾ | |
| 84¾ | *Beckhampton Inn | 22¼ | |
| | Forward to Bath, through Chippenham, 24½ m. | | |
| | To Swindon 11 m. | | |
| | To Oxford 41 m. | | |
| | To Wansdyke | | |
| | Cross the Kennet and Avon canal | | |
| 88½ | *DEVIZES | 18¼ | |
| | { To Ludgershall 20 m. | | |
| | To Salisbury 22 m. } | | |
| | To Chippenham 10½ m. | | |
| | cross the Kennet and Avon canal | | |
| 91½ | Summerham Bridge | 15¾ | |
| | { To Send 1 m. ; thence to Trowbridge 6 m. } | | |
| | London to TROWBRIDGE 98½ m. | | |

(Descriptive notes for this table, measured from Hyde Park Corner, include entries for A. Fonsident, Esq., Waltham; READING, Mrs. Cadoran, Prospect Hill; CALCOT GREEN; THEAL, Englefield House; WOOLHAMPTON; NEWBURY; SPEEN HILL, E. Brice Bunny, Esq.; SPEEN; HUNGERFORD, Denford House; FROXFIELD, A Crombieh, called the Devil's Den; FYFIELD; and SILBURY HILL.)

## Bottom table

**LONDON TO EXETER.**

| MEASURED from HYDE PARK CORNER | From London | From Exeter | |
|---|---|---|---|
| NEW INN, Fonthill Abbey | 77¼ | 87¼ | |
| *New Inn | 72¾ | 92 | |
| *HINDON | 70¼ | 94 | |
| MERE | 67¾ | 96¾ | |
| Willoughby Hedge | 63¾ | 100¾ | |
| *MERE | | 102¼ | |
| Zeals Green, Dorsetshire | 61¾ | 102¾ | |
| Bourton | 60¼ | 104¾ | |
| Bayford, Somerset | 57¾ | 107 | |
| *WINCAUNTON / WINCANTON | 56¼ | 108 | |
| Holton | | 110 | |
| WOOLHAMPTON | | 111¼ | |
| Blackford | | 111¾ | |
| Sparkford | | 113¾ | |
| Cadbury | 51 | 115¾ | |
| *ILCHESTER | 49 | | |
| | 48¼ | 121 | |
| *ILMINSTER | | | |
| Petherton Bridge | 37½ | 127 | |
| Cross the river Parret | | | |

(Descriptive column entries include NEW INN, Fonthill Abbey, seat of John Farquhar; MERE, with Castle; ZEALS GREEN, Stourhead, Henry Hoare, Esq.; BAYFORD; HOLTON; BLACKFORD, At Compton Pauncefort, J. H. Hunt, Esq., and Cadbury House, James Bennet, Esq.; CADBURY, Cadbury Castle, or Camalet; SEVINGTON, Hinton St. George, Earl Poulett.)

*Four pages from Mogg's 1822 edition of Paterson's Roads. (top) London to Bath via today's A4 to Beckhampton and A361 to Devizes, but refers to the alternative route from Beckhampton by today's A4 through Calne and Chippenham. (bottom) London to Exeter using mainly today's A303. (opposite top) Mainly the route of today's A343 and A354. (opposite bottom) London to Bruton and Chard. This today's B3089 from Barford to Hindon, but beyond Willoughby Hedge is now represented by the line of the old road (with 1750 milestones) by White Sheet Castle, Kilmington and Kingsettle Hill (the Harroway) to Bruton, then minor roads to Castle Cary, picking up the A359 to Sparkford*

174

## LONDON to EXETER, CONTINUED to the LAND'S END.

| MEASURED from HYDE PARK CORNER. | | From L. End | Place | From London | THROUGH ANDOVER, SALISBURY, and DORCHESTER. |
|---|---|---|---|---|---|
| | | 237¾ | Long Parish House / Hurstbourne | 58¾ | HURSTBOURNE, Hurstbourne Park, seat of Portsmouth. |
| | | 234½ | Down House | 61½ | |
| | | 232½ | *ANDOVER | 63½ | |
| | | 230½ | Little Hart | 65½ | |
| | | 228 | Down Farm | 68½ | |
| | | 225½ | Middle Wallop | 71 | |
| | | 229½ | Lobcombe Corner, Direction Post | 73½ | |
| | | 221½ | Winterslow Hutt | 75 | |
| | | 214½ | *SALISBURY | 81½ | SALISBURY, entrance of, The College, Wardham, etc. |
| | | 212 | Combe Bisset | 84½ | CASHMOOR INN, 1 m. |
| | | 205 | *Woodyates Inn, Dorsetshire | 91½ | |
| | | 200 | Cashmoor Inn | 96½ | BLANDFORD, Branston |
| | | 195 | Tarrant Hinton | 101¼ | |
| | | 192½ | Pimperne | 103¼ | |
| | | 187½ | *BLANDFORD | 108¼ | WINTERBORNE WHITCHURCH |
| | | 185 | Winborne Whitchurch | 111¼ | MILBOURNE |
| | | 181½ | Milbourne / Piddletown | 114¼ | |

## LONDON to BRUTON, CONTINUED to CHARD.

| MEASURED from HYDE PARK CORNER. | From Chard | Place | From London | THROUGH SALISBURY. |
|---|---|---|---|---|
| DINTON, Dinton House / FONTHILL | 143¾ | Hyde Park Corner to Barford, Wilts., page 64 | 87 | DINTON, Marshwood House. SPARKFORD, Hazel Grove House, Rev. Henry Bennett. |
| | 56¾ | Dinton | 89¼ | ILCHESTER. |
| | 54¼ | Teffont | 91¼ | |
| | 52½ | Chilmark | 92¾ | |
| | 51 | Fonthill | 95 | |
| | 48½ | Berwick St. Leonards | 95¾ | |
| | 47¼ | *HINDON | 96¾ | |
| | 44½ | Willoughby Hedge | 99¼ | |
| CASTLE CARY | 32 | *BRUTON, Somerset, page 72 | 111¼ | ILMINSTER. |
| | 30¼ | Pitcombe | 118¾ | |
| GALHAMPTON | 27¼ | Ansford Inn, or *CASTLE CARY | 116 | |
| | 26¼ | Sparkford | 117½ | |
| | 23¾ | | 120½ | |
| *ILCHESTER | 17¼ | *ILCHESTER | 126¼ | |
| | 11½ | Petherton Bridge | 132¼ | |
| | 8½ | Sevington | 135¾ | |
| | 6¾ | White Lackington | 137¾ | |
| | 5 | *ILMINSTER | 138¾ | |
| | 9½ | *CHARD | 140¾ | |
| | | | 143¾ | |

Kingsettle Hill and Bruton. A note pointed out that at Willoughby Hedge you could proceed to Mere, but need rejoin the upper road again near Kilmington, while at Hardway (village) you could bypass Bruton and continue instead through Shepton Montague.

On his route from London to Exeter, via Andover, Salisbury, Blandford and Dorchester, there is a fascinating little aside before the Bridport reference: 'The traveller in a chaise, who has occasion to go from Bridport to Weymouth, by turning off on the right, about $3\frac{1}{4}$m before Dorchester, will save a change of chaise, a turnpike, and about 4m of distance.' Presumably

*The Pheasant Inn, Winterslow, largely rebuilt, but formerly the Winterslow Hut, an important coaching inn between Andover and Salisbury. William Hazlitt, the essayist, lived and wrote there in 1819*

he was referring either to the road (now B3159) branching at Winterborne Abbas, or what is now a bridleway leaving the A35 at 637905 to join this at Rew Manor and continuing through Martinstown and Upwey.

Unfortunately, Paterson is remarkably inconsistent where turnpike gates are concerned. Thus, on the Andover-Dorchester sections of his London-Exeter road only one is specifically mentioned, that at Longbredy (now vanished beneath the A35). There are references to Winterslow Hutt, Cashmoor Inn, Tarrant Hinton, Penn Inn and Hunter's Lodge, where turnpikes probably existed, so one is left to wonder why that at Longbredy should be singled out.

Cary's 1806 *Traveller's Companion* is not much more forthcoming, although when giving an itinerary from Salisbury to Bruton by what he calls 'Another Road' turnpike or toll gates are noted at Fisherton and Willoughby Hedge. This route also used the Harroway 'over the Downs' to 'Hutt' near Kilmington, probably at 810316 where a track comes in from Kingston Deverill.

Paterson's later editions include details from the 1821 census, listing, for example, inns which supply post-horses, such as The Antelope and King's Arms at Dorchester, The Bear, Crown, Golden Lion and King's Head at Weymouth, the Crown at Blandford, and the White Hart at Salisbury, among many others. Indeed, almost every market town, and many villages along the main roads, offered this facility. Charges for the hire of horse, also given in Paterson, provide a ready reckoner, showing the cost for a pair of horses at 12d-18d a mile for distances of 5-20 miles. Two pairs were charged double,

The King's Arms, Dorchester, an important coaching inn. George III stopped here on his way to Weymouth

(below) The White Hart, Salisbury, built about 1820 and listed in Cary's road-book

and a single horse half that for a pair. These tables of charges were, incidentally, given in English and French.

Postage rates for the carriage of mail were also related to distance:

*The Crown at Everleigh, Wiltshire, which was highly praised by William Cobbett in 1826*

| Single Letter Rate | | 50-80 miles | 8d |
|---|---|---|---|
| Up to 15 miles | 4d | 80-120 miles | 9d |
| 15-20 miles | 5d | 120-170 miles | 10d |
| 20-30 miles | 6d | 170-230 miles | 11d |
| 30-50 miles | 7d | 230-300 miles | 12d |

The carriage of mail formed the life blood of the single generation of coaching prosperity, and although this was centred on London, nevertheless flourished in the provinces, including Wessex. The true coaching inn was probably its most outward and visible sign, and in order to achieve good time-keeping along a route conveniently spaced posting-houses were needed at which horses could be changed. All depended on this. Extensive stabling, and large numbers of horses, postilions and ostlers were essential. To innkeepers this meant a large capital outlay, on which they naturally wanted some return, preferably through increased trade at the bar. But this would mean delay, and delay could not be permitted for the mail, so one outcome of this was that coachmasters, whose main profit came from the mail, either leased or bought inns along the various routes.

The Annual Register for 1775 revealed that there were 400 coaches on the roads, and 17,000 four-wheeled carriages. Sixty years later the number of coaches alone had risen to 3,000, employing 30,000 men, and requiring 150,000 horses, and it has been estimated that the most important inn in almost any market town would have 50-60 horses 'on call' in its yard to meet the demands of the mail-coach, stage-coach, and other services.

Inns and roads were interdependent. The inns thrived on travellers' custom, while the roads could not have carried the volume of traffic they did

(above) *Coaching inn notice at Hindon, probably early nineteenth century*

(left) *Coaching sign at the King's Arms, Calne, Wilts*

without the inns, whose services were essential to travellers and coachmen alike, when average speeds were at best little more than 8 miles an hour. Along an important route such as the Bath road they had to cater for travellers of every rank and type. The Castle Inn at Marlborough, formerly a home of the Seymours, was let to Lord Northumberland in 1752, for conversion into an inn. A few years later portable coal stoves were installed — 'Mr White begs leave to acquaint the Nobility and Gentry travelling the Bath and Bristol Roads, that, as Winter is coming on, he has erected some of Mr Buzaglo's Warming Machines.' In 1773 the White Hart, at Marlborough, was offering stiff competition while at Salisbury another White Hart, with its nine bays and pillared portico was built about 1820 to challenge its rival The Antelope. Both were listed by Cary.

It may have been an eighteenth-century innovation to identify inn names by painted signs. Before the increase in travel arising from the turnpikes, it would scarcely have been necessary. Heraldic emblems could readily be recognised by people who could not read or write, and in any case the visual attraction of a well-painted sign would doubtless add some *cachet* to an inn. Publicity about an inn's coach services took a number of forms, including small printed handouts, as illustrated by the example from the Crown at Blandford, and the more ostentatious, elegantly-painted board displayed outside the King's Arms at Calne. Both of these show the extensive network of services offered in modest market towns around the 1830s. It is by implication that the coaching inns underline the importance and widespread

(above) *The Brace of Pheasants Inn, Plush, Dorset*

(right) *The Amesbury Turnpike Trust, formed in 1761–2 and one of the earlist to feel the effects of railway competition.* (Reproduced by courtesy of Dr J. Chandler and the South Wiltshire Industrial Archaeology Society)

influence of the turnpike roads of the day. Although these roads did not reach into the remoter parts of Wessex, the large number of market towns scattered regularly throughout the area ensured that, if a village or hamlet was not served by a turnpike and a stage-coach service, carriers' carts or private post-chaise would provide the necessary local links. In the country areas much more modest inns met the needs of the local people — the Brace of Pheasants at Plush in Dorset, The Wagon and Horses by the Bath road at Beckhampton, and rare names in Wessex, the Woolpack at Sutton Veny near Warminster, the Packhorse at South Stoke on the edge of Bath, and another Packhorse on the London road in Chippenham.

Change lay just around the corner. By 1841 Brunel had opened his railway line from London to Bristol, and within 20 years the main network embraced most of Wiltshire and Dorset. The railways had a dramatic effect, not only upon the landscape, but on the towns and villages through which they passed, as well as on those which they missed. They changed many market towns — Dorchester, Sherborne, Bridport, for example — into bustling centres of population and trade, while other places such as Beaminster and Cerne Abbas, which they avoided, declined into the pleasant small country towns they are today. At the same time the country railways in particular gave a hitherto undreamed-of mobility to local society.

## The End of the Turnpikes

The records of the Amesbury Turnpike Trust vividly illustrate this. During the period 1810-40, its revenues from tolls had steadily increased from about £500 annually in 1805 to £700 in 1825, and exceeded £1,000 in the peak years 1836-9. Within another 2 years the Amesbury Trust was feeling the effects of railway competition. In 1842 only a single long-distance coach, the *Swiftsure*,

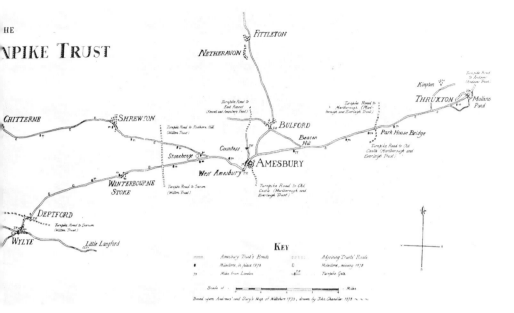

KEY

|  | Amesbury Trust's Roads | | Adjoining Trusts' Roads |
|---|---|---|---|
| • | Milestone, in place 1978 | □ | Milestone, missing 1978 |
| 7½ | Miles from London | | Turnpike Gate |

Scale of ·————·————·————·————·————· Miles

Based upon Andrews' and Dury's Map of Wiltshire 1773, drawn by John Chandler 1978

---

*An eighteenth-century milestone of the Amesbury Turnpike Trust at Winterbourne Stoke, Wiltshire*

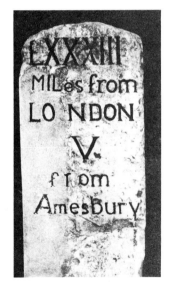

passed through the Wiltshire town, and then on a very curtailed route. No more did it run from Barnstaple to London, but only from Warminster to Andover Road Station (Micheldever). Five years later it no longer used the Amesbury Trust roads, but ran only between Salisbury and Warminster, along the course of the modern A36.

Revenues in 1845 had dropped to £370. In the following years, in common with many other Turnpike Trusts, it could not afford to maintain its roads. The General Highway Act of 1835 had abolished Statute Labour, and parishes had been given the right to combine into Highway Boards. Another Act, of 1841, empowered justices to levy rates in an attempt to relieve the increasingly impoverished Trusts, and this effectively meant the end of the tollgates, and over the next 50 years, many toll houses were sold and converted to other uses. In the late 1880s County Councils assumed responsibility for the roads, and the last turnpike gate was removed in 1895.

Over most of Wessex, from about 1860 onwards, as turnpike acts became due for renewal, the various Trusts were wound up, to be replaced first by Highway Boards, later by the County Councils. The Amesbury Trust received no receipts from tolls in 1868, and paid no salaries that year. Three years later, on 1 November 1871, it officially ceased to exist, and on the previous day an auction of all its property was held at the George Inn, Amesbury; three of its toll houses were sold for £70 each, one for £60 and one for £40. Similar closing scenes of the many Turnpike Trusts in Wessex occurred throughout the region. In the opening sentence of *The Woodlanders*, Hardy wrote,

> 'The rambler who, for old association's sake, should trace the forsaken coach-road running almost in a meridional line from Bristol to the south shore of England, would find himself during the latter half of his journey in the vicinity of some extensive woodlands....'

He was referring to that section of the Old Sherborne Road as it approached Minterne Magna from the north of High Stoy, which was turnpiked in 1752, and he had set the action of the story in the period 1876-9, almost 20 years after the railway had linked Sherborne and Dorchester, via Yeovil. Well may the old road be then described as forsaken. Indeed, for many roads described in this book, the last three decades of last century brought silence and stillness they were never again to experience, for the century's end saw the beginning of the motor age. Today, the quiet roads are most likely the oldest ones, those prehistoric ridgeways where men and livestock walked in the distant past.

# Bibliography

**General Books**

Addison, W. *The Old Roads of England*, 1980

Adlam, R. *The Book of Dorchester*, 1981

Atthill, R. *Old Mendip*, 1964

Bailey, C.J. *The Bride Valley*, 1982

Bettey, J.H. *Dorset*, 1974

Bettey, J.H. *Rural Life in Wessex, 1500-1900*, 1977

Bettey, J.H. *The Landscape of Wessex*, 1980

Bettey, J.H. *Wessex from AD 1000*, 1986

Bradby, E. *The Book of Devizes*, 1985

Burke, T. *Travel in England*, 1942

Burke, T. *The English Inn*, 1931

Chandler, J. *Endless Street: A History of Salisbury*, 1983

Cochrane, C. *The Lost Roads of Wessex*, 1969

Daniell, J.J. *The History of Warminster*, 1879

Darby, H.C. *A New Historical Geography of England*, 1973

Gitteridge, R. *Dorset Smugglers* 1981

Good, R. *The Old Roads of Dorset*, 1966

Havinden, M. *The Somerset Landscape*, 1981

Hawkins, D. *Cranborne Chase*, 1983

Hutchins, J. *History & Antiquities of the County of Dorset.* 3rd edition, 1861-73

Hutton, E. *Highways & Byways in Wiltshire*, 1917

Hyland, P. *Purbeck, The Ingrained Island*, 1981

Jervoise, E. *The Ancient Bridges of the South of England*, 1930

Oliver, Jane *Ancient Roads of England*, 1936

Olivier E. *Wiltshire*, 1951

Phillips, D. *The Great Road to Bath*, 1983

Pollard, E. Hooper, M.D. and Moore, N.W. *Hedges*, 1974

Stedman, A.R. *Marlborough & the Upper Kennet Country*, 1960

Taylor, C. *Dorset*, 1970

Taylor, C. *Roads and Tracks of Britain*, 1979

Timperley, H.W. & Brill, E. *Ancient Trackways of Wessex*, 1965

Treves, F. *Highways & Byways in Dorset*, 1906

Weinstock, M.B. *Old Dorset*, 1967

**Prehistoric Trackways**

Coles, J.M., Orme, B.J. Hibbert, F.A., and Wainwright, G.J. (eds) *Somerset Levels Papers 1*, 1975 and *Somerset Levels Papers 2*, 1976

Cox, R.H. *The Green Roads of England*, 1948

Dunn, M. *Walking Ancient Trackways*, 1986

Fowler, P.J. *Recent Work in Rural Archaeology*, 1975

Grundy, G.B. 'The Ancient Highways and Tracks of Wiltshire' *Arch. Journal* Vol 75, 1918

Jennett, S. *The Ridgeway Path*, 1976

Selkirk, A. & W. (eds) *Current Archaeology* No 84, 1982

**Roman Roads**

Berry, B. *A Lost Roman Road*, 1963

Crawford, O.G.S. *Archaeology in the Field*, 1952

Grundy, G.B. 'The Ancient Highways of Dorset, Somerset, & S.W. England'. *Arch. Journal*, 1937 & 1938

Leech, R. *Romano-British Rural Settlement in South Somerset & North Dorset* (Unpublished Ph.D. thesis, Univ of Bristol), n.d.

Margary, I.D. *Roman Roads in Britain*, 1973

Musty, J.W.G., Davies, D.A.L., Hunter, J.R. & Morgan, D. 'The Roman Road from old Sarum to the Mendips' *Wilts. Arch. Magazine*, 1958-60

Shurlock, B. *The Test Way & The Clarendon Way*, 1986

**Medieval Roads**

Beresford, M.W. 'The Six New Towns of the Bishops of Winchester' *Med Arch.* 3, 1959

Coleman, O. 'The Brokage Book of Southampton 1443-44' *Southampton Record Series*, 1960-1

Fowler, J. *Medieval Sherborne*, 1951

Grundy, G.B. 'The Evidence of Saxon Land Charters on the Ancient Road System of Britain' *Arch. Journal* 1917-18

Hindle, B.P. *Medieval Roads*, 1982

Hindle, B.P. 'Roads & Tracks', Chap 7 in *The Medieval Landscape* Ed.Cantor, L., 1982

Hindle, B.P. 'The Road Network of Medieval England & Wales' *Journal Hist Geog.* Vol 2, 1976

Hinton, D.A. *Alfred's Kingdom (Wessex & the South 800-1500)*, 1977

Jusserand, J.J. *English Wayfaring Life in the Middle Ages*, 1909

Miller, E. & Hatcher, J. *Medieval England*, 1978

Petteret, D.A.E. 'The Roads of Anglo-Saxon England' *WAM Vol 79*, 1984

Platt, C. *The Monastic Grange in Medieval England* 1964

Postan, M.M. 'Glastonbury Estates in the Twelfth Century' *Econ.Hist. Rev.*5, 1952-3

Power, E.E. *The Wool Trade in English Medieval History*, 1941

Stenton, F.M. 'The Road System of Medieval England' *Econ. Hist.Rev*, 1936

**Maps and Travellers 1540-1800**

Aubrey, J. *The Natural History of Wiltshire* (ed Britton), 1847

Aubrey, J. *A Wiltshire Collection* (ed Jackson) 1862

Bowden, P.J. *The Wool Trade in Tudor & Stuart England*, 1962

Bowen, E. *Britannia Depicta: 1720 Road Atlas of England & Wales*. Reprint, 1970

Bryant, A. *King Charles II*, 1931

Byng, Hon J. *The Torrington Diaries Vol 1* (ed Andrews C.B.), 1936

Camden, W. *Britannica*, 1590

Crofts, J. *Packhorse, Waggon & Post*, 1967

Davis, T. *General View of the Agriculture of Wilts*, 1794

Defoe, D. *A Tour Through the Whole Island of Great Britain*, 1724-6, 1971

Evelyn, J. *Diary 1640-1700*, 1819

Harrison, W. *Description of Britain*, 1586

Leland, J. *Itinerary 1535-43* (ed Smith, L.T.), 1964

Marshall, W. *The Rural Economy of the West of England*, 1796

Moir, E. *The Discovery of Britain: The English Tourists 1540-1840*, 1964

Morris, C. (ed) *The Journeys of Celia Fiennes*, 1947

Ogilby, J. *Britannia*, 1675

Parkes, J. *Travel in England in the Seventeenth Century* 1925

Pepys, S. *Diary, 1660-69*, 1927

Ramsey, G.D. *The Woollen Industry in the Sixteenth & Seventeenth Centuries*, 1972

Stevenson *General View of the Agriculture of Dorset*, 1812

Stukeley W. *Itinerarium Curiosum*, 1776

Timperley, H.W. *Vale of Pewsey*, 1954

Tunnicliff, W. A *Topographical Survey of the Western Circuit*, 1791

Woodforde, J. *The Diary of a Country Parson 1758-1802*, 1978

Various Quarter Sessions Records

**Drovers' and Traders' Roads**

Bonser, K.J. *The Drovers*, 1970

Hamer, J.H.' Trading at Saint White Down Fair, 1637-49' *Proc. S.A.N.H.*, 1968

Hamer, J.H. *Roads & Bridges of Lacock. WAM Vol 49*

Thirsk, J. (ed) *Agrarian History of England & Wales 1500-1640*, 1967

**Turnpike Roads**

Albert, W. *The Turnpike Road System of England, 1663-1840*, 1972

Baker, M. *The Bath Road, and The Exeter Road, in Discovering the Westward Stage*, 1972

Cary, J. *Traveller's Companion*, 1809

Chandler, J. 'The Amesbury Turnpike Trust', *Hist Monograph No 4 S. Wilts Ind. Arch. Soc*, 1970

Chubb, L. *Dorset Toll House Survey, for Dorset Countryside Treasures, Dorset C.C.* 1977

Cobbett, W. *Rural Rides 1830* (mainly Vol 1), 1948

Copeland, J. *Roads and their Traffic, 1750-1850*, 1968

Copeland, J. 'Sherborne Toll House,' *J. of Sherborne Hist.Soc.* Vols 1-6 1964-9

Gow, W.G. *Dorset Milestone Survey, for Dorset Countryside Treasures*, 1980

Hudson, W.H. *A Shepherd's Life*, 1910

Kay-Robinson, D. *Hardy's Wessex Reappraised*, 1972

Lane, M. *Jane Austen's England*, 1986

Mungay, G.E. (ed) *The Victorian Countryside*, 1981

Mogg, E. (ed) *Paterson's Roads*, 18th edition, 1822

Moorman, M. (ed) *Dorothy Wordsworth's Journal (1795-8)*, 1971

Pike, M. (ed) *The Piddle Valley Book of Country Life*, 1980

Plomer, W. (ed) *Kilvert's Diary*, 1871

Reader, W.J. *The McAdam Family & the Turnpike Roads*, 1980

Tristram, W.O. *Coaching Days & Coaching Ways*, 1901

Weinstock, M.B. *More Dorset Studies*,

Wesley, J. *Journal*, 1770

Various issues of the *Wiltshire Archaeological Magazine*

Various issues of the *Dorset Year Book & Dorset Magazine*, 1950-80

Various issues of the *Gentleman's Magazine*

Proceedings of Dorset Natural History & Archaeological Society

Proceedings of Somerset Archaeological & Natural History Society

Directories for 1826, 1830 and 1840

Minute books, accounts and plans of various Turnpike Trusts, in the County Record Offices of Dorset and Wiltshire.

# Index

Numbers in italics refer to illustrations or maps.